THE EVOLUTION OF GOTH CULTURE

EMERALD STUDIES IN ALTERNATIVITY AND MARGINALIZATION

Series Editors: Samantha Holland, Leeds Beckett University, UK and Karl Spracklen, Leeds Beckett University, UK

There is growing interest in work on transgression, liminality and sub-cultural capital within cultural studies, sociology and the social sciences more broadly. However, there is a lack of understanding of the problem of alternativity: what it means to be alternative in culture and society in modernity. What 'alternative' looks like is often left unexplored. The alternative is either assumed un-problematically, or stands in for some other form of social and cultural exclusion.

Alternativity delineates those spaces, scenes, sub-cultures, objects and practices in modern society that are actively designed to be counter or resistive to mainstream popular culture. Alternativity is associated with marginalisation, both actively pursued by individuals, and imposed on individuals and sub-cultures. Alternativity was originally represented and constructed through acts of transgression and through shared sub-cultural capital. In contemporary society, alternative music scenes such as heavy metal, goth and punk have spread around the world; and alternative fashions and embodiment practices are now adopted by footballers and fashion models. The nature of alternativity as a communicative lifeworld is now questioned in an age of globalisation and hyper-commodification.

This book series provides a stimulus to new research and new theorising on alternativity and marginalisation. It provides a focus for scholars interested in sociological and cultural research that expands our understanding of the ontological status of spaces, scenes, sub-cultures, objects and practices defined as alternative, liminal or transgressive. In turn, the book series enables scholars to theorise about the status of the alternative in contemporary culture and society.

Titles in this series

Amanda DiGioia, *Childbirth and Parenting in Horror Texts: The Marginalized and the Monstrous*

Samantha Holland and Karl Spracklen (Eds.), *Subcultures, Bodies and Spaces: Essays on Alternativity and Marginalization*

Stephen Brown and Marie-Cécile Cervellon, *Revolutionary Nostalgia: Neo-Burlesque, Retromania and Social Change*

THE EVOLUTION OF GOTH CULTURE: THE ORIGINS AND DEEDS OF THE NEW GOTHS

KARL SPRACKLEN
Leeds Beckett University, UK

and

BEVERLEY SPRACKLEN
Independent Scholar, UK

emerald
PUBLISHING

United Kingdom – North America – Japan – India – Malaysia – China

Emerald Publishing Limited
Howard House, Wagon Lane, Bingley BD16 1WA, UK

First edition 2018

Reprints and permissions service
Contact: permissions@emeraldinsight.com

British Library Cataloguing in Publication Data
A catalogue record for this book is available from the British Library

ISBN: 978-1-78714-677-8 (Print)
ISBN: 978-1-78714-676-1 (Online)
ISBN: 978-1-78743-930-6 (Epub)

Printed and bound by CPI Group (UK) Ltd, Croydon, CR0 4YY

ISOQAR certified
Management System,
awarded to Emerald
for adherence to
Environmental
standard
ISO 14001:2004.

ISOQAR
REGISTERED
Certificate Number 1985
ISO 14001

INVESTOR IN PEOPLE

Contents

Contents

Chapter 1

An Introduction

Definitions and Frames

What is goth? This book is an attempt to answer that question by exploring the history of the evolution of goth culture, that is, the origins and deeds of the goths. Goth, like culture or sub-culture or alternativity, is a problematic concept, having multiple meanings and uses. We want to avoid any attempt to provide a definitive story to what goth is, or where it started, because these are stories that are strongly contested by people who identity as goths. People who write popular narratives about the origins and deeds of the goths, what goth culture is or goth style is, may have some insider understanding, or they may be outsiders reproducing stereotypes about what the Internet thinks goths do and what they look like. We want to explore the construction of the collective memory of goth. That is, we want to explore what goths think are the important moments in their evolution and important aspects of their culture, and how that is reflected in wider accounts of that history and culture. Having said all that, for those unfamiliar with the history and culture of goth, a short explanation follows. First, gothic or goth emerged as a sub-genre label for a number of bands in the post-punk movement in the United Kingdom at the beginning of the 1980s. Since, it has survived and become globalised as a cultural practice associated with being alternative and transgressive. How that happened, what the evolution entailed and how goths and non-goths make sense of the history and culture will be made clear in the rest of the book. So, read on.

This book builds on work the authors have already published on goths and other alternative sub-cultures, some it by the two of us, some of it just by Karl alone or with others (Spracklen, 2014; Spracklen, Henderson, & Procter, 2016; Spracklen, Richter, & Spracklen, 2013; Spracklen & Spracklen, 2012, 2014). All our research is ethnographic and qualitative; we use our own ethnographic experience of being alternative combined with interviews of key respondents and content analysis. We follow a discourse-tracing approach (LeGreco & Tracy, 2009), which combines grounded theory with ideas from semiotics to try to make sense of how goths and others make sense of their histories, communities and cultures. In Spracklen and Spracklen (2012), we explore the paganism and Satanism on the fringes of one part of the goth scene and make the claim that such 'dark leisure' represents some authentic, communicative rationality in defence of the lifeworld (Habermas, 1984, 1987; Spracklen, 2009). In Spracklen and Spracklen (2014), we examine how the Whitby Goth Weekend has changed the perception of Whitby and the goth scene, and how the 'gothicness' of people attending the festival has been questioned by other goths (a theme we return to through this book). Spracklen, Richter, and Spracklen (2013) discuss the impact of gentrification and privatisation, what we defined as eventisation, on the spaces of alternative scenes in one city, and suggests that alternative scenes were shrinking. Karl Spracklen (2014) argues that the communicative rationality of goth and black metal has vanished in online spaces, and has written extensively on extreme metal's precarious status as a communicative leisure space (Spracklen, 2009, 2014, 2015a). Finally, Karl Spracklen, Henderson, and Procter (2016) explore how people remember being members of the F-Club, a crucial formative space for post-punk and goth in Leeds (again, which we will return to later in this book).

Goths have been the subject of a small body of work amongst sociologists (Hodkinson, 2002), cultural studies/gender theorists (Brill, 2008; Siegel, 2005) and popular music studies/musicology (van Elferen & Weinstock, 2016). Hodkinson's book on goths takes an ethnographic, sociological approach to understand social identity and belongingness in the scene as it was in the late 1990s, when his book's research was undertaken. It is an important starting point for research on goth; but it is dated, and limited in its lack of sustained critique of the commodification at work in goth. Siegel's book *Goth's Dark Empire* is highly problematic because of its false assumptions about what is part of goth, and what is punk or metal or something entirely unrelated. Brill's (2008) book *Goth Culture* is much better than Siegel, as it explores what goth actually is, though the emphasis on gender means only one part of goth's meaning is discussed. Finally, van Elferen and Weinstock's (2016) recent book *Goth Music: From Sound to Subculture* is only a brief (if useful) snapshot of goth's continued salience as a global, sub-cultural form. So, a book is needed that captures the history, sociology and philosophy of goth, and its meaning and history as understood by goths themselves – which is what you are reading right now.

This is a book about the nature of alternativity in goth sub-culture: where did the idea that goth is alternative and transgressive come from? And, is it still alternative and sub-cultural – or as one of us (Spracklen, 2014) has hinted in research in online spaces (as discussed above), has its transgressive nature suffered the 'heat death' of commodification? There is a growing body of work on transgression and liminality in cultural studies, which in turn is based on the theories of Bataille (1985, 1988), Turner (1969), Foucault (1986, 1991, 2002) and Lefebvre (1991, 1996, 2014), among others. This theory work is typified by the discussion in Partridge (2014) of the sacred and the profane in popular music, which he sees as a site of contestations over the meaning of good and evil between hegemons and musicians/listeners. In this cultural studies work, the problem of alternativity – what it means to be alternative in culture and society in modernity, what alternative looks like – is often left unexplored. There is a growing empirical and theoretical interest in transgression and sub-cultural capital in sociology and related social sciences; for example, in the work of queer theorists and gender theorists exploring embodiment, body modification and fashion (Holland, 2004; Winge, 2012; Yuen Thompson, 2015) as well as in popular music studies (Cohen, 1991; Hodkinson, 2002), youth studies (Bennett, 2000) and leisure studies (Rojek, 2000, 2010). These different explorations of alternativity and marginalisation demonstrate the salience of this book, and its relevance to scholars. But much of the work in these two approaches to alternativity often fails to adequately theorise the meaning of alternativity *qua* alternativity. The alternative is either assumed un-problematically, or stands in for some other form of social and cultural exclusion.

Alternativity delineates those spaces, scenes, cub-cultures, objects and practices in modern society that are considered to be actively designed to be counter or resistive to mainstream popular culture. The idea of the alternative in popular culture became itself a mainstream idea with the rise of the counter-culture in the 1960s America, though there were earlier forms of alternative cultures in America and other Western countries. Alternativity is associated with marginalisation, both actively pursued by individuals, and imposed on individuals and sub-cultures. Alternativity was originally represented and constructed through acts of transgression and through shared sub-cultural capital. In contemporary society, alternative music scenes such as heavy metal, goth and punk have spread around the world; and alternative fashions and embodiment practices are now adopted by footballers and fashion models. The nature of alternativity as a communicative lifeworld is now questioned in an age of globalisation and hyper-commodification (Spracklen, 2014). This book critically interrogates the alternative and marginal nature of goth, and narratives about goth.

The new goths take their name from the old Goths, the warriors who sacked Rome (albeit briefly), and established their own kingdoms across the European landscape in what historians call Late Antiquity. The origins and deeds of the old Goths were constructed by Roman historians in fear of the Goth as barbarian outsider; at the same time, the Goths were themselves the heroic subject of their own histories, constructed as stories of their mythical origin and the deeds that led them to be rulers of their own kingdoms in the post-Roman period (Heather, 1989, 1996). Who the old Goths were, their origins and their deeds, was a product of history, historiography and myth-making: by historians and by others, including writers and readers of the present era (Wickham, 2009). The existence of these old Goths and the adoption/adaption of the goth/gothic name by – or the imposition of the name on – the subjects of our book has led to the name being capitalised when people (goths and non-goths alike) discuss the new goths, that is, some people say Goth, not goth. We prefer goth, not Goth, because we are speaking of a culture, or genre, or space, or scene, or lifestyle or possibly sub-culture. It is a descriptor like punk, or skinhead, or indeed vandal (those modern-day hooligans named after the Vandal barbarians who, like the Goths, invaded the Roman Empire and carved their own kingdoms from it).

We use the late-antique framework of origins and deeds of the old Goths here to explore the controversies and boundary-making surrounding the genesis and progression of the modern gothic alternative culture. In this book, we argue that goth as sub-culture in the 1980s was initially counter-cultural, political and driven by a musical identity that emerged from punk. However, as goth music globalised and became another form of pop and rock music, goth in the 1990s retreated into an alternative sub-culture based primarily on style and a sense of transgression and profanity. By the 2000s, goth became the focus of teenage rebellions, moral panics and growing commodification of counter-cultural resistance, so that by the 2010s goth had effectively become another fashion choice in the late-modern hyper-real shopping malls, devoid generally of resistance and politics, but which still had some communicative rationality at work.

We use archival research, interviews with participants and content and semiotic analysis of relevant internet sites. The eight participants we interviewed (four males and four females) are all goths associated with the scene in the north of England, and are individuals who have long history of being goths. In no way are they representative of all goths, and we do not make any such claim anywhere in the book. But our respondents offer ways in which we can shed light on how some goths think about the origins and deeds of the new goths, the history and culture. As goths ourselves to a greater or lesser extent, we have our own history, memory and awareness of what it means to be a goth.[1] Combining our positional stance with our respondents' thoughts and memories with the other data, we make the case that goth has changed its meaning for its participants, and for wider society, though its short existence. The book engages with the work of other researchers and authors on goth, before developing a new theory of alternativity as a communicative lifeworld standing in opposition to the instrumentality of the mainstream. As such, goth, like punk, is in danger of being co-opted altogether by capitalism.

The Structure of the Book

There are three aims that guided how we structured the contents of this book. The first aim is chronological and ethnographical. We wanted to make sure that it would be read as a conventional research monograph that explores the history of goth from its origins to the present-day, which includes wider discussions about goth culture and the philosophy and sociology of goth. So, we have included chapters in a roughly chronological order: on the origins of goth and the early deeds of the goths, then chapters about the evolution and globalisation of goth culture, then the commodification of goth and the (possible) end of goth in this century. Our second aim was to make sure that we highlighted two key elements of British goth culture, namely the well-known and contentious band 'The Sisters of Mercy' and the similarly contentious 'Whitby Goth Weekend'; so, we have these two unique case studies as separate chapters alongside inter-disciplinary explorations of the sociology of goth online, goth fashion and the moral panic about goths in mainstream society. Our final aim was to develop new theoretical frameworks that allow commodification and alternativity to be explored, so we have a chapter developing that as well as a chapter review of literature.

The book begins, then, with that review. Chapter 2, 'Academics and Popular Writers on Goths', is a literature review that will examine and critique other writing on the goth scene. This work allows us to situate this book in the work of others who have also written about goths, from academics to popular writers. The review will begin with academic writing on goth. This section of the review will focus, in particular, on the key research monographs on goth, from the work of Hodkinson (2002) through Siegel (2005) to Brill (2008) to the more recent book by van Elferen and Weinstock (2016). We will argue that while their work is invaluable, it is either too grounded in small parts of the goth phenomenon, or too reliant on the work of cultural theorists to make sense of the everyday practice of goth. In the second section of this chapter, we will explore the work of popular authors on goth, from the work of authors such as Mick Mercer to Wikipedia. In writing about academics and popular writers on goth, we will sketch out the salient features of the history, culture and sociology of goths.

Chapter 3, 'Constructing a New Theory of Alternativity', is where we do the important theoretical work that allows us to develop a critical lens through which we can make sense of the rest of the book. This short chapter will develop a new theory of alternativity through combining the work of Adorno (1991) and Adorno and Horkheimer (2016), Habermas (1984, 1987), Butler (2006) and Lefebvre (1991, 1996, 2014). Although Adorno and Habermas are part of the same Marxist tradition of critical theory, and Butler and Lefebvre belong to a post-Marxist, post-structural epistemology, the four theorists may seem strange when analysed together. We situate ourselves firmly in the epistemology and ontology of Adorno and Habermas, although we accept that humans can still make choices to resist, even if such resistance is shaped by the power of hegemony. We will show that Butler and Lefebvre offer new theoretical insights into the nature of alternativity, transgression and resistance, which can be added to Marxist critical theory so long as the epistemological relativism of post-structuralism is not brought with it. This new critical lens will allow us to make sense of the origin and deeds of the goths, and the move from being defined through alternative space to being a commodity, a social media meme and fashion choice.

Chapter 4, 'The Origin of the Goths', deals with the complex history of the invention of the goths. We approach this origin story through the memories of our respondents and the wider goth community, as well as through popular narratives. We will use these multiple data sources from our research to sketch out the origin of the goth scene in the late 1970s and early 1980s Britain. As with the barbarian Goths of the first millennium, we will show that the genesis of the goth scene was partly a result of musicians thinking about how to be alternative and real, and partly a result of promoters and journalists seeking to label 'new' music and scenes. We will situate goth in the post-punk music scene in the United Kingdom, as a radical musical counter culture committed to radical politics.

Chapter 5, 'The Early Deeds of the Goths', is, like Chapter 4, constructed from our multiple data sources: from the memories of our respondents, popular narratives of the history, primary sources such as music magazines and more credible histories of the period. This chapter will show how goth developed as a discrete musical sub-culture in the 1980s in the United Kingdom and beyond, and became an accepted part of the alternative music scene. We situate goth in this period primarily as a sub-genre of post-punk, alternative music that shared many similar fashions and ideologies with the wider alternative scenes especially in the United Kingdom and Germany. We show that this post-punk, alternative politics in the goth scene was challenged by bands that abandoned goth for a contemporary hard rock sound, and by goth rock bands such as 'The Mission' who discarded the radical politics and took the goth sound and aesthetics into the charts and the mainstream at the end of the 1980s.

Chapter 6, 'The Sisters of Mercy: A Case Study', is the first case study of the book, and covers the most important goth band in the 1980s: the Leeds band 'The

Sisters of Mercy'. If The Sisters of Mercy were not the inventors of goth aesthetics and goth sounds, they are clearly the band that became famous world-wide for being the popularisers of goth. This band came to exemplify the goth look and the goth sound, and came out of a crucial local scene where goth was allegedly first used to describe the music. The band became hugely successful in the commercialisation of goth rock, but subsequently the band's leader, Eldritch, publicly disowned the goth name. The band's history and its status in the collective memory of goths and those interested in eighties popular music more generally is still significant, even if Eldritch might argue otherwise. The band was *the* goth band, the band that made the scene around the F-Club so important in goth memory, the band that made Leeds the goth capital of England and arguably the world. This chapter will explore the band's story and liminal state through published interviews with band members, reviews and features by journalists, ethnography online and the interviews with our goth respondents undertaken by the authors.

Chapter 7, 'The Goths and the Globalisation of Popular Culture', explores the trends that made goth music, culture and aesthetics cross from the post-punk scene in the United Kingdom into Europe, America, then the rest of the world. In this chapter, then, the globalisation of goth sub-culture is re-constructed. We will explore how goth initially spread as a form of alternative culture in the 1980s, and continued to maintain its alternative status once its moment of fashionability had passed in the early 1990s. By using our multiple data sources, we will explore how goth was transformed in the process of globalisation, thus becoming an identifiable form of popular culture from the 1990s onwards, and seen as both an alternative space operating underground and far from the mainstream – while, at the same time, being an alternative space that embraced mainstream cultural practices and habits, as well as one that became increasingly defined by the stereotypes imposed on it by mainstream cultural commentators. In this chapter, we will explore the connections between goth and metal, and how metal started to claim some practices and forms from goth, from wearing black to transgressing everyday cultural norms.

Chapter 8, 'Goths as Harbingers of Doom, and Moral Panics About Them', explores the ways in which goths have been stereotyped as dangerous outsiders. In this chapter, the reception of the globalisation of goth culture in hegemonic, mainstream public discourse and spheres is explored. The chapter will examine how goths came to be seen as dangerous outsiders by moral majorities in different nations around the world. Much of the data for this chapter will be found from online sources such as new sites and conservative religious campaigns against goths – both Christians in the West and Muslims in the East. We will explore how some of the stereotyping about goths has operated in a general way to stigmatise all those considered alternative, transgressive or deviant – and consequently, goth has come to mean anyone in black, with emos and metallers being lumped together under the goth category.

Chapter 9, 'Goth as Virtual Identity and Virtual Culture Online', argues that goth survived through the 1990s and 2000s partly due to the rise of digital leisure and digital culture – but the Internet by its nature has changed goth identity and culture. This chapter will explore the rise of .alt culture on the Internet in the

1990s through to the 2000s, and the ways in which goth culture has been continually reconstructed and its core identity reproduced. Using online ethnography, we will show how goths struggled to define gothness that was both inclusive of others seeking belonging, while being exclusive in the forms and myths associated with being a goth. We will show that goth has essentially changed from being a music sub-culture into one defined by some loose idea of darkness and transgression found online.

Chapter 10, 'Whitby Goth Weekend: A Case Study', tackles a topic we have touched upon in our previously published research (Spracklen & Spracklen, 2014). The second case study will be the history of the Whitby Goth Weekend, its status in British popular culture and the attitude towards it from goths. Whitby Goth Weekend is one of the most important events on the goth calendar, and historically it has appealed to goths across the country and the globe. Whitby Goth Weekend takes place in the town of Whitby on the coast of Yorkshire, famous for its ruined Abbey, its seaside resort delights and its key role in Bram Stoker's *Dracula*. In that book, it is the place where Dracula first appears on British soil, when the ship that is carrying him is caught in a storm. Unfortunately, it is also the place where Lucy Westenra is convalescing, and she is soon in Dracula's control. Bram Stoker also stayed at Whitby when he was writing the book. The chapter will explore how the weekend has become both a way of creating a 'Gothic' status for Whitby, and a way for everyday individuals to play as goths for the weekend. We will argue that while the Weekend is seen as important in the memory of our goth respondents, they question its continued relevance and fear it has been taken over by people who want to be steampunks, or people who just want to listen to eighties rock bands.

Chapter 11, 'Goth as Fashion Choice', will look at the importance of fashion and style in the rise of goth. In this chapter, we will begin with a discussion of the change and continuity in goth fashions and goth aesthetics since the formative years of the 1980s. We will show how the goth aesthetic borrowed from punk, post-punk and hard rock; then, we will show how goth and metal have had a symbiotic relationship in terms of transgressive, alternative fashions. In the second section of the chapter, we will show how goth in this century has become primarily a fashion choice, with gothness being performed as pantomime by amateurs, or as professional career choice by models. We will briefly discuss the development of steampunk out of goth, and show how goths have resisted or embraced the steampunk aesthetic. In the final section of the chapter, we will then describe the ways in which goth fashions and styles have become co-opted by mainstream fashion, and mainstream popular culture.

Chapter 12, 'The End of Goth?', is the most controversial chapter in the book. In this final substantive chapter, we will take the pulse of the goth scene today, and show how its commitment to alternativity, and its self-imposed marginalisation, is being threatened existentially and materially by the forces of instrumentality that govern late modern global capitalism. We will explore how goths today make sense of goth ideology and style through our interviews with our goths and online ethnography, and argue that although goth is alive and well in its radical, communicative state, it is at risk of becoming side-lined, or taken over and changed into something more corporate.

Chapter 13 is our short conclusion, in which we return to the big themes of goth's radical politics, its communicative leisure and culture. We want to show how goths are actively engaged in resisting attempts to subvert their alternative space, and they are involved in boundary work, memory-making and community action to maintain that. But there is a danger that such work will fail as the idea of the alternative changes in wider society. In the final part of our concluding chapter, we make a short return to our new theory of alternativity, and explore what it suggests what the future of goth may be.

Note

1. We both grew up in Leeds, and have a long-standing interest in goth as partici-pants in the eighties onwards. Both of us stepped away at different times, but we have retained interest in goth since we started to live together in 1997 in Bradford. Beverley became a tribal-fusion dancer, and achieved some recognition in that scene with the goth troupe Tanzhexen. Karl became a full-time academic in leisure studies.

Chapter 2

Academics and Popular Writers on Goths

Introduction

All research monographs have to include a critical discussion of what others have written on the topic. This review allows us to situate this book within the work of others who have also written about goths, from academics to popular writers. This chapter is a literature review that examines and critiques other writings on the goth scene. We do not want to limit the review to academics, as we believe there are interesting books written about goth by journalists, popular music writers and goths themselves. The review begins, however, with traditional academic writing on goths. The review is not a systematic one, and we do not claim to have attempted to survey every academic paper written on goths. Although there has not been a great deal of academic analysis of the goths, we are lucky to have a number of interesting research monographs. This section of the review focusses in particular on those research monographs on goth; from the work of Hodkinson (2002) through Siegel (2005) to Brill (2008) to the more recent book by van Elferen and Weinstock (2016). We will argue that although their work is invaluable, it is either too grounded in small parts of the goth phenomenon, or too reliant on the work of cultural theorists to make sense of the everyday practice of goth. In the second section of this chapter, we will explore the work of popular writers on goth; from the work of authors such as Mick Mercer to the collective effort of the editors on Wikipedia. In writing about academics and popular writers on goth, we will sketch out the salient features of the history, culture and sociology of goths as (re)constructed in their narratives.

Academic Writers on Goths

There is a small but significant number of academic papers that discuss one aspect of goth or another. Our own work, for example, has explored goth authenticity in parts of the goth scene in the north of England (Spracklen & Spracklen, 2012, 2014), eventisation (Spracklen, Richter, & Spracklen, 2013), the heat-death of goth (Spracklen, 2014) and memories of the F-Club in Leeds (Spracklen, Henderson, & Procter, 2016). Goulding and Saren (2009) have discussed the construction of gendered identity at Whitby Goth Weekend through the consumption of goth goods; in another paper, they show how consumption creates goth identity at the event more broadly (Goulding & Saren, 2010). And gender and sexual politics are at the heart of a research paper by Wilkins (2004) on the goth club scene somewhere in the United States of America. These, and other papers,[1] will be cited throughout this book. Other work on goth includes the edited collection by

Goodlad and Bibby (2007), but this has a broad and loosely defined definition of goth, and many of the contributions lack explanatory weight. However, the four research monographs on goth are the focus of this section. We will discuss these in the order of their publication, so we can see the epistemological development of 'goth studies'.

Paul Hodkinson

Paul Hodkinson's book *Goth: Identity, Style and Subculture* is the oldest of the four books, published in 2002. As a book published in the Berg series called 'Dress, Body, Culture', it has a strong focus on goth fashions as well as goth music and goth community networks. The book is based on Hodkinson's PhD thesis, an ethnography of goth identity, style and sub-culture, with the fieldwork – participant-observation, interviews, questionnaires, content analysis – undertaken in the 1990s in the United Kingdom (and online). The published version of this research feels very much like a PhD thesis transformed into a book, with the presumed removal of a traditional introduction and methodology. The publishers claim on the back of the book that:

> no-one has conducted a full-scale ethnographic study of this fas-
> cinating sub-cultural group. Based on extensive research by an
> 'insider', this book is the first.

Hodkinson's book is certainly an outstanding ethnography of goth sub-culture in the 1990s. Like all good ethnographers, Hodkinson immerses us immediately into the scene's key signifiers and myths. We are told a story of Hodkinson travelling with other goths to the Whitby Goth Weekend. He tells us about the music on the stereo of his friend's car: The Mission. We see one of his friends through his eyes, an exemplar for all goths in the United Kingdom in the period: wearing eye-liner, dressed in tight black jeans, wearing a purple velvet shirt (Hodkinson, 2002, p. 1). Hodkinson (2002) mentions being part of a national internet 'discussion group' for goths (p. 1). Hodkinson (2002) and his friends arrive at Whitby and he tells us about the spectacle he sees on the streets and in the pubs: the 'blues, pinks, purples, reds and greens among the crowd are offset by an excess of black' (p. 2). He mentions a variety of styles of make-up, hairstyles and clothing without actually telling us what they are – but reassures us that they are 'consistent' within the diversity of goth fashions. He continues to show us the business of the event, and tells us about the bands coming from 'Britain, Scandinavia and the United States of America to perform there (Hodkinson, 2002, p. 3). He shows us how the goth sub-culture is taking control of its own space through having a network of small labels, fanzines, mail-order catalogues and other sellers of goth fashions and music.

Hodkinson wants to defend the idea of sub-culture, and wants to argue that goth is a genuine and sustainable sub-culture, not something as ephemeral as a passing high-street fashion craze. He situates his own work in the ideas of Thornton (1995) and Muggleton (2000), and in response to debates in sociology, cultural studies and youth studies about the meaning and value of sub-culture in the contemporary world (Maffesoli, 1996; Redhead, 1997). For Redhead (1997), as for Maffesoli (1996), sub-culture is too closely associated with structuralist Marxist criticism to be useful in understanding what they both believe to be a period of postmodern epistemological fuzziness. This postmodern turn in the sociology of youth and culture in the 1990s demands that we reject all notions of fixed group identity (the goths, goth sub-culture and goth scene) in favour of a multiplicity of intersecting, liquid and transient identities. Thornton's work on club cultures generates the notion of 'sub-cultural capital', extending the Bourdieusian framework of capital, habitus and field (Bourdieu, 1986) to sub-cultures so that sub-cultures can be spaces of agency and identity-making beyond the restrictions imposed on them by Marxist theorists such as Hall (2016) and Hebdige (1979). Muggleton (2000) is a postmodern theorist who retreats from rejecting the idea of sub-culture by arguing that there can be a postmodern sub-culture, because sub-culture is a form of fragmentation. As he says (Muggleton, 2000, p. 158; cited in Hodkinson, 2002, p. 23):

> Subculturalists are postmodern is that they demonstrate a fragmented, heterogeneous and individualistic stylistic identification. This is a liminal sensibility that manifests itself as an expression of freedom from structure, control and restraint, ensuring that stasis is rejected in favour of movement and fluidity.

Hodkinson's research, then, is an attempt to make sense of these two different conceptions of what sub-culture is, and a defence of goth as an authentic sub-culture (in whichever of the two forms of sub-culture one might choose to apply). A theoretical framework is put together to make sense of the research, but this has the inherent contradiction at the heart of the whole book: Hodkinson's two forms of sub-culture seem to be locked into a paradox of meaning, being both post-structural and structural. This is not something the book ever resolves successfully, but Hodkinson is aware of the contradictions in his social and cultural theory, and continues to tease at the tension of this paradox all the way through to the conclusion.

The seven ethnographic chapters of the book provide the evidence that goth in the 1990s is a thriving sub-culture, with its own sub-cultural capital and possibly its own fragmented, postmodern sub-cultural transience. Hodkinson shows us how goth is a global network of local scenes, connected by the business of underground labels, musicians, promoters, journalists, internet posters and fans. He situates goth as a style emerging in the post-punk scene. He argues successfully that goth is recognisable as a sub-cultural style, and he maps out the fashions, forms, signs and signifiers through which it becomes identifiable. The 20 photographs he supplies map various ways of (re)presenting goth in the 1990s: from wide-brimmed cowboy hats and crushed velvet, through Victorian dresses to PVC and cyber-goths; goths in New Rock boots lined up outside The Elsinore pub in Whitby; shops, stalls, fliers and fanzines. He writes about the symbolic boundaries of the community, about the tension between being a sub-culture that is tolerant of diversity and alternative sexualities while being suspicious of fakes and other outsiders invading the scene and its spaces. He explains about the importance of the Whitby Goth Weekend alongside discussions of the importance of other spaces and events: club nights, gigs and social get-togethers. He explores how being goth provides a strong sense of identity, community and in-group belonging through attending goth events and discussing goth with other goths, and the development of friendships in the wider global network. He discusses the complex problem of the internal commodification of goth by goth insiders, the individuals who set up labels, events, shops and other business that 'sell' goth sub-cultural identity to goth consumers – and he suggests that these individuals are successful when they are seen to be contributing to the scene and having appropriate sub-cultural capital themselves. Goths in Hodkinson's fieldwork are shown to be keen consumers of goth products, supporting the people who set up the small businesses that provide the products if they but wary of overt commercialisation of the scene.

Hodkinson then moves onto exploring how goths communicate with other goth in the sub-cultural space. He identifies two forms of media – traditional and online – and devotes one chapter of the ethnography to each of them. As goth in the 1990s is no longer a part of the mainstream in the United Kingdom and North America, the traditional media of the goth scene are featured stories in heavy metal magazines (where goth is seen as an adjunct or outshoot of metal), fanzines, flyers and posters. It is fanzines that provide the most important crucial 'traditional' media for the goths Hodkinson interviews, as they provide curated information about new bands, new releases, new fashions and information about events. They are spaces through which goths can learn about being goth, and the symbolic boundaries of goth. However, online media is also important for Hodkinson's respondents. Despite the relative infancy of the Internet in this period, already it has become a crucial resource for connecting goths and allowing goths to communicate with one another. Hodkinson shows us how goths were keen adopters of this new technology, and his respondents are keen to show him that they are 'web-savvy'. His respondents identify email, new groups, discussion groups and websites as digital media resources for enhancing their belonging, community and identity as goths. These goths are beginning to break with reading fanzines for news on events, and turning to reading news groups and discussion forums instead. Hodkinson sees the rise of the Internet as an opportunity for goth to be a truly world-wide global sub-culture, one where finding information about being goth is easy, and believes that the ease of access will not make the sub-culture any less robust.

Overall, despite the strength of the fieldwork and the ethnography, there are some problems with Hodkinson's book. First of all, it is now about 20 years since he did the fieldwork, and things have changed dramatically for goth and wider society. Secondly, the theoretical framework never quite resolves the question of whether goth is an authentic sub-culture with its own field, habitus and capital, or whether it is postmodern with looser arrangement of belonging and authenticity. The book is itself a product of its times, and the debate about postmodernity and postmodernism is less pressing. Thirdly, the book could have spent more time discussing the historical development of goth in the 1980s, the radical politics of goth and the globalisation of goth. That said, this is an important contribution to our academic knowledge and to what we might call 'goth studies', and it is a book we will return to throughout this book.

Carol Siegel

Carol Siegel's *Goth's Dark Empire* was published in 2005, so it belongs to the years when goth had globalised, and when goth was the subject of rising moral panics. Siegel decides to use the capitalised form of the word goth ('Goth'), which allows her to conflate goth culture with Gothic fiction and the Gothic more generally. Siegel is not a goth herself, but she tells us she has spoken with hundreds of goths across the United States of America (Siegel, 2005, p. 3). In the Introduction, she sets out her view about goth culture clearly enough (Siegel, 2005, p. 2):

> American academics' lack of interest in Goth is that they have, for the most part, seen the subculture's radical engagements with gender and sexuality as an ephemeral trend, a superficial experimentation with images rather than substance... I disagree with this assessment of Goth because I agree with Michel Foucault, Gilles Deleuze and Félix Guattari that physical pleasures – particularly the consensual sadomasochism (S/M) I find intrinsic to most Goth subcultures – can function as radical technologies of resistance to the oppressive regimes of sexual normalcy upon which the maintenance of consumer capitalism depends.

The comment about sadomasochism being 'intrinsic to most goth sub-culture' is an incredible claim to make right on the second page of a monograph. We have no doubt that the people she spoke to her were truthful about their exploration of sexuality. But her respondents all seem to be fans of one American band, Nine Inch Nails (Siegel, 2005, p. 3), which crossed from goth to metal and industrial. This is one small part of the wider goth scene in America, and one smaller part of the global goth sub-culture at the time she was writing. Siegel seems to be happy to make this huge problematic generalisation the hypothesis, and the proof and the explanation of her entire book. Siegel at least sets out her theoretical framework early enough. She is a post-structural feminist inspired by the work of Foucault (1998a, 1998b) on the role of alternative sexuality as a space for resistance, and Deleuze and Guattari (1983, 2013) on the role of desire and pleasure as revolutionary drives. This framework limits her ability to see anything else about goth other than a new presentation of the sexual revolution.

Siegel (2005) tells us of the first time she realised there was something about the meanings attached to goth sub-culture, when she saw goths 'streaming like black smoke down the freeway overpass' (p. 6). She thinks of her young self-citing T. S. Eliot's 'The Waste Land' and sneering at the commuters rushing to work and chasing money, and sees in the goths in front of her 'an alternative to the life-in-death that is the bland conformity' of the mainstream, 'corporate American culture' (Siegel, 2005, p. 6). She stares at the white corpsepaint and the ripped clothing and decides right there what was going on. This is a playful adoption of death and the markers of death, as a way of rejecting the mainstream. She boldly claims, in a passage worth citing in full (Siegel, 2005, p. 7):

> Had death also, though so differently, undone them? If so, in what sense? Certainly they had an intimate relation to death. My own youthful sense of self was constructed along lines dictated by my assimilation of the rhetoric of sexual liberation expressed in sixties favorites, such as Norman O. Brown's 1959 Life against Death, in which refusal to submit to the deathly demands of an oppressive culture meant coming alive sexually, and vice versa. So it was both exciting and unsettling to me to see the Goth' perversely eroti-cized embrace of death. Here, it seemed, was a new take on the old sexual revolution.

In seeing the goths as sexual radicals fighting the oppressive gender order and the starched morals of American society, Siegel distorts the polysemic nature of goth, and misunderstands the boundaries of goth. In the rest of the book, we are taken on a tour of all the parts of the broader goth culture she likes, because they are the parts where her theoretical framework can be confirmed. In the search for examples of goth songs that exemplify what she thinks is the 'essence of Goth', she chooses a cover of Rod Stewart's 'Do You Think I'm Sexy' by the Revolting Cocks, a band that are actually just a deliberately silly industrial rock side-project other industrial rock musicians. The book is strongly influenced by Siegel's own personal and professional interest: English literature. She writes about authors who write things that appeal to the goth scene, or who explore dark and trans-gressive themes. She focusses her analysis on authors that have appeal beyond goth sub-culture, such as Angela Carter, Anne Rice and Poppy Z. Brite. The latter two do have significant appeal in the goth sub-culture, and we accept that Rice has had an influence on the rise of vampirism in goth – but the rise of vampirism is equally down to the appearance of the television programme *Buffy the Vampire Slayer* (Spracklen & Spracklen, 2012). But they are only one small part of the picture, and Siegel is not capable of seeing any of the blood-drinking and fetish-ism in Rice and Brite as ironic. Hence, she is not capable of thinking of goth as playful, or performative – if the goths dress in bondage gear on a night out, they must be bondage users at home. Ironically, Siegel comes to the same conclu-sion about goth as the moral majority in her home country: goths are immoral deviants. In most of the book, Siegel does not attempt to engage in understand-ing goth culture through exploring what her goth respondents have told her, or through exploring wider goth culture and spaces – apart from one chapter where she tries to defend goth from charges of racism by introducing goths she knows who are nor white.

Overall, this is a frustrating book. Siegel gets many of the facts about goth music and the history and evolution of goth culture wrong. She tells us that goths are drawn to Gothic architecture because there is some kind of essential relationship between the medieval churches and the modern music sub-culture. She thinks there is a relationship between black metal and goth – which there is in terms of lyrical themes, in fashions and make-up, and the crossover appeal of bands such as Cradle of Filth – then, makes the strange claim that the relationship is demonstrated by 'the self-placement of both styles within the larger category Darkwave' (Siegel, 2005, p. 5). Where is the evidence that goths and black metallers are placing their music in this category? None is presented to us. And the claim is a nonsense, because darkwave[2] is just one sub-gene of goth music. Black metal is not a style in the category of darkwave – it is metal, uncompromisingly so (Spracklen, 2006, 2014).[3] The back cover gets it wrong from the start when it says goth 'came to prominence with punk bands such as Marilyn Manson'. Then it tells us that 'in the early years of the twenty-first century... Goth virtually disappeared'. Siegel uses this mis-reading of the rise and evolution of goth culture throughout the book. Goth existed long before Marilyn Manson, and became well known around the world before Marilyn Manson. Marilyn Manson are not a goth band, and are not a punk band, though their lead singer, Marilyn Manson, copied goth fashions because goth in its cyber-goth dance phase was still popular in alternative spaces at the time.[4] Goth did not disappear, and no one thought it had disappeared, so Siegel is setting up a false mystery to solve.

Dunja Brill

Dunja Brill's book *Goth Culture: Gender, Sexuality and Style* came out in 2008. It was published in the same Berg book series as Hodkinson's book, and is almost entirely about style: fashions, make-up, clothing and the performance of gender. Like Hodkinson's book, this is a well-written ethnography based on participant-observation, photography and interviews with key informants. Brill completed a PhD at the University of Sussex in 2005 entitled 'Between subversion and stereotype: the "Goth" movement as a case study of gendered representations in subcultural media and style', which was published a year later in Germany (Brill, 2006). In *Goth Culture*, Brill tells us that much of the research for the monograph took place in the period when she must have been competing her PhD, so the monograph must be a re-working of the original thesis, or a re-use of data collected for the PhD. For the purpose of our analysis, all we need to know is that there is a relationship between the PhD and the 2008 monograph, which explains the richness of the ethnography and the literature review chapter that positions her work in the same debates as Hodkinson's book. Brill agrees with him that goth is a sub-culture, one where Thornton's sub-cultural capital can be gained, and where community and identity are forged through practice, aesthetics and other symbolic boundaries. Unlike Hodkinson, Brill privileges critical theories of gender and wants to interrogate the construction of masculinity and femininity in the sub-cultural space. Brill is strongly critical of Siegel for her random methods and her 'uncritical raving about supposed gender subversion' (Brill, 2008, p. 34). But she is equally critical of Thornton (1995) for uncritically reproducing gender stereotypes and power hierarchies, and also claims that Pini (2001) is guilty of the same reification of masculinity and femininity. For Brill, then, her research is about both the construction masculinity and femininity, the and gender as object and subject.

As with Hodkinson, Brill immediately sets the scene by narrating two moments from her field diary, or at least two memories recollected for the purposes of the research. The first anecdote is being in a club in Berlin in 1992 and seeing (Brill, 2008, p. 1):

> Theatrical, mysterious figures and shapes slowly moving in the fog. Most wear velvet dresses or capes, elaborate make-up and long black hair, and even when the fog lifts for a moment it is often hard to tell whether these strange, beautiful, black-clad creatures elegantly swaying are male or female. In fascination, I watch a girl with pale make-up, dark lipstick and heavy black eyeliner, wearing a hooded velvet cape around her frail body. Only when my eyes are caught by the waving movements of the rather large, bony hands sticking out of the wide black sleeves do I realise that 'she' is actually a boy.

Brill does not say why she is in the club in the first place. We suspect she already had some knowledge of goths and goth music, because goth music was not hidden away in the underground in 1992 and goth bands were entering the charts in Germany and elsewhere, but it is an arresting image with which to begin the book. In the next anecdote, it is 2003, and in Brighton Brill sees:

> A man with a crew cut… stomping back and forth in a martial manner to the sound of distorted electronic beats. Next to him, there is a girl dressed in a tight black PVC corset, miniskirt and high-heeled platform boots, whose tiny-stepped, wriggly dancing somehow calls to mind a dark, lascivious nightclub sequence from a David Lynch movie.

This is another striking image. Brill is sophisticated enough to understand that a subtle shift had occurred between the early 1990s and early 2000s, namely the development of forms of goth music such as EBM influenced by dance, and the decline of 'classic' goth rock fashions for cybergoth and industrial/martial looks. Brill is an insider, though she claims her academic status allows her to have a critical distance from the subject. She is clearly sympathetic to goth, but does not let that stop her critiquing aspects of goth culture. The book begins with a quick run-through of the history of goth, and the development of goth styles and subgenres. Unlike Siegel, Brill knows her history and sociology of goth, and her German roots allow that history and sociology to reflect the more accepted nature of goth in Germany, as opposed to the (often) liminal status in the United Kingdom and the United States of America.

The ethnographic analysis in the book is based on six chapters, through which Brill distributes 20 pictures that cover every shade of gender performativity, fashion and style in the goth spaces she is observing. Among these pictures, she shows us men dressing as masculine men, women dressed in what she calls hypersexy fetish style, alternative trans femininity, representations of gender blurring and fluidity, and erotic performances. She takes us through how style in the goth scene is connected to status. She then explores female style in goth and subjectivity, and masculinity as style. Through this work, Brill maps the potentiality of goth as a space and sub-culture for alternative and transgressive agency and meaning-making. She explores queer sexualities to see how liberated and progressive the political ideology of sexuality is, and goes on to show how goth 'works to privilege heterosexual and primarily male-defined desire' (Brill, 2008, p. 145). She explores how goth is presented in the media, especially the German media, and finds it reproducing the hegemonic gender order, even though there may be spaces where that is not the case. In her concluding comments, recognises some freedoms and possibilities, but she writes (Brill, 2008, p. 186):

> Goth falls short of realising its professed Utopian ideals… In the common practice of Goths, the traditional gender binary is not so much disrupted or transcended as shifted in the direction of femininity… Goth men are encouraged to refuse certain pressures of hegemonic masculinity in their style practices and their means of status achievement. Goth women, by contrast… remain tied to a fairly restrictive standard of (hyper)femininity for winning approval and status.

This was absolutely the case at this moment in goth's evolution. Later in this book, we will return to this question of whether goth reproduces or transgresses the gender order, especially in its current form.

Isabella van Elferen and Jeffrey Andrew Weinstock

Isabella van Elferen and Jeffrey Andrew Weinstock have published the most recent research monograph on goth, their book *Goth Music: From Sound to Subculture*, published in 2016 by Routledge. The research monograph is the first in goth studies to actually use music theory, and musicological analysis, to explore how goth music is made. The two authors are perfectly matched to undertake such a musicological analysis. The first author, van Elferen, is a well-known academic musicologist and an active participant in the goth scene. She is the author of a related book *Gothic Music: The Sounds of the Uncanny* (van Elferen, 2012), a musicological analysis of goth music as well as music associated with 'Gothic' novels, films and television programmes.[5] The second author, Weinstock, is well-known and respected goth DJ who understands the history of goth and the music of the most obscure sub-genres. With these credentials, they have a strong and coherent understanding of the history of goth. They map its rise and its evolution, and its relationship to other social trends such as digital culture, concisely but precisely in a short introductory chapter.

The authors are critical of every previous book on goth for failing to focus on the music. They are astounded that Hodkinson ignores the music even though chooses to hand out questionnaires to people attending the Whitby Goth Weekend, an event that is essentially a music festival. They are dismayed that Siegel spends most of her book analysing novels, and are incredulous about Siegel's list of goth bands in the appendix, which includes only a narrow range of first-generation bands. They note that Brill fails to explore fully the musical differences of the sub-genres of goth music in which different fashions have been favoured, which Brill says are probably influenced by the music. They dismiss the edited collection by Goodlad and Bibby, as we do, for its wide-ranging definition of gothic, but then also note it has only three chapters from 22 that deal with music specifically (van Elferen & Weinstock, 2016, p. 4).

Whereas this critique of the other books is fair – Hodkinson, Siegel, and Brill do fail to include any musicological analysis – this does feel like an unwarranted and over-wrought dismissal. Not every book about a subject can include every way in which that subject can be analysed. Academic authors have to make choices about the disciplinary lenses through which we investigate issues. We have to make decisions about the epistemological frames, the methods of data collection and analysis. All disciplines and subject fields have particular rules about what constitutes 'proper' research, and in many of those disciplines and subject fields are constantly negotiating those rules. Good academics need to try to write in an inter-disciplinary way, something we are doing in this book, with our attempt to write a history, a philosophy and a sociology of goth. In popular music studies, there has been a long struggle between musicologists and sociologists to own the rules of studying popular music, so we can understand where van Elferen and Weinstock are coming from (Tagg, 2011).

Using Actor-Network Theory (Latour, 1987, 2005), the authors make the bold claim that goth music is its own agent working on goths and the goth scene and helping construct the meaning and reality of goth (van Elferen & Weinstock, 2016, p. 7):

> Our claim that music is central to goth social reality thus goes significantly further than to insist that goth subcultural events always involved music or that music is a privileged topic of goth conversation and debate. Instead, the argument is that qualities and composition strategies characterized as goth provoke specific affective responses that then are endowed with personal meanings inserted into shared fantasy structures.

To make this claim, the authors divide the analysis into 4 chapters, with a full musicological analysis of 12 songs chosen to represent the different aspects of goth. They start with exploring playlists at two large goth music events and contextualising goth. They then move on to a Latourian analysis of goth music networks, and a 'hauntology' of the uncanny and other-wordly sounds. They then explore goth music chronotopes and what they suggest is goth's yearning for other worlds and other times that never existed. Finally, they discuss the social and cultural contexts in which goth music and goth desires are (re)produced.

We find many problems with van Elferen and Weinstock's monograph. We are not convinced that the 12 songs are suitably representative to be able to move to much generalised points about what goth music makes goths feel and desire. We are not convinced by the hauntology or the Latourian analysis – it is the makers of the music who are the agents of its making, or those who change the music in transmission or in reception. But the book is useful as a corrective to the socio-logical focus of Hodkinson and Brill, and serves as a source later on in our book when we try to compensate for our lack of musicological skill and precision.

Popular Writers on Goth

For the rest of this chapter, we explore how popular authors have constructed the history of goth and the evolution to goth culture. On traditional published sources, we limit ourselves to the books that have reached a global audience, and ones that are purely about goth. We are aware that there are many other sources published in traditional book form, but we have not explored them here as they have had limited reach in goth culture itself. All the books here have been read by our goth respondents, or have been mentioned by them. We end this section with a brief overview of what the Internet tells us about the origin and deeds of the goths, focussing on the Wikipedia as a multi-authored and multi-edited source of received opinion.

Mick Mercer

There is no doubt that the most influential popular author on goth is Mick Mer-cer. He started out writing his own punk fanzine before getting paid work as a freelance writer – then a staff writer and then ultimately an editor – in a number of British music newspapers and magazines from the late seventies onwards. His presence on the punk, post-punk and alternative desks of the music press allowed him to witness and report on the rise of goth rock. His first book on goth (called *Gothic Rock*) was already published in 1988, a few short years after the rapid rise of the first wave of British goth rock bands. As such, it is an accurate account of the birth and evolution of goth rock, and its popular, mainstream status in the sec-ond half of the eighties. The continued growth of goth culture alongside goth rock and goth music encouraged Mercer (or his publishers) to revise and reprint the book in 1991 (now titled *Gothic Rock: All You Ever Wanted to Know… But Were Afraid to Ask*). For young goths, musicians and journalists, this book was essential at the time for making sense of the new scene, its sounds, its bands, its aesthetics, and its emergence. We remember reading it ourselves in its revised version.

Mercer's third book on goth was published in 1997, and was amusingly called *Hex Files: The Goth Bible*. The book title punned on *The X-Files*, the popular mystery television series of the period, but the word Hex represented the weird and magical turn of goth culture towards paganism (Spracklen & Spracklen, 2012). And calling it the 'Goth Bible', while probably just a way of saying it was an essential read, suggests that it is some kind of anti-Christian, pro-Satan mock-ery of the 'good' Bible. Mercer's first two books started with the music inspired by the UK post-punk scene, but this book travelled far and wide to identify different goth fashions, and different sub-genres of goth music.

His fourth book came out in 2002, and attempted to capture the millennial zeitgeist with a title called *Twenty-First Century Goth*. This book followed the evolution of goth onto the Internet and around the world. It is an interesting primary source for how goth looked at the beginning of the 2000s, although most of the websites, as is the fate of the Internet in the age of social media, have disappeared. Overall, it feels as if Mercer had run out of inspiration but for whatever reason he had to write yet another goth book. After its publication, he turned from trying to map the complexities of global goth culture to focussing on the bands and musicians. His fifth and so-far-final book on goths, *Music to Die For*, came out in 2009. It is an outstanding, idiosyncratic discussion of all the goth music he loves, extending the idea of goth to some new spaces and fusions, such as country goth music. The book draws on extensive interviews with the musicians themselves, and allows them to tell their own stories while providing a context and framework to their place in goth.

Gavin Baddeley

Gavin Baddeley is journalist and writer who has explored Satanism, paganism and the weird in a series of books (Baddeley, 1999, 2000, 2002, 2006). The book that made him well-known in rock music scenes around the world was his 2000 *Lucifer Rising*, in which he shows the long and sustained influence of various forms of Satanism on rock music. As someone who describes himself as a Priest of the Church of Satan on the back cover, we might think Baddeley's history is biased. But he is sensitive to the many complex ways in which rock music has shaped ideas from Satanism. In this book, he only spares two pages to write about what he calls goth rock, which he notes is because 'the modern gothic counterculture is pre-occupied with appearance rather than the Satanic aesthetic' (Baddeley, 2000, p. 178). He mentions the band Fields of the Nephilim, inspired by Lovecraft, Crowley and Eastern mysticism; then, he discusses Inkubus Sukkubus, though he admits that band is inspired by Wiccan paganism rather than the individualism and elitism of contemporary Satanism.

Baddeley's 2002 book on goth, *Goth Chic: A Connoisseur's Guide to Dark Culture*, is an attempt to write a history of the influences on goth, the combination of styles in literature, architecture and art that came to be called the Gothic. He writes every well about the Gothic revival of the nineteenth century, its rejection of science and modernity, and its embrace of Romanticism. He explores Gothic fiction and its continued importance in the twentieth century. He then connects these historical movements to the goth rock scene, making the claim that the romantic, death-loving, modern-hating philosophy of Gothic transferred into goth rock through the deliberate adoption of Gothic tropes: in dress, in lyrical themes, and in imagery on album covers. There is no doubt that there is some connection between the Gothic in art, and goth culture. Certain individuals are drawn to goth music for the same reason individuals were drawn to the doomed figures in the fiction of Goethe, or the dead or dying in the paintings of the Pre-Raphaelites – because some people feel the need to be outside of the mainstream, and wish to reject its norms and values through self-destruction, or through resistance. Since the rise in popularity in goth, many goth musicians have explored the connection to the Gothic directly, but not every goth band is Gothic. There is no Gothic aesthetic in the EBM dance scene. The most famous bands in the last 20 years or so that exploit Gothic imagery and themes are not even goth in their musical style, My Dying Bride being death/doom metal, and Cradle of Filth being black metal. And, the key bands involved in the construction of goth were not inspired by insipid Romanticism, as we will show later in this book. In other words, Baddeley has confused the Gothic with goth, so is probably the person to blame for the same assumption made by Siegel (2005), and the popular assumption today that goths love everything Gothic and that is why they go to Whitby dressed as Victorians (Spracklen & Spracklen, 2014).[6] In fact, Baddeley's claim is probably the reason most goths themselves see goth as Gothic: the book has constructed the myth of the (Victorian) Gothic goth in the minds of modern-day goths.

Dave Thompson

In 2007, the music journalist, Dave Thompson, published *The Dark Reign of Gothic Rock: In the Reptile House with the Sisters of Mercy, Bauhaus and The Cure*. The book makes the claim that the only authentic goth music and goth subculture was that which emerged from post-punk in the United Kingdom in the early 1980s. The modern goth culture, for Thompson, is a triumph of style over substance, with hundreds of mediocre artists and bands simply producing ersatz versions of songs written by the big UK post-punk bands. For Thompson, there is no proper goth because the bands of the eighties disappeared (like Bauhaus) or evolved their sound (The Cure, The Sisters of Mercy). This book has an interesting exploration of the roots of the goth rock sound and aesthetic, with Iggy Pop being identified as key influence on the black fashions, the thin faces and the dark tones. While we agree with him that goth rock started in their post-punk scene, and also that the scene lost its radical punk politics when it entered the mainstream and globalised, we believe that goths after the 1980s are not always reduced to being copy-cats or fakes.

Natasha Scharf

The second decade of this century has seen another popular book published that explores the history and culture of goth: Natasha Scharf's 2011 *Worldwide Gothic: A Chronicle of a Tribe*. Scharf is another journalist working and writing for various alternative music magazines in the United Kingdom. The book correctly locates the origins of goth in the British post-punk scene, and then charts the rise and evolution of goth as it grows globally, while passing out of the mainstream. Scharf notes how goth was the subject of a number of moral panics in the late 1990s and early 2000s, and was even linked to fascism through the rise to notoriety of neo-folk (Scharf, 2011, pp. 93–94). At various stages of the narrative, Scharf (2011) points out that the mainstream media assumed goth had died, which is clearly not true. For example: (p. 43):

> If the UK media were to be believed, by the early 1990s the goth scene was little more than a decaying lump of blackened goo… but in reality, the really exciting stuff was only just beginning; a new dark rose was growing out in Europe and beyond, its petals opening further and further outwards.

Here, Scharf is referring to the rise of goth bands, new sub-genres of music, clubs and festivals in Europe, especially in Germany. She shows how goth continued through the 2000s as a vital alternative, underground sub-culture, though it changed into a number of different forms defined partly by music but mainly by fashion. The book is filled with pictures of goths at festivals, goth bands in various poses and goth models. All the models are sexy females, and those pictures all confirm Brill's (2008) argument about the limitations of goth for femininity. This is also the first popular book to mention the presence of steampunk among goth's cultures, and includes two photographs of the new sub-culture (Scharf, 2011, p. 117): a steampunk man with three steampunk women at Wave Gotik Treffen; and the two principal songwriters of the spoof[7] steampunk punk band The Men That Will Not Be Blamed For Nothing.

The Internet and Wikipedia

These days, traditional books and magazines have come to be challenged by the Internet and Wikipedia as a source of information about anything (Spracklen, 2014, 2015a, 2015b). On the Internet, there are literally millions of websites that mention goth sub-culture. On the day we are writing this chapter (18 August 2017), a Google search for that term brings up 5,1000,000 hits. The first page directs us to a peculiar range of websites. At the top of the hit-list is the Wikipedia page on goth sub-culture. The next two hits are to the same website, which has not been updated since 2009 (www.gothicsubculture.com), which was evidently set up to debunk scare stories circulating in the United States of America. It takes its information about the origins and definitions of goth from the FAQs list of the defunct alt.gothic newsgroup, and these are reasonably accurate. The next hit is for a social anthropology class on goths at a subscription-only learning resource (http://study.com/academy/lesson/what-is-the-goth-subculture.html). Then there is a page defending and describing the lifestyle and spirituality of goth at a Canadian website promoting religious tolerance (http://www.religioustolerance.org/goth.htm), which tries to tell believers that goths are just like you. Next is a sympathetic piece written in *The Independent* newspaper to celebrate World Goth Day in 2017, which even manages to interview Paul Hodkinson (http://www.independent.co.uk/life-style/world-goth-day-2017-pop-sub-culture-what-is-it-darkness-music-clothes-style-cure-dracula-tim-burton-a7038176.html). Then, Google's algorithms came up with http://www.whatisgoth.com/, where the author writes:

Put simply, a Goth is someone who finds beauty in things others consider dark. They love all that is dark and mysterious. That doesn't mean Goths are evil, it just means they have a different perspective to many. And it also doesn't mean Goths are unkind, violent or lacking in humour, in fact quite the opposite is true. Goths love to laugh but their humour is more of the black comedy sort. They aren't sad because they like dark things – dark things make them happy and inspire them. Goths are often intelligent, romantic and artistic realists. Being Goth is not about how one dresses. Most of what you can find written about Goth is that it was something that was born out of the Punk movement in the late 70's and that most Goths wear black. I disagree. Goth isn't something that was created in the 70's because it always was.

A saner perspective on goth follows at the penultimate hit on the first page of the search, which is a mish-mash of ideas taken from various sources (http://subcultureslist.com/gothic-culture/). The final hit on the first page of the search takes us to a blog where someone is upset about modern-day goths for excluding other alternative people from the goth inner circle, for only being interested in fashion and misery (http://www.rebelsmarket.com/blog/posts/5-things-wrong-with-goth-subculture-right-now).

Anyone searching for goth on the Internet in 2017, then, will be taken to these kinds of websites: learning guides, old websites not updated, newspaper articles, weird blogs with angry authors, and Wikipedia. The importance of Wikipedia as a primary source for information about goth can be seen in Spracklen (2014), which reviews websites that were in use in the months in which that particular research project was undertaken. Wikipedia was important in 2014 as a reliable source of goth music and fashion; other websites reviewed in the paper are wikihow.com's 'how to be a goth' page, which includes egregious, almost self-parodic content; and goth.net, a website that had information on what goth is, and fairly active forums where goths could talk to each other. In this rapidly changing digital age, the forums on goth.net are no longer actively used: most information about goth culture now is shared on social media such as Facebook and Instagram.

Wikipedia is constructed by anyone who wants to sign-in and edit a page (Tkacz, 2014). But signing in and editing is only the first step of how the community activism of the site operates. Any new edits on a page are supposedly scrutinised by other users, who can flag edits that are partial, incorrect or irrelevant. There are groups of editors who discuss and approve changes anyone makes to pages by re-editing the text themselves. Wikipedia insists that factual claims are backed by secondary sources. What this means in practice is that other websites serve as sources for Wikipedia – there is no quality control over using only reliable, academic sources such as journal articles or research monographs, and references to these academic sources only appear if someone who knows about them is editing the page. The page we are looking at on the afternoon of 18 August 2017 was last updated on the morning of the same day, so it is being curated and edited by some active users. This page (https://en.wikipedia.org/wiki/Goth_subculture) starts with the following paragraph:

> The goth subculture adopts dark fashion elements such as black clothing, dyed black hair, dark eyeliner, black fingernails and black period-styled clothing and a focus on gothic rock and a range of other music genres. The goth subculture, began in England during the early-1980s where it was developed from the gothic rock scene, itself an offshoot of the post-punk genre. Notable post-punk groups that presaged that genre include Siouxsie and the Banshees, Joy Division and Bauhaus. The goth subculture has survived much longer than others of the same era, and has continued to diversify and spread throughout the world. Its imagery and cultural proclivities indicate influences from the 19th century Gothic literature and gothic horror films.

Wikipedia is better than the person who wrote the above-cited blog. This is an accurate account of the formation and fashions of the sub-culture; however, the influence of Gothic art is overplayed, and hence the page goes on to include a section that describes Gothic literature. This is the claim made by Baddeley, which appears in the other websites we have visited. Wikipedia, then, is something that tells us what the common narratives or myths are about the origin and deeds of the goths – this is the history of the goths believed by the goths and their sympathisers. This is the history that is followed by sites such as subcultureslist.com, what we will call, through this book, following Butterfield (1968), the Whig interpretation of goth history: goth history written by goths that reveals present-day concerns and memories coloured by nostalgia. That is, this the collective memory of the genesis and deeds of the goths shared by goths and other interested outsiders. We will explore the genesis and deeds in turn; but before we do, we will construct or theoretical framework – the purpose of the next chapter.

Notes

1. For example, Carpenter (2012) on the origins of goth in the music of Bauhaus, or Skutlin (2016) on goth in Japan.
2. Now to be fair to Siegel, dark has been used in Germany in some spaces to stand for all alternative music, including goth and extreme forms of metal, with a 'dark' theme. The British death/doom metal band My Dying Bride, for example, which is popular in Germany, played the 'dark' festival Wave Gotik Treffen in 2016. We will discuss this evolution of goth culture as 'alternative' and in symbiosis with metal in Chapter 7.
3. Although there is a link between black metal and goth, as we explore later.
4. And Marilyn Manson are in fact the inheritors of goth, as we discuss, again, later in the book.

5. We have not included this book in our list of research monographs about goth because it is actually about the wider Gothic aesthetic, and only connects to goth culture through the analysis of goth music, and the claim that the Gothic directly inspired goth.
6. We will come back to this point throughout the rest of the book, but especially in the chapter on Whitby Goth Weekend.
7. The Man That Will Not Be Blamed For Nothing were set-up by two stand-up comedians to mock steampunk fetishes about the British Empire, imperialism, and steam technology. They started out playing punk songs about women in goggles, and Isambard Kingdom Brunel. Ironically, they now headline steampunk festivals. We discuss them when we talk about steampunk.

Chapter 3

Constructing a New Theory of Alternativity

Introduction

This is where we do the important theoretical work that allows us to develop a critical lens through which we can make sense of the rest of the book. This short chapter will develop a new theory of alternativity through combining the work of Adorno (1991) and Adorno and Horkheimer (2016), Habermas (1984, 1987), Butler (2006) and Lefebvre (1991, 1996, 2014). While Adorno and Habermas are part of the same Marxist tradition of critical theory, and Butler and Lefebvre belong to a post-Marxist, post-structural epistemology, the four theorists may seem strange combined together. We situate ourselves firmly in the epistemology and ontology of Adorno and Habermas, although we accept that humans can still make choices to resist, even if such resistance is shaped by the power of hegemony. We will show that Butler and Lefebvre offer new theoretical insights into the nature of alternativity, transgression and resistance, which can be added to the Marxist critical theory so long as the epistemological relativism of post-structuralism is not brought with it. This new critical lens will allow us to make sense of the origin and deeds of the goths, and the move from being defined through alternative space to being a commodity, a social media meme and fashion choice. Before we combine them into our theory of alternativity, we will briefly overview each theorist's work and position them with wider debates about modernity and postmodernism.

Adorno and Habermas: Structural Theorists, Structural Theories

Theodor Adorno remains a star around which the planets of social theory and cultural theory orbit (Adorno, 1991, 2002, 2005; Adorno & Horkheimer, 2016). He was one of the founders of the Frankfurt School, which developed critical theory in Germany in the inter-war period. Adorno was a structural Marxist; but unlike Marx, he believed the conditions of modernity had allowed capitalism and fascism to take control of the political sphere through control of the cultural sphere. This is the same control, named hegemony, which Gramsci (1971) was writing about in his *Prison Notebooks*. Both Adorno and Gramsci – and others in the Frankfurt School such as Horkheimer (2013) and Benjamin (2015) – were responding to the rising threat of totalitarianism in their home countries of Germany and Italy, and the failure of the proletariat to rise up against the bourgeois reactionaries of this counter-revolution. For Gramsci, the problem was that the working classes were being fed a diet of lies and propaganda by the state-controlled media. That is, the ruling powers in most modern nation-states were able to shape what their citizens believed about their lives in such a way that the citizens were not aware they were unequal and without power. This hegemony was most obviously represented in the anti-Semitism of the Nazi propaganda, but hegemonic power could make normal and invisible patriotism, racism, the gender order and the monarchy in nations, which claimed to have a free press such as Great Britain (Grant, 1994).

Adorno was interested in how culture operated to make people unfree in modernity. Like Gramsci, he knew his classical literature. He knew that the elites in Classical Greece and Rome maintained their political power over their citizens by learning and perfecting the arts of rhetoric. He knew that Roman rulers at the height of the Republic were told that they had to lavish money on games and donate to public works and temples to prove their benevolence while simultaneously satisfying needs and desires (Dunkle, 2008; Spracklen, 2011). By the time of the Roman Empire, the veil of worthiness around such elite sponsorship of welfare and spectacle had been discarded, and the whole was seen as a way of diverting attention from hegemonic control like the magician's sleight of hand telling the audience to look at the card and not the other card palmed in his hand. With all political power in the hands of the Emperor, there was no space for political discourse, free thinking and disagreement. Juvenal, the Roman satirist, wrote that the people of Rome in his day were happy to be given dole (bread) and entertainment (circuses) as diversions from engaging in political debate (Juvenal, Satire 10.77-81, in Braund, 2004).

Adorno wrote *The Dialectic of Enlightenment* with Horkheimer (Adorno & Horkheimer, 2016) to map out the problem of modernity. The Enlightenment had promised rational solutions to political problems to inequality and social injustice; but in the twentieth century, the rationality of science and technology only seemed to serve capitalist gain and the hegemonic interests of nation-states. Rather than an increase in liberty, equality and fraternity, the modern age had led to increased oppression and constraint, rising inequality, and wars of imperial aggression and state-sanctioned genocide. How had the Enlightenment failed? Adorno and Horkheimer argued that the old elites in the West had made a pact with the new elites of bourgeois capitalism to ensure the continuance of their rule. Modern capitalism in America and Europe, rather than being disassociated with the State and suspicious of its restrictions, worked to ensure the masses were kept in their place through instrumental controls, technological bureaucracies and the cultivation of the culture industry and its technologies: the commodification and commercialisation of art and other cultural forms.

The culture industry was already a sprawling, moneymaking enterprise by the 1940s, when Adorno and Horkheimer were working on their book. The wealth of the West, taken from imperial conquests abroad and the exploitation of workers in mills and factories back home, had led to enormous investment in new science and technology in the nineteenth century. This led to a mass market in cheaply published books, newspapers and magazines. Many of these were radical or stimulating, but most were reactionary in their politics, and salacious in their coverage of crime and sex (Rabinowitz, 2016). The culture industry of the press extended to the theatre through the distribution of crude, populist sheet music, the rise of the music hall and the rise of the actor as celebrity, famed more for their love life than their acting (Inglis, 2010). Music was also being co-opted by the same hegemonic pressure, as Adorno explored in his book on the subject (Adorno, 2016), with the construction of the canon of classical music supposedly indicating high art and authentic art, and the production of popular music as a form of consumption, artifice and simplification. For Adorno, this was a trick of the culture industry on both the bourgeois aesthetes of classical music, and the working classes dancing in their music halls. Classical music's authenticity was constructed by the culture industry to dupe the bourgeoisie, who learned to stay still and silent and associate movement with the brutes of the lower classes. However, Adorno reserved most of his critique for popular music, especially the jazz music that had become popular in the twentieth century, and the music that was broadcast by the new technologies of radio and record to audiences far removed from the music's construction. All this pop music was empty of aesthetic value, and was designed to stimulate raw emotions of happiness and sadness and to stupefy and control.

In a later essay on the culture industry, Adorno (1991, pp. 98–99) writes:

> In all its branches, products which are tailored for consumption by masses. And which to a great extent determine the nature of that consumption, are manufactured more or less according to plan… The customer is not king, as the culture industry would have us believe, not it subject buts object. The very word mass-media, specially honed for the culture industry, already shifts the accent onto harmless terrain… The culture industry misuses its concern for the masses in order to duplicate, reinforce and strengthen their mentality, which it presumes is given and unchangeable.

Many later theorists and researchers in sociology and cultural studies have rejected Adorno's view of the culture industry (Cohen, 1991; Gracyk, 1992; Longhurst, 2007; Redhead, 1997; Thornton, 1995). In popular music studies, for example, people such as Bennett (1999, 2000) want to show that pop music can be meaningful and the site of agency and meaning-making. This is what Hodkinson (2002) thinks about goth – it is something that transcends the Adornian pessimism and takes on pop as hegemonic control. Adorno has been dismissed for being a snob, someone who believes in the authenticity of high culture over low culture (Gracyk, 1992), someone who would rather see children taken to see Sophocles rather than Disneyworld.

We believe there is a great deal of truth in the work of Adorno. It will come as no surprise to those who have read the first author's previous work on leisure (Spracklen, 2006, 2009, 2011, 2015b) to read here that we think Adorno's work is important where it is developed in the theoretical framework of his mentee and colleague, Jürgen Habermas (Habermas, 1984, 1987, 1989, 1990).[1]

Habermas rejected the pessimism of Adorno and believed it was possible to build a better society through democracy, protest and reform – but he agreed with Adorno that elites, in their interests, controlled culture and society in modernity. The point of difference between Adorno and Habermas is histori- cal and philosophical: Habermas accepts that rationality has led to the instru- mentality of modernity and the commodification of culture, but he claims the Enlightenment constructed a public sphere that allowed – and still allows – human agents to think freely about the world and their place in it. There are, then, according to Habermas, two forms of thinking and acting in modernity: communicative and instrumental.

For Habermas (1984), communicative rationality and communicative action are necessary for the construction and maintenance of the lifeworld: the society and culture we choose to create as freethinking, democratic agents. In the public sphere, historically in the Enlightenment, the bourgeoisie then other urban dwell- ers such as the working classes had the opportunity and the freedom to think for themselves (Habermas, 1989). Communicative rationality is the pursuit of think- ing and reason in a free and public debate. In the lifeworld, it becomes possible for every human to be treated equally and for every human to access knowledge and debate things for themselves. In history, we see the Enlightenment lead to a plethora of ideas about how to construct a fairer society, how to improve the world and find out the truth about the universe (Spracklen, 2011). These ideas are freely shared and freely checked by others in the debate. This is how science works and shapes the modern world. It is the way liberal democracy emerges with its bills of rights and checks and balances between interests. In the lifeworld, it is communicatively rational to arrange our culture and out leisure in the ways in which we desire them. Communicative rationality, then, leads to communicative action and free choice in the things we do when we are not working. Communica- tive rationality is predicated on discourse and interaction, with rules of fair play and equality, but communicative action does not always have be so ethically and politically charged.

Habermas takes his account of the unfortunate consequences of the Enlight- enment from Adorno and Horkheimer. What is crucial in the narrative Haber- mas (1989) develops is the evolution of the modern state and all its failings from the public sphere. That is, historically the public sphere sows the seeds of its own demise because it allows the modern state to appear, which destroys or sub- verts the public sphere. The Enlightenment set the stage for the removal of the old elites associated with Christianity, kings and feudalism. The Enlightenment nurtured the interests of new bourgeois elites in towns and cities, and led to the rise and growth of science, technology, industry and capitalism. The Enlighten- ment then, led to the construction of new ways of thinking, what Habermas (1984, 1987) identifies as instrumentality, following Weber (1964), or instrumen- tal rationality. The communicative rationality of the public sphere and science, the reason that leads to science and the nation-state, becomes instrumental in its logic. In the period of high and late modernity at the end of the nineteenth- century Habermas (1984, 1987) shows that two ways of thinking instrumentally become dominant. The first is the construction of bureaucracies in governments, which turn people into passive citizens receiving orders and being monitored by security agencies. The second form of instrumentality at work is the reduction of all social activity and moral value to the bottom-line of an accounting ledger. In this world of what we might now call neo-liberalism, capitalist corporations become as powerful as – then more powerful than – nation-states. In this stage of modernity, capitalism and the pursuit of profit and growth are the only things that matter to policy-makers, and in this state the lifeworld of human action is in real danger of being colonised by instrumental rationality (Habermas, 1984, 1987, 1990). In this state of modernity, the nation-state uses all its powers of surveillance to ensure its citizens consume and take part as rational actors in the free market, but any attempt to build communal, social or communicative spaces is discouraged. People who try to resist the market and the instrumental logic of popular culture are often made illegal or suppressed, but in the global North they are tolerated but marginalised.

With only the pessimism of Adorno about the fakeness of the culture industry, and its role in disciplining and controlling the masses, we would have to view goth and alternativity more broadly as a con. We would have to say that the idea of being alternative is a trick of instrumental logic: people buy their goth identity and feel like they are individuals, but they are not making any real choice except, perhaps, over whether to buy the New Rocks or an imitation model. Worse, we would have to say that there is no possible space for goth to be an alternative or counter culture, that it was – and can only ever be – part of the machinery that enslaves us and fools us into thinking we have power and agency over our leisure lives. However, with the alignment of our theoretical framework with Habermas, we can suggest that goth may be something that is freely chosen as an expression of communicative rationality, a form of resistance to define and protect the life-world. That resistance and agency may have been shaped by the history of the culture industry and the rise of instrumentality; it may or may not be completely lost by the commodification of goth, and the commodification of alternativity (as we will explore more fully towards the end of the book) – but that counter-hegemonic resistance may still shape the meaning and purpose of goth history and goth culture.

Butler and Lefebvre: Post-Structural Theorists, Post-Structural Theories

Adorno and Habermas have come to be labelled as structural Marxists because they believed in reason and our ability to make sense of the history and evolution of society. They believed that class structures define the tensions of modern society, and believed it was possible and necessary for sociologists to identify the hidden hands that controlled the world. They were strongly criticised in the 1970s through to the 2000s by a range of philosophers and sociologists – nearly all French – who loosely aligned with what we call post-structuralism. Derrida (1976) argued that it was impossible to read the true meaning of any text, and argued that the social world and the natural world were just different kinds of text. Lyotard (1984) said that social structures had dissolved as society entered the post-modern condition. Foucault (2002) argued that meaning in history and in science could only ever be partial, and was always the subject of power struggles. Latour (1987) suggested that nature was the consequence of consensus in science, not the arbiter of scientific debate, suggesting that all scientific knowledge is socially constructed. Bauman (1992) in his postmodern phase argued that society had become fluid as modernity entered postmodernity, or what he later called liquid modernity (Bauman, 2000): the end of class divisions, the rise of global flows and the decline of the industrial base in the West. Some of this post-structural argument came from the philosophy of science, where the case for scientific realism and the scientific method was attacked by the work of Kuhn (1962) and Feyerabend (1975).

For a period in time, Habermas fought back against the rise of un-reason and irrationality. He did not believe that it was impossible to find the truth, or that every person's truth is equally valid. It was demonstrably false to believe these things, and he accused post-structuralism and postmodernism for being distractions from fighting for social justice in the world (Habermas, 1981, 1990). In consequence, many post-structuralists attacked Habermas, using *ad hominem* arguments commenting on him for clinging to out-moded, Eurocentric notions of truth, and the name of the Enlightenment became a sneer of contempt (Bauman, 1992). Therefore, it may seem strange that we are about to connect his ideas to two of the post-structuralists. However, it is necessary if we are to understand transgression and space. Foucault (1973, 2006) argued that madness and transgression were cultural constructions, products of the increasing scientisation and rationalisation of modern life. For Foucault, and for radical psychologists such as Laing (1990), there was no real deviance, no real mental health problems. These mental problems were only a failure of modern nation-states to recognise (or allow) the diversity of human thought and human behaviour. Other academics started to use these insights to explore the construction of deviance and transgression, and the importance of such behaviour in the development of human beings.

Judith Butler is our first important post-structural theorist. Her work on gender and performativity (Butler, 2006) has been very influential among sociologists, cultures studies researchers and others interested in sex and sexuality (in leisure studies, for example, see Williams, 2009). Butler's theories build on the idea of performance, associated with Goffman's (1971). He argued that individuals follow scripts and stage directions to perform social identity. Butler suggests that gender is itself a performance and it cannot be anything else other than something performed by individuals. Drawing on radical feminist theories, Butler shows that the hegemonic power of heterosexual men is expressed through the performance of heteronormativity. This performance is undertaken by men and by women. For men, being heteronormative is to play a traditionally dominant role, stereotypically articulated through masculine sports and leisure pursuits such as watching football, shooting guns and drinking beer. For women, heteronormativity is to play a traditionally subservient role, domestic, private, being pleasing to men and allowing men to have their fun. Where Butler differs from radical feminist theory is in her belief in the power of individual agency to undermine such performativity. It is perfectly possible, she claims, for individuals to transgress this heteronormative order. Butler uses drag as an example of such transgression: homosexual men and women can and do subvert heteronormative performances by playing grotesque caricatures of the other gender, so lesbian drag-kings, for example, smoke pipes and wear moustaches, and drag-queens hide behind garish make-up, boas and sequins.

Butler is undoubtedly a post-structuralist. Her work draws heavily on the post-structural psychodynamics of Lacan (2007), who brings Freudian theory into postmodern theory. Butler is post-structural feminist because she believes the gender order is not fixed. Women, men and transpeople have the ability to transgress heteronormativity, so they have the ability to use their agency resist the gender order. Alternativity for Butler is transgression of what is considered acceptable, the norms and values of the mainstream. The performance of alternativity has transformative, counter-hegemonic potential.

Henri Lefebvre is the second post-structuralist[2] from whose work we want to draw some key ideas. Lefebvre wrote extensively across a range of sociological fields, but we want to take two of his contributions into our new theory of alternativity. First, Lefebvre argues that sociologist have downplayed the importance of everyday life as a site for social control and social activism. In *The Critique of Everyday Life*, he attempts to undertake a critical theory of everyday life, and shows through his analysis how the un-importance of everyday life such as leisure and popular culture actually makes it very important: everyday life is a formal space where capitalism operates to keep people in their place in society, and where people can try to find meaning after the existentialist crisis of alienation in modernity (Lefebvre, 2014). So being a goth, that is, being alternative, might be a way of finding meaning in this capitalist world.

The second contribution that interests us is hinted at in the last paragraph: Lefebvre's argument in *The Production of Space* that space is only ever understood as a social construction. Humans make spaces through deciding what they mean, the rules of entry, and through defining the symbols that define the boundaries of any given space. Historically, Lefebvre sees different modes of production constructing different forms of space – this spatialisation reaches its apogee with urbanism and the rise of modern society. At this point, capitalism shapes spaces in cities to more efficiently bring raw material and workers to factories, and to take finished goods to markets (Lefebvre, 1991). In the post-structural and post-industrial space of contemporary society, we can see how spaces are increasingly controlled and privatised by nation-states concerned with disorder, and for the benefit of capitalist elites who want to extract profit from those spaces by any means necessary (Elden, 2004; Spracklen & Lamond, 2016). What Lefbevre does is to provide the tools for scholars in critical urban studies and cultural geographies to question the idea that space is simply something objective and material. In our work on Leeds (Spracklen, Richter, & Spracklen, 2013), for example, we explore how alternative spaces have become privatised and eventised, and how alternative people have been forced to the margins of the city centre.

A New Theory of Alternativity

We are explicitly aligned with the Frankfurt School and their critical reading of Marx. To paraphrase Marx, we believe that history and social structures shape and limit our world and our choices; but as humans, we still have the desire to make free choices – and sometimes we can make them. We situate ourselves firmly in the epistemology and ontology of Adorno and Habermas, although we accept that humans can still make choices to resist, even if such resistance is shaped by the hegemonic powers of global capitalism and nation-states. Taking the ontology of Adorno, we admit that the culture industry is all-powerful, and its historical development shows how any alternative culture is swiftly co-opted, commodified and discarded as an unfashionable relic. Popular music, of which goth is one sub-genre, is a key space for the reproduction of hegemony in popular culture, and it is easy to dismiss alternative music sub-cultures as examples of Adorno's epistemological argument about *ersatz*, artificial forms of rebellion.

However, we believe, following Habermas, that there is another way of looking at the alternative in popular culture. Habermas tells us that communicative rationality and communicative action are possible even in the contemporary world, though such free and democratic agency is marginalised by the rise of the instrumentality of global capitalism and modern nation-states. This communicative action operates to maintain the life-world, the space in which we are free to be human and thrive in the Aristotelian sense. Alternativity has always been a way of expressing communicative rationality – rejecting the system, resisting the gender order, transgressing norms and values – and in history, we can see alternative counter-cultures serving to maintain and sustain the life-world of the public sphere, whether that was the radical Jacobins of the Enlightenment (Israel, 2001) or the hippies and punks of the twentieth century (Hebdige, 1979). Alternativity in its authentic form, then, has to be communicative, not instrumental.

Butler and Lefebvre offer new theoretical insights into the communicative nature of authentic alternativity, transgression and resistance. Butler allows us to think of being alternative as a *political performance*, a form of direct action where alternativity is made visible and public as challenge to the instrumentality of the mainstream. Lefebvre allows us to see that communicative alternativity is a form that is made in everyday life and in public spaces, and in the public sphere, so that the liminal coming to the centre challenges the spatialisation of global capitalism. Butler and Lefebvre's ideas can be easily added to our Adornian–Habermasian critical theory so long as the epistemological relativism of post-structuralism is not brought with it. We do not believe there is any paradox in this – Butler and Lefebvre wanted to be able to challenge the gender order, the mainstream and capitalism, so they are part of the critical tradition stretching back to Marx. This critical lens of communicative alternativity as authentic, and instrumental authenticity as part of the culture industry, is new, and our contribution to social and cultural theory. It allows us to make sense of the origin and deeds of the goths, and the move from being defined through alternative space to being a commodity, a social media meme and fashion choice. We will start to explore the tension between the two models of alternativity in our history and sociology of goth, which is the topic of the rest of the book from the next chapter onwards.

Notes

1. Part of the following discussion of Habermas is based on Spracklen (2017a).
2. Although Lefebvre distanced himself from post-structuralism, he was one of the main instigators of the post-structural turn in French social and cultural theory (Elden, 2004).

Chapter 4

The Origin of the Goths

Introduction

In a feature written by Alex Ogg for *The Quietus* on 8 April 2009 (Ogg, 2009), Ian Astbury, the singer in Southern Death Cult, says:

> It was (NME writer) David Dorrell, later manager of Bush, who was the instigator [of the term goth]. It came from Andi of Sex Gang Children. He lived in this Victorian apartment block in Brixton. We referred to him as Count Visigoth and his followers, the gothic hordes. And Dave Dorrell was around Brixton at the time, and it kind of became a joke. Just sort of teasing Andi, because he had the curtains drawn all the time and was always wearing a Chinese robe. At that time you would see girls with teased black hair, occasionally you'd see a girl wearing bat earrings or something, principally followers of Siouxsie And The Banshees, and that's what it derived from. And then I think David wrote an article referring to 'goth' in that way. That was pretty much it. Anything that looked dark with spiky hair was called goth.

Ogg's (2009) article is an extended interview with Mick Mercer, taken on the occasion of the publication of *Music to Die For* (Mercer, 2009). We assume the quote is from Mercer's archives, and in the article, Ogg suggests the quote and others like it comes from that book. However, we have read the book very carefully and cannot find the quote. But we trust Ogg not to have made up the quote as he was a key figure in punk and post-punk fanzines, and has become an academic scholar of punk and post-punk. If he says Mercer gave him the quote, we believe him – and we trust Mercer to have interviewed Astbury around the time he was researching the 2009 book, even if he did not end up using that quote in the published version.

Astbury's origin narrative basically says the goth name started out as a joke comparing the hangers-on surrounding Andi from Sex Gang Children with the 'gothic hordes' of the first-millennium, barbarian kind. These hordes are described as following Andi, who Astbury claims was nick-named 'Count Visigoth', another reference to the barbarian Goths. Astbury then tells us that a journalist used the joke 'goth' name in an article, thus creating from a bad joke a serious music culture. The date is uncertain but it must have been some time in 1981 or 1982. This chapter deals with the complex history of the invention of the goths. We approach this origin story through the memories of our respondents and the wider goth community, as well as through popular narratives. We will use these multiple data sources from our research to sketch out the origin of the goth scene in Britain in the late 1970s and early 1980s. As with the barbarian Goths of the first millennium, we will show that the new goths were partly defined by their supporters, and partly by their distractors. That is, we will show that the genesis of the goth scene was partly a result of musicians thinking about how to be alternative and real, and partly a result of promoters and journalists seeking to label 'new' music and scenes. We will situate goth in the post-punk music scene in the United Kingdom, as a radical musical counter-culture committed to radical politics. To begin the history, it is necessary to explore punk, and what came to be known as post-punk.

Punk Rock as Year Zero, Post-Punk as the Morning After

Punk has been the subject of an enormous range of academic and popular literature. It is so important to the history of rock that entire academic networks exist to critically assess the importance of punk in history and culture, and the journal *Punk and Post-Punk* is dedicated to research on punk. There are essentially two historiographies of punk. The first is the kind written by journalists such as Burchill and Parsons, writing and reflecting during the period (1978); however, it is also present in some punk scholarship studies today. Punk is seen as a great cleanser in British rock, a rejection by the youth of Britain of an older generation's fake values. In its early seventies form, punk stood against the overly fanciful tunes of progressive rock, against the laziness of transatlantic cock-rock bands and their drug-addled superstars (Bestley, 2011; Savage, 2002). Punk rejects the falseness and pacifism of the hippie movement, and insists on honesty, self-expression and activism. Its politics swings from anarchism and socialism to libertarianism and fascism – what these have in common is a rejection of the mainstream consensus of 1970s popular culture and politics in the United Kingdom. Punk in this mythology is fundamentally about the individual standing up and speaking out against the mainstream: punk is communicatively rational, and forms a communicative alternativity that represents a complete rejection of that mainstream (Bestley, 2011).

The second type of punk historiography argues that the dramatic disjuncture with the past does not fit the facts of the bands and youth movements that preceded punk, and the sub-cultural resistance in punk was always subject to takeover and commodification (Hebdige, 1979; Savage, 2002). There are clear links between punk in the United Kingdom and the bands of the pub-rock scene, bands playing simple pop songs loud and fast (Frith, 1986, 1998). There are clear links between punk in the United States of America and earlier scenes and bands (such as The Stooges) associated with bikers and other 'deviant' sub-cultures (Frith, 1998). The ideology of rejecting the mainstream and working independently of the music industry is something already present in the counter-cultural movement in both countries. In this regard, bands such as Hawkwind and The Pink Fairies were involved in what punks would identify as their own Do-It-Yourself or DIY culture: running free or low-priced festivals and gigs; printing their own flyers and posters and encouraging the production of fanzines (Bestley, 2011; Triggs, 2006).

Related to these second types of historiography are those that suggest punk was not a great break with the mainstream at all, that is, punk was constructed, or at least shaped and promoted, in the mainstream culture industry (Adorno, 1991; Hebdige, 1979). Punk started out as a loose network of journalists, label managers and promoters looking to find the next new thing to make money from, something such networks had always searched for in pop and rock music since the construction of the culture industry (Fraser & Fuoto, 2011). The small number of punk bands and their fanzine-editing supporters were found as the next big thing and projected in the music press, the national newspapers and television as that next big thing (Savage, 2002). The thrill of rebellion exemplified by The Sex Pistols singing about 'the fascist regime' over heavy guitar chords ensured that punk was identified with by millions of youthful listeners fed up with the norms and values of Western society. Those who argue that punk was transformative, or truly counter-hegemonic and communicative, generally accept that it was swiftly commodified when bands such as The Damned, The Sex Pistols and The Clash signed big-money deals and engaged in the behaviours and practices of every mainstream rock and pop band despised by the first generation of punks. One way to deal with this was to accept it and see punk as one other form of rock music, one that performed a certain musical style, alongside a strong DIY aesthetic and some radical politics central to song lyrics and press interviews. Another way to deal with the corporate takeover of punk was to retreat into the fanzines and the DIY counter-culture entirely, rejecting offers of deals and the payola of the industry to have complete control of records and gigs, as typified by Crass in the United Kingdom (Dunn, 2012). The third way was to find a new sound and a new look, based in the radical ideology of punk: this is what has become known as post-punk (Crossley, 2015).

There are a number of related themes in the emergence of post-punk. Firstly, the first post-punk bands were searching for new sounds. Digital synthesisers had become widely available in the late 1970s, and drum machines quickly followed with, for example, the Roland TR-808 being released in 1980 (Wang, 2014). A wide range of pop music genres adopted these two technologies because they allowed artists and producers more control over live and studio performances. Digital synthesisers allowed one keyboard player to reproduce a multitude of instruments, and to create new sounds and effects (Fraser & Fuoto, 2014). Drum machines solved the ongoing problem of finding drummers who could be accurate in every performance space, and allowed artists to be more flexible about how they composed new songs. Many post-punk bands and artists embraced these technologies, and what was at the time called New Wave typified by Gary Numan and the Tubeway Army. Others in the search for a new sound in post-punk went the other way and tried to find musical inspiration in previous musical genres or musical spaces; thus, Southern Death Cult explored tribal drumming and rhythms; the Mekons moved towards folk and Americana over a period of time; and Siouxsie and the Banshees tapped into the sound-scapes of The Velvet

Underground for their debut album. The Banshees could embrace this art-music because post-punk rehabilitated some of the music that punk had disowned. What counted as proper music was music written and performed by artists who were rebels in their own spaces, and post-punk could use any musical influence if the ideological case could be made to the listeners. So, the debut album of The Cure is able to have a cover of arch-hippie Jimi Hendrix's 'Foxy Lady' because they make it sound like something completely new and dangerous.

The second theme associated with post-punk is its emergence as a clear and distinct youth sub-culture, with its own fashions. As explored in the outstanding book *Some Wear Leather, Some Wear Lace* (Harriman & Bontje, 2014), the post-fashion aesthetic was something that is undoubtedly a formative influence on the look of what we think of as goth, especially eighties goth; for example, the women have make-up that copies and adopts the look of Siouxsie from the Banshees, and have combed-back, black or multi-coloured hair; they are dressed at times in black, with goth-like frills and lace accessories, though they wear a wide range of colours and styles. Post-punk crossed over with the theatricality of the New Romantics, and both scenes allowed men to wear make-up and dress in extravagant costumes in public. Post-punk became a way of dressing and performing in an alternative style. As most of the contributors to the *Some Wear Leather, Some Wear Lace* collection point out, the clothes they wore were generally adapted at home by family members, or by themselves: this was not a sub-cultural aesthetic bought from a high street or shopping mall.

The third theme associated with post-punk was a continued commitment to the radical politics of punk. The Mekons and Gang of Four, both formed in Leeds in 1977 by students who knew each other very well, are widely recognised as two of the most important bands in the British post-punk scene, gaining global fame at the time (Brown, 2015b). They are both still well-known today, and have continued to perform and release albums (although with different line-ups), and continue to innovate (especially The Mekons, as already mentioned above). When they were first being noticed on the local scene and in fanzines, they were uncompromising in their left-wing, radical politics. Both groups wrote songs with uncompromising radical messages against the inequity of modern society. Inevitably, their reputation grew and they found themselves facing the question about selling out. In an article[1] and interview with Jon King and Andy Gill (the key music-makers in Gang of Four at the time) called 'Gang of Four: Dialectics Meet Disco' (Mary Harron, *Melody Maker*, 26 May 1979), they justify signing to a major label:[2]

> Neither Jon or Andy talks much about specific political issues, and I don't think even they are sure if they are Marxists or not. Where Marxism – or, rather, Marxist aesthetics – do operate is in their attitude to rock. Andy says, 'It's not a group's function just to be entertaining. A group should entertain and try and change things. You can't change the actual status quo, the power structures, but you can change the way people think'. They do not mean by shouting political slogans, because that doesn't

change the way people think, but through music that disrupts conventional attitudes and ways of seeing. In March the Gang Of Four signed a record contract with EMI, who are certainly pillars of capitalism. The Gang Of Four say that as all record companies are part of the same system, you might as well sign with one that can pay you the £30 a week it takes to live. They had reached the stage where they could hardly afford to go on without a contract, but in any case, signing with a big label fits in perfectly well with what the Gang Of Four are trying to do, which is to channel revolutionary messages through a capitalist medium. This, of course is not easy to do. Shortly after signing, the Gang Of Four had a conflict amongst themselves – and with the company – over what the single should be. The obvious choice for airplay was 'Waiting For My Elevator' which is a wonderful jump-up-and rock 'n' roll song, but not particularly representative of what the Gang Of Four are trying to do. Andy Gill said at the time that he was alarmed at how easy it was to rationalise this choice in terms of ideology, on the grounds that it would break them into the market and they could then use this to get their message through. Eventually they decided on 'At Home He Thinks He's A Tourist', which is more musically adventurous – thus providing an example of how attitudes that belong to art can benefit rock.

The Mekons signed to Virgin for their 1979 debut album, and similar arguments about the need to subvert capitalism from within were made by them and their supporters. Both bands continued to try to act as fairly as possible, performing social justice through their support of left-wing political campaigns and by refusing to compromise for Establishment censors, such as the moment Gang of Four walked out of the BBC television show *Top of the Pops* when the producers tried to get them to change the lyrics of 'At Home...'. Post-punk, then, stuck to the individualism of punk, but grafted to it a radical, Marxist (or post-Marxist: Kruse, 1983) ideology: using music to challenge capitalism, performing solidarity and communality, and embracing the view that being alternative to the system – religion, capitalism, the State, the West, the culture industry – was the only option. It was in this post-punk space that goth was constructed.

The First Goths

The Cure, Siouxsie and the Banshees, Joy Division and Killing Joke

We have already mentioned about The Cure and Siouxsie and the Banshees. Both bands were post-punk, and interested in experimentation and progression. Both became bands strongly associated with goth rock in the 1980s, as witnessed in all the popular literature of the first generation (Mercer, 1988; Scharf, 2011;

Thompson, 2007). Their singers, Robert Smith and Siouxsie Sioux, have literally been goth rock pin-ups. The two bands recorded a number of key albums
in the late 1970s and 1980s that have come to define the goth-rock sound. They
toured together, and Smith even played guitar for the Banshees, so their fan base
was essentially the same group of post-punks finding solace in their dark performances. Carpenter (2012, p. 30) cites a review in by Nick Kent in *New Musical
Express* as proof that:

> The Banshees were labeled 'gothic' almost from the start. A July
> 1978 review of a Banshees gig in London unequivocally consid-
> ers the band gothic, and regards them as kindred spirits with cer-
> tain proto-gothic bands: '[p]arallels and comparisons can now be
> drawn with gothic rock architects like the Doors and, certainly,
> early Velvet Underground'.

It has to be noted that at this point, the description 'gothic rock' points to a
sound the journalist thinks he has heard in The Doors and The Velvet Underground – music that is undoubtedly dark, but not very gothic. But the point is this:
in 1978, well before the story of goth being invented in 1981/1982 as a joke by Ian
Astbury on a journalist, there is a feeling that some post-punk bands are invent-
ing a dark aesthetic and a dark sound, coupled with strongly romantic or morose
lyrics. In this period, The Banshees and The Cure are selling records to a new
generation of people who want to be identified as something alternative, something true to the alienation felt by punks and post-punks. When The Cure borrow
from Camus's (1946) classic tale of existential crisis in their first single 'Killing An
Arab' at the end of 1978, they are voicing the angst felt by their keen listeners. In
Camus's story, there is nothing else, no hope of any feeling of emotional resolu-
tion, no chance to be human for Meursault other than killing someone.

More evidence that 1978/1979 is a key moment in the invention of goth is
the rapid rise to prominence of Joy Division. This Manchester-based band, led
by Ian Curtis before he committed suicide in 1980, was ensured a notoriety and
afterlife because of that tragic act, and because it was the band from which New
Order arose (Crossley, 2015; Fraser & Fuoto, 2014). But they were already well-
known and receiving critical acclaim before Curtis died. In 1979, they released
their debut album Unknown Pleasures, and Max Bell in *New Musical Express* on
14 July 1979 reviews it as follows:

> Never funny peculiar, funny ha-ha or clever-clever – the lot of most
> of the bands trying to slip into the current avant-garde – their music
> clearly fuses all the frayed ends with a new, unforced simplicity, a
> direction beyond expectancy. Joy Division's atmosphere is uncom-
> fortably claustrophobic in meaning, but its structures and dynam-
> ics are accessible. Although the band and their producer Martin
> Hannett have constructed something memorably psychotic, I'd
> hesitate to linger on their background of mental institutions and
> the vocabulary of the psychologist – for fear of encouraging images

of contrived banshee rant and postured metal machine thrashing, all of which has its place but is not the guiding experience here. Joy Division music worries and nags like the early excursions of the better known German experimentalists. Investigate these confined spaces, these insides of cages, this outside of insanity. They all bring to mind endless corridors where doors clank open and shut on an infinite emotional obstacle course ... The root causes of Curtis' lyrical 'insights' – industrial and urban decay – are ignored in favour of the end result; the noises are human and the effect is shattering, literally... In many other hands Joy Division's relentless litanies would appear pompous, tasteless or just plain vicarious; The Sex Pistols, for example, turned out to be all three. But Joy Division are treading a different tightrope; what carries their extraordinary music beyond despair is its quality of vindication.

This sounds like what goth rock claims to be, although Bell did not use the word. Bell tries to reference what this is related to (art music, alienation), and what it is not (punk, contrived posturing, 'thrashing' and 'banshee' rants). This is gothic post-punk. Later that year, in a feature on Joy Division's label Factory Records written by Mary Harron (*Melody Maker*, 29 September 1979), gothic finally emerges in print sounding something like it is still understood in relation to goth rock:[3]

> [Joy Division's] songs are a series of disconnected images; Ian Curtis says he writes the lyrics to an imaginary film. The purpose of this surrealistic montage is not to convey a message, but to arouse strange feelings. One clue to Joy Division lies in their album's title. Another is the description given by Martin Hannett, who calls them 'dancing music, with gothic overtones'. Unintentionally, Bernard Albrecht gave an excellent description of 'gothic' in our interview, when describing his favourite film, Nosferatu. 'The atmosphere is really evil, but you feel comfortable inside it.' All the fear and excitement of a nightmare, with the comfort of being awake. 19th Century gothic tales used ruined castles and vampires as symbols of vague subconscious terrors. Joy Division are 20th Century gothic, and their images of assassins, imprisonment, pursuit, draw off the modern nightmare. To me, it's the totalitarian state.

Joy Division's music is described as 'gothic' by their producer, Martin Hammett, who is the person responsible for the bleakness of the sound. The person who handily supplies a definition of 'gothic' is Bernard Albrecht, otherwise known as Bernard Sumner, the guitarist of Joy Division, which forever links goth with Nosferatu and horror films more generally with their shared uncanny feeling. But it is Harron, the author, who provides more considered critique. For her, Joy Division do not represent the Romantic stereotypes of the nineteenth-century

Gothic revival. This is modern gothic, that is, to make sense of and fight against the evils of capitalism and over-powerful nation states. This is goth: beyond punk and fighting the radical cause of the alternative against the mainstream.

Joy Division's second album *Closer* was released in July 1980, months after Curtis's suicide. The album became a huge hit and served as a fitting finale to the band, and an emotional tribute to the singer. The mainstream media started to take an interest in this gloomy post-punk, indie goth-rock movement, but no had yet defined the entire movement as goth – although Carpenter (2012) notes that Bauhaus's music was described as 'gothick' in the music press in that year. As people were coming to terms with the end of Joy Division, Killing Joke released their self-titled debut album in August. The band's key members were all left-wing radicals, inspired by punk and aligning their lyrics to punk's rejection of mainstream politics and the evils of modernity. The debut album's cover was a black-and-white picture taken by famous war photographer, Don McCullin, of rioters fleeing an attack by the British Army in Northern Ireland. Killing Joke were not yet defined as gothic, and there is a strong debate to be had about whether they were ever goth or gothic at all – but the album caught the twentieth-century gothic mood of the time. The album is existential art, the communicative alternativity trying to fight the all-powerful system. The post-punk sound-scape in the debut album, the speed-drenched rage of the lyrics, the mournful guitar, and the almost machine-like rhythm section, points to what goth rock was about to be defined.

Bauhaus

Bauhaus formed in 1978 in Northampton, fronted by charismatic Pete Murphy. Their first single, 'Bela Lugosi's Dead', was released in August 1979, and has since become a song identified as the first goth rock song. As Hodkinson (2002, p. 36) describes it, after skirting through Joy Division and Siouxsie and the Banshees:

> The most important starting point for goth, however, was probably provided by the images and sounds of Bauhaus – notably the single 'Bela Lugosi's Dead… The performance of this song, and indeed much of the band's set, contained most of the distinctive themes which still pervade the goth scene, rom macabre funereal musical tone and tempo, to lyrical references to the undead, to deep-voiced eerie vocals, to a dark twisted form of androgyny in the appearance of the band and most of its following.

Carpenter (2012) is strongly critical of Hodkinson and the popular writers who pin-point the song as the *primum movens* of goth rock. Although the song references the actor who became famous for his portrayal of Count Dracula, and it was marketed with a gloomy cover, Carpenter argues the song remains fixed in post-punk experimentation and the desire to be novel and authentic. He uses interviews with the band and musicological analysis to show that the song was situated in the glam rock of Gary Glitter, and the reaction of the post-punks who started to follow Bauhaus forced Murphy to adopt a 'gothic' stage presence. Carpenter (2012, p. 42) ends his analysis by asking:

> How did 'Bela Lugosi's Dead' became the 'ground zero' of gothic rock? While Bauhaus may not have intended to give birth to gothic rock, its musical and visual tropes may indeed have made it inevitable that the band, with Bela Lugosi as its vampire mascot, would be identified as the first gothic band; certainly, one could argue that Bauhaus was the genre's first 'star' act. In the end, as Peter Murphy recalls, the members of Bauhaus played the role of gothic rockers for their audience, and, for both the fans and the band, the vampire-as-rock-star identity – an alluring if paradoxical blend of glam and gloom, forged in the kitschy gravitas of 'Bela Lugosi's Dead' – was authentic and definitive: 'If taking on this Nosferatu role on the stage were not real to us', asks Murphy rhetorically, 'then how could it have been to the audience?'

A love of gothic horror and vampires was not something new in popular music. Black Sabbath famously named themselves after a horror film, and spawned a long line of heavy metal bands inspired by all aspects of horror from Satanic black magic to the cartoon-like monsters of American television and movies (Weinstein, 1991). In America, the Misfits formed one year before Bauhaus and made a series of singles and albums combining punk with bats, vampires and the undead, in a genre they dubbed 'horror punk'. Bauhaus may well have seen the Misfits and copied their proto-goth combination of corpse paint, dark eye make-up and black clothes with skeletons. The song 'Bela Lugosi's Dead' is clearly inspired by the same American horror popular culture that inspired the Misfits. Bauhaus may have not noticed the Misfits at all, and it was just a happy coincidence their song was recorded after the Misfits changed their image. Bauhaus became popular very quickly, and broke up under the pressures of that fame in 1983. They never wrote anything as cartoonishsly grotesque as 'Bela Lugosi's Dead' again, but it remained the crowd-pleaser; everybody knew the song. But even as early as 1980, their live shows were challenging the punks who were watching with scorn and suspicion the band's uncompromising alternativity. Phil Sutcliffe, in *Sounds*, 24 May 1980, wrote (Sutcliffe, 1980):

> The band, who I'd never seen before, have an aggressively weird stage act using lots of make-up, freak hairstyles and darkness cut by strobes, back-lighting and a floodlight occasionally fired at the audience. I didn't exactly cotton on to what their intentions were but I expect you could say broadly they were artistic or stylistic. A large and active section of the audience, skin/punk crossovers in appearance, weren't into such sophistication though. They took everything personally, i.e., if they didn't fancy the look or the sound of the group they wanted to hurt someone – if no musician

came to hand, well, the nearest person in the crowd who wasn't actually a close friend would do ... So Bauhaus didn't have a particularly happy night – though whether their problems were caused by 'integrity' or bad judgment I'm not too sure. They began quite encouragingly ... There was that four-square drumbeat, the bare bones of a scratching rhythm guitar once in a while twanging a lead line of such garage simplicity it took me back to the Ventures ... Over these spartan outlines singer Peter Murphy gave vent to a voice of operatic bravura, approximately Tito Gobbi meets Iggy Pop. It was an interesting sound (gaudy-ghoulie rock?) and I could have been a lot more fascinated if I'd been catching more than the odd snatch of their allegedly well-wrought lyrics ... this was where the twats opened up with the spit and water pistols. And I don't think Murphy advanced the cause of civilisation by exchanging insults and threatening them with the mike stand. By the end of a lengthy 'Bela Lugosi's Dead' he was soaked and in danger of being stiffed himself by an electric shock.

While Bauhaus were in the process of defining goth rock, it was being rejected by the more fundamentalist punks: the skinhead-punks who just wanted to spit and to fight. Goth rock was already becoming something constructed by those who rallied against it as much as supported it: just like the original Goths, gothnness was defined by insiders and by outsiders in a shared process of boundary construction. The reporter in this review still is not convinced he is watching goth rock, but his term for it is fairly close. Joy Division, Killing Joke and Bauhaus in 1980 are all defining goth rock and being watched by young people who want to be like Meaursault, who want to reject modernity, the norms and values of their parents, and the foolishness of the Cold War and the threat of Nuclear Holocaust. Other musicians, along with people who want to be musicians and who are realising this movement is important, are also watching the bands in 1980. The Sisters of Mercy were formed in Leeds in that year. We devote an entire chapter to The Sisters of Mercy, but we will also bring them into the story in the next two chapters. The Sisters of Mercy came out of the F-Club, and this the most important space where goth was formed, defined and limited.

The F-Club, John Keenan and Futurama

The F-Club and the Futurama festival, both set up and run by Leeds promoter, John Keenan, have become entrenched in the shared memory of post-punks and goths as spaces where goth rock was born in the form it is now known. In this extract from a blog[4] by fan, The Sisters of Mercy, Futurama and F-Club are reconstructed as spaces in which The Sisters of Mercy (TSOM in the blog) and goth emerged as if by magic:

Of all the TSOM [*sic.*] gigs played in their maiden year as a 'live' band in 1981, by far and away the most populous and important was Futurama 3, the third edition of the 'World's First Science Fiction Music Festival', the first two versions of which had been staged in Leeds's cavernous and dilapidated Queen's Hall in the preceding years. Organised by legendary Leeds promoter John F Keenan, who was the man behind the seminal late 70's F Club punk gigs where Eldritch met Marx, and who still organises gigs in the city to this day, the third edition of Futurama took place in the slightly incongruous surroundings of Bingley Hall, Stafford. I got in touch with John Keenan and asked him about the change of venue from the previous years, and he told me that the move had not been intentional. 'The 1980 Futurama was very success-ful, and I was looking forward to establishing the event. Unfortu-nately, I went on holiday after the show to wind down for a while. When I came back, John Curd, a promoter from London, had booked the Queen's Hall for the following September with a copy-cat, two-day indie festival called "Daze of Future Past". It was my first introduction to the unscrupulous world of the music business. It took me a lot of ringing around to find another venue. It was an enjoyable event, fun to do, but with all the messing about it didn't make any money. Eventually, John Curd's company, "Straight Music" (ha!), went bust and I moved back to the Queen's Hall in 1983'. Early adverts for the gig fail to list TSOM amongst the par-ticipants, as they were a late addition to the bill, but later posters and flyers did indeed list them, and ... they had a half-hour mid-afternoon slot many hours before the big names (Theatre of Hate, Bauhaus, Gang of Four, all of whom ironically were also to go on to appear at the 'Daze...' event) took to the stage on Saturday 5th September 1981. Again John Keenan can clear up the mystery of the band's last-minute appearance on the programme: 'Andy and Craig were friends of mine, I used to see them every week at the F Club. When I first started compiling the 1981 festival, they weren't ready. Nearer the date they came and asked if I could put them on, and I fitted them onto the bill.'

This micro-history tells us everything important about the F-Club in the gene-sis of goth rock. The blogger tells us John Keenan was very cannily nurturing two of the members of The Sisters of Mercy (Andrew Taylor, aka Andrew Eldritch, and Craig Adams). They were his friends, and he was waiting until they had prac-tised enough and had the right songs before he would allow them onto the bill of his Futurama festival. The blogger tells us that Andrew Eldritch had met Gary Marx, the other co-founder of the band, at the F-Club. The blogger then gets an insight into why the third festival had to shift away from Leeds: a rival promoter putting on a similar-sounding festival at the old venue. We then see that The Sis-ters of Mercy are low on the bill, and the big names include almost-goth Bauhaus, experimentalists Theatre of Hate and the left-wing activists Gang of Four, all of whom had played the F-Club. Gang of Four were long-standing members of the Leeds post-punk scene, as we have mentioned in this chapter – and they were regular punters at the F-Club. The blogger then includes an anecdote about Andrew Eldritch re-called by Gary Marx:

> Marx also recalled a classic bit of early Von banter, the first attempt at distancing himself from the nascent gothic movement. 'My memories are of playing very early in the day and Andy walking onstage and yelling "Bring out your dead" to the few Bauhaus and Theatre of Hate fans scattered around the largely empty hall.' Marx is almost correct in his assertion, although Eldritch in fact uttered the immortal words after the set-opening Floorshow.

The F-Club is mentioned in Scharf's (2011) popular history, and of course in Mercer's (1988) and Thompson's (2007),[5] but Hodkinson (2002) overlooks it. There is no mention of it in Siegel (2005) or Brill (2008), either, though that is not too surprising as one is about a narrow American interpretation of goth, and the other is about contemporary goth culture. In their research on memories of the F-Club among those who attended it in its various incarnations and locations across Leeds, Spracklen, Henderson & Procter (2016, pp. 154–155) claim:

> The F-Club definitely engendered a long-lasting alternative scene in Leeds. Going to events under its banner allowed our respondents to meet other fans, other musicians and fanzine journalists. Most of our respondents moved into the student centre of Leeds, Leeds 6, even those who did not come to study but to work. Leeds 6 became a centre of alternative life for most of our respondents, and some are still involved in events in the area and live nearby. Being part of this alternative scene meant adhering to the DIY ethics of punk (Gordon 2014; O'Brien 2011). Many of our respondents were involved as musicians, promoters or writers – beyond just being fans. The musicians were particularly driven by collaboration and cooperation (Gordon 2014), and many of the well-known F-Club bands reflect this in their public history. As punk shifted to post-punk and goth, some of our respondents remained true to the original punk ethic – especially the two respondents from punk bands, who continued playing punk until the other things in their lives got in the way (one of these respondents, SW, actually became a high-ranking police officer). But most of our respondents followed the alternative scene in Leeds as it shifted from punk to post-punk. As RT suggests above, this then became the goth scene. The alumni of the F-Club continued to be active in this new alternative scene through the 1980s.

John Keenan started promoting gigs in Leeds in 1977, determined to bring punk and other alternative acts to a city that had a big student population alongside the local people excited by punk's rise to the mainstream.[6] In the first year, he took bigger bands such as The Buzzcocks and The Damned to Leeds Polytechnic, but then set up the F-Club as a branded, membership night at The Ace of Clubs. Here, he could organise gigs for smaller, newer acts. In 1977, this was where Siouxsie and the Banshees and Gang of Four headlined separately in the same month, and where The Mekons supported The Rezillos. In 1978, the F-Club moved to Chapeltown, then to Brannigan's in the centre of Leeds: the Banshees played once, Joy Division played twice. In 1979, Joy Division returned, and The Cure played. What is noticeable, though, is the sheer diversity of acts on the bill over the three years Keenan has made available: this is alternative music that embraces punk, post-punk, new wave, synth-pop, indie and folk rock. The 1979 gigs show Keenan starting to run the Sheepdog Trials, nights for up-and-coming local acts, and we can see The Xpelaires, the former band of The Sisters of Mercy bassist Craig Adams, among them. In Spracklen, Henderson, and Procter (2016), the respondents all remember this diversity. This was a space where alternative was broadly defined as opposition to mainstream pop, and mainstream popular culture – and after the election of Margaret Thatcher in 1979, opposition to the neo-liberal, parochial mess of Thatcherite policies.

Similar to Gang of Four, The Mekons and The Sisters of Mercy, the F-Club, as it moved into the eighties, was a space for other bands to coalesce. Soft Cell, fronted by Marc Almond, came from out of this environment with their proto-gothic synth-pop sound made famous by their cover of Tainted Love in 1981. The March Violets, close friends of The Sisters of Mercy formed in 1980 and played their first gig in 1981, and its members were regulars at the Club. Simon Denbigh of The March Violets had moved from Bradford to Leeds to be a student because he was a fan of The Mekons and Gang of Four. At Leeds University, he ran the Music for the Masses Society[7] (which put on gigs and club nights) and shared a house with Craig Adams.[8] Other local post-punk/goth rock bands were formed in this F-Club/Leeds/Yorkshire space in this period, such as Salvation, Skeletal Family, Danse Society, New Model Army, and of course, Southern Death Cult. Other venues and spaces were coming to be associated with this alternative music scene, such as The Faversham pub and The Phono (Le Phonographique), where the disc jockeys (DJs) played music that was clearly defined as gothic to the local goths by 1984.[9] In this same year as The March Violets formed and The Sisters of Mercy played Futurama, UK Decay were described as 'punk gothique' in an article in the music press (Scharf, 2011).

When the Futurama festival returned to Leeds in 1983, it was then identified as Gothic in a review in the *Yorkshire Evening Post* headlined 'Two days down in Gothic city' (Corry, 1983):[10]

> Two days of non-stop music … most of it poundingly aggressive. That's the first impression – there was a heavy emphasis on the Gothic bands with a distinct lack of light relief … Now Bauhaus have gone [headliners Killing Joke] have assumed the mantle of Gothic Kings, but they won't have the crown long unless they pull their socks up.

At a panel on Leeds Goth in Perspective in November 2016, Keenan revealed that he had fed the *Yorkshire Evening Post* the line about Gothic City, and the genre description Gothic. In other words, Keenan is claiming he invented or popularised goth by being the first to get goth into the mainstream news.

The Batcave, Specimen, Alien Sex Fiend, Sex Gang Children and Southern Death Cult

In 1982, a new club appeared in London called the Batcave, and it lasted for three years (Mercer, 1988; Scharf, 2011; van Elferen and Weinstock, 2016). Ollie Wisdom and John Klein, both from the band Specimen, set up and organised the club. Their band was formed in Bristol in 1980, playing a theatrical cross between punk and glam rock. They moved to London in 1982 to join the growing alternative, post-punk, sub-goth rock. Their decision to set up the Batcave was a shrewd one, as they attracted the same kind of broad-based post-punk alternative people, who danced to a wide range of alternative music. The club put on gigs by the same bands as the F-Club and Futurama, such as Bauhaus, but it was soon widely known for its DJ-led club nights, and was the London focus for the alternative scene in the wider region (Scharf, 2011).

Apart from Specimen, there are two other bands strongly associated with the Batcave. Wikipedia claims that Alien Sex Fiend were actually founded in the club in late 1982, as Nik Wade (aka frontman Nik Fiend) worked there.[11] This may or may not be true, but it is clear that the band were closely associated with the club. They were on the Batcave compilation in 1983, before signing to Cherry Red and releasing a string of spooky-goth rock singles and albums through the 1980s. The other band in the collective memory of goth associated with the Batcave were Sex Gang Children. Formed in 1982, they were the band that this chapter started with, when Ian Astbury told the tale about the front man Andi Sex Gang having a following of goths. Their presence on the scene, making their first single, attracted attention in October 1982, when they were interviewed in *ZigZag* magazine (Wilde, 1982a):

> Dave [Roberts]: 'Talking of our appeal, so many bands are surface covering... image... and little else – we have nothing to do with them. I hear us and I just hear Sex Gang Children. I hate the idea of movements and cliques which just do more harm than good.'
> Sex Gang Children opt for the outside and refuse to be drawn... the tidy, ordered unchallenging unchallenged refuge of the twilight punk zone is not their sordid affair, so resist the temptation to lead them astray.

They are suspicious of bands who focus on aesthetics over the substance of music and lyrics. They do not want to be part of a scene, but they already know they are part of it: Wilde identifies goth rock as 'the twilight punk zone'. Sex Gang Children in this interview want to be seen as serious musicians playing positive music. Their answers echo those made at the same time by Southern Death Cult (Morley, 1982) in an interview in *New Musical Express*:

> Barry [Jepson] says: 'We respect what Sex Gang Children and Danse Society and those other groups we are being attached to are doing for what it is, but we're not a part of it, we don't feel that it's the same.'
>
> Ian [Astbury] says: 'I don't think they feel that they're part of anything either. "It", this thing that's apparently about, it's just some guy's been sat at a typewriter and he's decided there's a new wave.'
>
> Perhaps it's enough to indicate; there's an audience falling about waiting for something that is solid and directly related to their experience, something that comes in at an angle, inside out, all skin and nerves, and (here it comes...) I suggest, blandly, to Barry that what 'it' is could be the most logical, the purest extension or fulfilment of the energy The Sex Pistols unleashed and he will say, in his way: 'Possibly... but that might well be a high thing to lay claim to...'
>
> Ian says: 'Oh god, they might think of some shit name for whatever it's supposed to be...'

Southern Death Cult were formed in Bradford in 1981 by F-Club attendee, Ian Astbury. Their first and only single Moya/Fatman was released in December 1982. Their sound – the tribal drums, the guitar lines and the bass – was definitely goth rock, thought they did not call it that, and it could equally be post-punk. The lyrics of the band's songs reflect Astbury's concerns about alienation, modern society and the destruction of Native American culture. Astbury had been a follower of Crass and was a hard-line punk, with suspicions about the culture industry and the music press in the United Kingdom. The band supported Bauhaus on a UK-wide tour and gained both a loyal fan-base and positive media support. They started work on a debut album in 1982; but in early 1983, the band split and Astbury reformed as Death Cult. In the interview above, we can see the frustration the band members feel about being associated with a fashion, a trend and a scene of some kind. The interviewer's remark that audiences need to have something to identify with, this 'it' that Astbury is concerned about, is obviously a reference to the way audiences needed to know what the name of this thing we call 'goth' was. Astbury's answer is amusingly prophetic, because the 'shit name' goth got has led to all sorts of confusion, as we will show later.

Before goth was settled on, some of the early bands and the UK press tried to label it as 'positive punk'. Richard North of the band Blood and Roses wrote an article that identified what we now call goth as positive punk in February 1983 for *New Musical Express*. The article talks about the same existentialist search for belonging and refusing to be part of the herd found in the interviews with Sex Gang Children and Southern Death Cult (both of whom feature heavily in the article he wrote). At the end, he suggests:

> So here it is: the new positive punk, with no empty promises of
> revolution, either in the rock'n'roll sense or the wider political
> sphere. Here is only a chance of self awareness, of personal revo-
> lution, of colourful perception and galvanisation of the imagina-
> tion that startles the slumbering mind and body from their sloth.
> Certainly this is revolution in the non-political sense, but at the
> same time it's neither escapist nor defeatist. It is, in fact, 'politi-
> cal' in the genuine sense of the word. Individuality? Creativity?
> Rebellion? The synthesis comes at the moment when you do the
> one thing, the only thing, when you know you're not just a trivial
> counter on the social chequerboard. Here are thousands doing
> that one thing: merging an explosive and cutting style with a
> sense of positive belief and achievement, and having fun while
> they're doing it.

The communicative alternativity of post-punk has been passed to goth in this paragraph. The twentieth-century gothic of Joy Division is now understood to be an identifying feature of goth or positive punk as it is called here. But positive punk failed to catch on, and goth took over.

Conclusion

Goths themselves have a shared mythology about their genesis: this is the Whig interpretation of Goth genesis, which gives the point of origin to Bauhaus but neglects the importance of Joy Division, and the Leeds scene around the F-Club. As with the history on Wikipedia cited in the previous chapter, there is a truth to be found in following the evolution of the music genre. We hope we have revealed some of that actual story here, rather than merely repeating the Whig-gishness of collective memory. There is a move to label a sound and the lyrical content of the Banshees as early as 1978 as 'goth'. Goth then re-appears in the summer of 1979 with the release of Joy Division's debut album. In the interview with the band and the record label, it is clear that the band and their producer have deliberately tried to construct something gothic. But this is not the gothic of nineteenth-century art, of vampires and castles – this is what Mary Harron calls 'twentieth-century gothic', a state of alienation and rejection of the main-stream, rejection of modernity. This is a form of communicative alternativity, which we have shown came from post-punk. Bauhaus and Killing Joke cap-ture the mood and the community, but what that community is hovers between labels. We can see Ian Astbury from Southern Death Cult being worried about being pinned to a particular genre label in 1982, being fearful of what might happen if the scene is pinned with an inappropriate name. There is an attempt to describe the genre and the spaces as positive punk, as the music and the message moved towards what we now call goth in 1982 and early 1983. This is music that uses dark themes to help the listener endure the horror of modern life, and find rapture and belonging in finding others like them. This is music very much like doom metal, where similar themes operate to give listeners catharsis and release (Yavuz, 2017).

But positive punk did not survive. When John Keenan branded the 1983 Futurama 'Gothic', this became the accepted word for the music and the people. The music press started to use the word 'goth', and goths stared to identify as goths. Around this moment in time, other nightclubs appear beyond the Phone and Batcave with goth playlists, goth dancers and goth-sounding names. Our multiple data sources repeat this essential origin myth: what Wikipedia believes is essentially what our respondents told us, and which is also the story present in popular sources (more or less). It is the same story told, more or less, by Hodkinson (2002) and van Elferen and Weinstock (2016), though only partially by Siegel (2005) and Brill (2008). As with the barbarian Goths of the first millennium, the new goths were partly defined by their supporters, and partly by their detractors. The genesis of the goth scene was partly a result of musicians thinking about how to be alternative and real (evidently Joy Division and UK Decay, quite probably Siouxise and the Banshees, Bauhaus and the other band sisscussed here) and partly a result of promoters like Keenan and journalists like Harron seeking to label 'new' music and scenes. But, it is impossible to deny the historical fact that goth was situated in the post-punk music scene in the United Kingdom, and was a radical musical counter culture committed to radical politics even as it found its name and identity. As positive punk, goth may have remained a small, now forgotten sub-genre of post-punk, which fell to pieces under the pressure of its own ideological commitments. But, goth expanded and managed to take over the world. In the next chapter, we will show how that journey started, and will briefly situate The Sisters of Mercy as the aesthetic and ideological source. Then, we will return to the status of The Sisters of Mercy, who are crucial to the whole story, in a separate chapter of their own.

Notes

1. All articles and interviews taken from the music press in the United Kingdom have been found by using the archives at rocksbackpages, accessed via Leeds Beckett University's subscription service. The archives do not include page numbers, so we have not used them.
2. Cited in the references as Harron (1979a).
3. Cited in the references as Harron (1979b).
4. http://sistersfan.blogspot.co.uk/2016/09/love-for-party-futurama-1981.html, accessed on 04 August 2017.
5. Whose book has The Sisters of Mercy in its full title.
6. Information about the first three years of Keenan's promoted gigs has been taken from his own website: www.livealeeds.com.
7. http://sistersfan.blogspot.co.uk/2011/12/music-for-masses.html, accessed on 02 September 2017.
8. http://teamrock.com/feature/2014-03-27/the-story-of-the-march-violets-the-batfish-boys, accessed on 20 September 2017.

9. https://blackveilgothic.wordpress.com/tag/le-phonographique/, accessed on 17 September 2017.
10. Mis-remembered as 'one day' here: http://www.dazeddigital.com/music/article/30658/1/what-was-it-like-to-be-a-goth-in-80s-yorkshire. We are grateful for John Keenan providing us with a photocopy of the clipping (at the panel mentioned in this chapter). There is no date or page number on the photocopy he gave us.
11. https://en.wikipedia.org/wiki/Alien_Sex_Fiend, accessed on 01 September 2017.

Chapter 5

The Early Deeds of the Goths

Introduction

In the collective memory of Western popular culture, the 1980s are reduced to a set of stereotypes continually affirmed as true representations of the essence of the decade – the fashions and hairstyles of American television programmes such as *Dynasty*; the styles and scripts of the blockbuster movies of the time, such as *The Breakfast Club*; and, in the United Kingdom, the ideology and iconography of divisive Prime Minister Margaret Thatcher (Bale, 2015; Robinson, 2016). There is a style of music known as eighties music, associated with the New Romantics or the PWL Studio, but felt in the pop music charts at the time: using drum machines or drums engineered in the studio to sound artificial, and synthesised guitars and strings (Kallioniemi, 2017). The eighties goth-rock sound borrows from the trends that were occurring in pop music at the time, and the bands who became famous embraced the behaviour, sounds and visual images of the mainstream rock bands. The eighties style is also associated with the mullets of rock and metal bands, or the hair-metal or glam-metal bands produced to a sheen by big labels (Kummer, 2017). In the collective memory, the eighties as a fictive decade is encapsulated by one word – excess. Goth imagination feeds on the same stereotypes:[1]

> Eighties UK bad boys The Mission are heading down under for their 30th Anniversary tour this November, the first time they've set foot in Australia since 1990. Known as the kings of excess, the band's memory of their last trip is hazy as they embraced the rock n roll lifestyle while the world fell in love with goth rock gems like Wasteland, Stay with Me and Butterfly on a Wheel. '30 bloody years! Who would've thought it, eh?' said vocalist Wayne Hussey. 'As we were well renowned for our, ahem, lifestyle choices, shall we say, I remember Melody Maker ran an office pool betting which member of The Mission would die first. I seem to remember Mick was the favourite with yours truly running a close 2nd. Well, we're still here, alive and well and still going strong'.

In this paragraph, we can see a number of ideas about the eighties and goth at work. First, The Mission are firmly fixed as a product of the decade. They are then described as 'bad boys', before we are even told they played goth rock. The lead singer, guitarist and songwriter, Wayne Hussey, is quick to embrace the eighties stereotype of excess by re-telling the tale that the band was so infamous for their decadence that journalists were running a sweep-stake on which member of the band would die first – from driving under the influence or an over-dose, or choking on alcohol-scented vomit or even from catching some strange sexual disease. The last trip is hazy because the band were all living the eighties stereotype to the full. Hussey's tale is recounted without question because he is the embodiment of eighties goth-rock excess. We all want to read stories like this and point at the bad behaviour of this wild decade; but of course, this is a collective fantasy. It is a logical error to reduce a decade of popular culture to a few words, images and sounds. The final years of the 1970s have more in com-mon with the beginning of the eighties than the latter years have with the end of the decade.[2] Popular culture everywhere is a combination of the dominant, the residual and the emergent, experienced inter-sectionally, across class and every other social category.

This chapter is the second of the chapters discussing history, exploring both the emergence and evolution of goth rock in the post-punk scene in the United Kingdom, and the memory of that emergence and evolution in popu-lar culture. Like Chapter 4, this chapter is constructed from our multiple data sources: from the memories of our respondents, popular narratives of the his-tory, primary sources such as music magazines and more credible histories of the period. This chapter will show how goth developed as a discrete musical sub-culture in the 1980s in the United Kingdom and beyond, and became an accepted part of the alternative music scene. We situate goth in this period primarily as a sub-genre of post-punk, that is, as alternative music that shared many similar fashions and ideologies with the wider alternative scenes espe-cially in the United Kingdom and Germany. We show that this post-punk, alternative politics in the goth scene was challenged by bands that abandoned goth for a contemporary hard rock sound, and by goth rock bands such as The Mission, which discarded the radical politics and took the goth sound and aesthetics into the charts and the mainstream at the end of the 1980s. But, this popularising of goth rock allowed goth to survive in its British heartland, and in a wider global space, as we will show in Chapter 7. In the first section of this chapter, we return to The Sisters of Mercy and Leeds. Then, we will discuss the rise of The Sisters of Mercy alongside the rise of The Cult, The Mission and the Fields of the Nephilim; we shall also discuss how that rise pushed goth into the mainstream – creating goth bands, making other bands turn into goth bands and engaging millions of young fans – even though it became unfash-ionable in the taste-making class of the UK music press. In the final section of the chapter, we will reflect on the wider alternative political struggle against Thatcherism, and how goth rock might be explained as a site of resistance against the Tories.

Back to Leeds in 1983: The Sisters of Mercy and Beyond

We have to briefly discuss The Sisters of Mercy again, although we devote a full chapter to them after this one. Put simply, The Sisters of Mercy found the right formula for goth-rock's sonic, visual and lyrical aesthetic – making them the source of goth as people think of it in this century. The 1982 version of the band introduced a drum machine, a second guitarist and the bass player, Craig Adams. This widened sonic template was introduced in the twelve-inch EP *Alice*, recorded in 1982, released in early 1983 and produced by John Ashton of post-punk band, The Psychedelic Furs. The cover of the record is a gold painting and text on a black background. It is on the band's own label Merciful Release. The first song, 'Alice', is all you need to listen to if you need a definition of how goth rock sounds, and what you need to do if you want to be a goth rock band – the simplistic mechanical sound of the drum machine, the prominent clean bass lines, the jangly guitars and the angry but mournful baritone singing about a woman in a party dress taking pills and believing in Tarot. The second song on *Alice*, 'Floorshow', starts with the tribal sound of Southern Death Cult, but the drum machine and Eldritch's voice turn the song into the archetype for every amphet-amine-fuelled goth-rock dance track. As with 'Alice', the lyrics are seemingly scornful of the people in the post-punk scene, but could be read as a celebration of the sweat and the movement of the audience. The third song, 'Phantom', is an instrumental track that plays like a mash-up of the soundtrack to a Spaghetti Western. Then, the final song is a cover of The Stooges song '1969', a sign of the band's confidence: this is their first EP, and they are telling us about one of the sources of their sound and look.

On stage, The Sisters of Mercy perfected the goth fashion and style: all (mainly) in black, black dye in their hair, sunglasses, black hats and cigarettes – hidden behind clouds of dry ice. In 1982, they started to pick up gigs nation-wide as the supporting act to established punk and post-punk bands such as The Clash and The Psychedelic Furs, as well as headlining their own one-off gigs locally.[3] By the spring of 1983, they had started to headline their own gigs nationally, though they continued to pick up gigs further down the bill. They played dozens of gigs across the United Kingdom and then toured extensively in Europe and the United States of America. This was all supported by the release of The Reptile House EP and The Temple of Love on Merciful Release, and extensive support in the British music media. The band recorded their first British Broadcasting Corporation (BBC) session with John Peel as early as August 1982 and then did another BBC session for David Jensen in March 1983.[4]

Around The Sisters of Mercy in Leeds and the wider West Yorkshire metro-politan county[5] area, other bands were being formed or re-constituted as goth rock bands. We have already mentioned The March Violets, close friends of Craig Adams, Andrew Eldritch and Gary Marx. They signed to the Merciful Release label and followed the rising fortunes of their friends as promoters, journalists, disc jockeys (DJs) and goth fans explored the new Leeds goth scene. The March Violets copied The Sisters of Mercy in adopting the new technology of drum machines. But other bands retained live drumming on record and at gigs, such as Skeletal Family. The name of the band is undoubtedly and shockingly gothic. Skeletal Family were formed at the end of 1982 in Keighley, up the valley of the River Aire that passes through the centre of Leeds. Keighley was where the classic early line-up of The Sisters of Mercy had played their first gig in March 1982, where they headlined as 'Leeds [*sic.*] Cult Band' with The March Violets in support[6] – it is possible that members of Skeletal Family had attended that gig, but they were clearly the people who attended gigs and clubs in Leeds at places such as the F-Club. When The Sisters of Mercy toured the United Kingdom in the second half of 1984, they took Skeletal Family as their support act.

Just south of Leeds is Barnsley, a city in the heart of the coal-mining areas. Still in the old West Riding of Yorkshire, but in the (then) recently created metropolitan county of South Yorkshire, Barnsley was where The Danse Society were formed as early as 1980. Their first album released in September 1982 showed the influence of Bauhaus on their particular emerging goth rock sound. But, The Danse Society also heavily borrowed stylistically and visually from The Sisters of Mercy. They also followed the punk/post-punk ideology of communicative alternativity through constructing their own DIY label. Just like Southern Death Cult and The Sisters of Mercy (in 1982), at the time of their first album The Danse Society situated themselves in the wider alternative sub-culture of the time, resisting for a time the attention of major labels and being suspicious of the media (Dunn, 2012; Savage, 2002). In 1983, however, they signed with a major label ahead of their second album, and managed to get into the UK charts. This second album, however, was perceived by some music critics as being without any real worth – already, even before goth rock was fully formed and chart-friendly, goth was becoming unfashionable (Frith, 1998; Hodkinson, 2002; Scharf, 2011).

Salvation are another key goth rock band from Leeds during this period. Like The Sisters of Mercy, Salvation have a name that borrows from Christian culture, but a name that also serves to align with the communicative alternativity of post-punk and positive punk. They achieved a measure of success when they worked with Wayne Hussey as a producer and mentor, who joined The Sisters of Mercy in the latter half of 1983, and who was one of the founding members of The Mission in 1986 after The Sisters of Mercy fell to pieces in 1985. Salvation owed Andrew Eldritch and the 1982 classic version of The Sisters of Mercy for their initial formation, but that relationship proved problematic. On their official website,[7] they re-call and construct their genesis and early formation in unambiguous terms:

> 1983… Danny and James get together to experiment and make noise. James liked Metal Machine Music, Danny liked Cabaret Voltaire. James had a bass guitar and Danny had 2 synths…they made Noise! Then guitarist Mike joined the band…he had pedals…loads of 'em! They linked them up, drum machine to synths – via pedals and through echo chambers then pressed Play! Eureka, they were a Band! At the time, Danny was working with The Sisters of Mercy and Übermeister Andrew Eldritch took the trio to Bridlington to record the first Salvation single for his label Merciful Release. K.G. Studio was 100 yards from the beach and had already played host to the Sisters. It was snowing and the band were skint! Andrew knew that the band didn't have any money and so, asked to be paid in kind with West Yorkshire's finest stimulants. 3 sleepless nights and the Girlsoul EP was born! The Sisters' connection guaranteed healthy sales and soon the band and Eldritch

were back behind the mixing desk; this time at Stockport's Strawberry Studios. 48 channels, all the latest technology! No excuses, they had to sound good! They recorded 6 songs for a prospective album on Merciful Release but Machiavellian machinations saw it being shelved and Mike decided to leave the band.

Lead singer, Danny Mass, was working as a roadie for The Sisters of Mercy when Salvation were formed. The website says he liked Cabaret Voltaire – a band from Sheffield that make experimental industrial music in the seventies, but which aligned with the New Wave, post-punk alternative scene by the early eighties – but the band set out to make gothic rock that cleaves close to the format established by Danny's boss. In this extract from the band's biography, we see that Andrew Eldritch signed them to Merciful Release and produced their first single and EP, but the relationship somehow broke down. We are only left with to wonder what Machiavellian machinations were taking place, but the band were temporarily left without a record deal and a label. The above-mentioned extract confirms the collective goth memory of the early goth-rock scene being subject to excessive use of amphetamine. Speed was ubiquitous in the alternative scene in the late seventies and eighties in the United Kingdom, and The Sisters of Mercy even recorded the song 'Amphetamine Logic' for the *First and Last and Always* album (although the song was re-titled 'Logic' on the sleeve of the album). Speed was the drug of choice for bikers and Motorhead's Lemmy, so it was no surprise people in the post-punk/positive punk/goth scene would use it, as bikers and Lemmy were seen as standing for everything against the hippies. More pragmatically, speed allowed people to dance for longer, and allowed the early goth rock nights – at the Bat Cave in London, and at the Phone in Leeds – to attract large numbers of speed freaks who did not care they were getting covered in other people's sweat (Klee, 1998).

After the breakdown of the relationship with Andrew Eldritch and Merciful Release, Salvation re-formed with a new guitarist and managed to restart their career. As we have already mentioned, they found a mentor in Wayne Hussey, who by 1985 was locked in a struggle with Eldritch over the direction and status of the band (see Chapter 6 for more details). Working with Salvation allowed Hussey to show his importance in the local goth rock scene at a crucial time, and Hussey invited Salvation to tour with his new band The Mission.

There were two other bands associated with the alternative/goth scene in Leeds that are worth mentioning here. The band 1919 defined themselves as post-punk, and originally came from Bradford, just to the west of Leeds. The gothic rock template established at the time heavily influenced their music, which still had a distinctive post-punk bass sound. They released a few singles and performed two BBC sessions for John Peel, but failed to make an impression on the charts or sign a deal with a major label, so the band changed direction and name by the middle of the 1980s. Being more working-class than the middle-class students at the universities in Leeds who filled out the ranks of The Sisters of Mercy and The March Violets, the members of 1919 could not afford to be anti-capitalist. The second band worth mentioning was New Model Army, who also came from Bradford. New Model Army were named after the radical soldiers of Oliver Cromwell, the men who discussed liberty and belief, and who fought to remove monarchy and oppression. New Model Army shared fans and alternative spaces in Bradford in the early 1980s with Southern Death Cult. Their earlier singles were solidly post-punk, and they never really sounded like goth-rock at any time of their career. But in the 1980s, they were seen as fellow alternative travellers to goth rock, and as a band that reached out to anyone who wanted to fight back against the evils of capitalism. That did not stop New Model Army from signing a major label deal, which brought the band scorn from the music press (O'Reilly & Doherty, 2006). But the band claimed to use that major-label deal as a way of getting their radical, anarchistic message across to more potential fans. New Model Army are the best example of a post-punk band that embraced communicative alternativity: when they were with a major label, they tried to do everything they could to circumvent the rules of the music industry; when they stopped being on the major label, they were early adopters of digital technology to build a closer relationship with their fans.

The goth scene in Leeds grew massively on the back of the rise of The Sisters of Mercy. As well as the Phono, alternative music nights started to appear at the University and the Polytechnic, with people turning up wearing gothic black fashions and having back-combed black hair – as recalled by some of our respondents. Young people started to choose to go to university in Leeds because they wanted to be associated with the goth-rock scene around The Sisters of Mercy and the Phono (Spracklen, Richter, & Spracklen, 2013). Young people in Yorkshire, such as the authors of this book, started to identify as goths to distinguish themselves as alternative and radical, but not indie – the music scene and fashion more usually associated with Manchester on the other side of the Pennines. By the middle of the eighties, independent record shop Jumbo records had started to sell fanzines, merchandise and, of course, records associated with goth – and alternative shops started to appear that sold gothic clothing and accessories alongside punk, post-punk and metal material. Goth had a clear and distinct sound, but its fashions and ideology still crossed punk and metal ones.

Goth rock elsewhere in the United Kingdom was fuelled by the continued rise of The Sisters of Mercy's classic line-up, from 1982 through to 1984. Local scenes emerged all over the country, with important scenes emerging around local bands and clubs in Nottingham, Northampton and other unfashionable provincial towns and cities (Mercer, 1988; Scharf, 2011; Thompson, 2007). The scene in London, focussed on the twin nodes of the Batcave and the positive-punk movement, followed the goth-rock template that had been fixed by The Sisters of Mercy and the Leeds scene, losing some of its diversity in the process (Thompson, 2007). As such, some of the prime movers of the London scene, and some of the London music media, were already rejecting goth: it had gone from being a radical, post-punk experiment to an exercise in uniformity; it had also become too popular, and too provincial, for the metropolitan taste-makers (Mercer, 1997, 2002; Scharf, 2011).

With The Sisters of Mercy touring heavily in Europe, it was inevitable that the continent would see goth-rock scenes and goth culture established by the middle of the 1980s. In Europe, possibly the first goth-rock band was Clan of Xymox from The Netherlands, established as early as 1980 as an experimental, post-punk New Wave electronic band. They signed to the British indie label 4AD, which had other dark, alternative, 'goth' bands such as Bauhaus and Dead Can Dance on their roster in the early 1980s, and released their debut album Xymox in 1985. This album followed the gothic-rock sonic template very closely. Other bands came into existence in all the countries in Western Europe where the British bands – the Banshees, The Cure, Bauhaus, The Sisters of Mercy – found enthusiastic audiences, notably in West Germany, where gothic rock was embraced (and renamed darkwave) alongside heavy metal as a radical, alternative space for individualism and solidarity (Brill, 2008; van Elferen & Weinstock, 2016). In the first generation of goth rock in Germany, the band Pink Turns Blue serves as an interesting example. In an interview[8] published online, the context is described as follows:

> We all had different idols, but there aren't really any surprises here: Joy Division for Tom, Killing Joke and The Cure for Marcus, Siouxsie, and Joy Division and Bauhaus, and later Laibach for me ... I reckon [our sound and approach] was just the opposite of what all the light-blue and pink-white wearing disco-mainstream pop was about in the mainstream 1980s. We wanted depth, doubts, darkness, eeriness. We wanted to sulk. We wanted to probe the depths of darkness. This music was the soundtrack to the ones who wanted to live on the other side, who had a higher artistic or intellectual aspiration than what was being offered in the world of 80s Top 40 and pop music at that time. We wanted to appeal to the poets and the romantics of the age, not to the consumerist mentality that was so rampant then (and now).

The band does not mention The Sisters of Mercy – that absence of influence may be true, or it may be a deliberate renunciation of their influence on Pink Turns Blue. In their recollection of their influences, citing The Sisters of Mercy – the band that have distanced themselves from goth rock and sneered at every band that joined the 'goth rock bandwagon (see Chapter 6) – may be a step too far for Pink Turns Blue. They formed right at the peak of the influence of The Sisters of Mercy. The interview shows that all the other bands we have mentioned in this book were an influence on Pink Turns Blue. They were informed by post-punk's rejection of the mainstream and the darkness and eeriness of gothic rock.

Elsewhere, goth rock was emerging in this period in the United States of America, fuelled by the exposure of the British bands and the crystallisation of the sonic template. Again, as in the United Kingdom and Europe, some of the bands were existing post-punk acts while switching to a dark style, or bands from the horror-punk/death rock scene building around The Misfits, who were pigeonholed as goth by fans, DJs and the media. In the latter category, Christian Death serve as a key example, a band formed in 1979 that became gothic rock in 1984 after line-up changes (Mercer, 2009; Scharf, 2011).

(~~Death~~) (The) Cult, The Mission and Fields of the Nephilim

The Cult

In the last chapter, we left Ian Astbury of Southern Death Cult after he split Southern Death Cult to form Death Cult in April 1983. Southern Death Cult had aligned with the positive punk movement, and made a show of their working-class, northern English roots in Bradford. Death Cult was a product of London, and the ruthless ambition of Astbury, the people around him and his label – the independent Situation Two, a subsidiary of the bigger independent label Beggars Banquet (Hesmondhalgh, 1997). Death Cult was a simple contraction of the original name, but is designed to evoke a gothic sensibility – it instantly saw the band labelled as gothic, and goth-rock fans associating themselves with the band. Astbury co-founded Death Cult with Billy Duffy, the Manchester-born guitarist for the London-based post-punk band Theatre of Hate. It is unclear how the two met each other, but they evidently trusted and respected each other enough: Duffy may well have seen Astbury performing with Southern Death Cult, and will have read about him in the music press; Astbury probably saw Duffy playing in London, the city where he now lived. The two complemented each other extremely well: Astbury was the flamboyant, romantic radical, and Duffy was the pragmatic professional who had grown up with the big seventies rock bands as his first musical inspiration before becoming a punk.

They hired their rhythm section from a Harrow-based post-punk band – Ritual – that was in the process of collapsing after making music that could be identified as goth rock. On drums, Death Cult had Ritual's Ray Mondo, a migrant from Sierra Leone who brought a tribal drumming style to the band; on bass, Death Cult hired Jamie Stewart, who has actually been Ritual's guitarist. Death Cult toured across Europe and the United Kingdom though the second half of 1983 and released an EP, gaining favourable coverage in the press and fanzines. Then Ray Mondo was sacked and replaced with Nigel Preston, then the drummer for Sex Gang Children, who had worked with Billy Duffy as the drummer for Theatre of Hate. This version of Death Cult released a single and toured again until the end of 1983, all the while writing and rehearsing new songs for their planned debut album.

Then in January 1984, they launched the new song 'Spiritwalker' on *The Tube*, with host Jools Holland announcing the band had just re-named itself The Cult. This clip is a perfect snapshot of the broad alternative music scene at the start of 1984.[9] The song is immediately in the goth rock sonic template, but still has echoes of Southern Death Cult's post-punk, tribal vibe. Billy Duffy is dressed all in black, with greased-back black hair – and he is playing jangly goth guitar. Jamie Stewart is half-dressed in black, and has goth boots and a scarf around his waist, but he has put on stonewashed white denim jacket. Nigel Preston looks like he is wearing the clothes he wears when he gets a pint of milk from the local shop. In the middle, Ian Astbury is wearing black trousers, too, and he has hair dyed white and black, but he has matched this with a red British soldier coat and Native American face paint. The audience are also a mixed crowd – while there are people who definitely look like what we think of as eighties goths (big make-up, big hairs, black clothing and lacing), there are people who look like punks (including one with a perfect mohican), psychobillies, and greasers and moshers, as well as some people who look like they got onto the set by mistake.

'Spiritwalker' was released in April 1984 and reached number one on the UK indie charts following extensive media interest. In September 1984, the debut album *Dreamtime* was released and reached number 21 in the UK Album Chart. The band continued to tour and recorded a BBC session, then at the beginning of 1985 went into a recording studio to record 'She Sells Sanctuary', quite probably the most famous goth-rock song. 'She Sells Sanctuary' reached number 15 in the UK Singles Chart. The video for the song begins with Ian Astbury briefly wearing the full goth-rock uniform, with a black hat, and black clothing with tassels, pulling gothic-rock shapes as he moves to the floating line of the song's opening riff. Then, when the song properly begins, we see him on stage with the rest of the band, dressed in white, white and black – but with black hair. This time Jamie Stewart looks completely goth, as does Duffy, though the guitarist has allowed himself to have blond hair. After 'She Sells Sanctuary', the band went back in the studio to create their second album *Love*, with a new drummer in tow. When this was released in October 1985, it was another huge hit, in the United Kingdom and around the world. Although the band were exploring and developing their musical taste in the songs on the album, it is still undoubtedly a product of goth rock. The album cover is all black, and the band do not deviate far from the goth-rock sonic template, or Astbury's post-punk rallying calls.

On the back of this album, The Cult started to tour worldwide, and to headline their own tours – though they took an offer from Wayne Hussey to support The Mission when they were still called The Sisterhood at the beginning of 1986. With yet another new drummer, the band started to plan the follow-up to *Love* with that album's producer Steve Brown, but both Astbury and Duffy were unhappy about the production on this new album when they heard the final mix of the songs they had recorded. They wanted to sound like a hard rock band, and crack the American market. So they hired Rick Rubin, and his production skills and a sense for what makes a good hook ensured that the next album, *Electric* (1987), saw them conquer America. The band still looked alternative, but they all dressed as bikers and moshers, and the songs and the videos tapped into stereotypes of American popular culture (outlaws, the West, the open road, bikes and open-top cars) so carefully that one could have thought they were from the United States of America, and were not interlopers. After *Electric*, Astbury and Duffy and moved to California, where they found another drummer and a replacement for Jamie Stewart, and found yet more success with the producer Bob Rock on their 1989 album *Sonic Temple*. Then, The Cult had become a stadium rock band with massive anthems, and even a classic rock ballad, and they toured with Aerosmith and Metallica. Extensive touring and the lifestyle associated with it strained the relationship between Astbury and Duffy, and subsequently the band's next album, *Ceremony* released in 1991, was less successful that *Sonic Temple*. The band continued on into the 1990s and brought in Craig Adams – bass player from The Sisters of Mercy and The Mission – to perform live and on the eponymous album released in 1994, but came to a halt in 1995. They have since re-formed, broke up and re-formed a number of times, and have released some albums, but none with the intensity of *Dreamtime*, the gothic majesty of *Love*, or the swagger of *Electric*.

The Mission

The Mission are important in this story of the early deeds of the goths, and their evolution, because they took goth rock to festivals and arenas around the world. They were also the direct inheritors of The Sisters of Mercy's fan-base and aesthetic, though they ditched the cynicism and radical politics of Andrew Eldritch for more stereotypically gothic lyrics about love and death (Farnell, 2009). The Mission's co-founder, Wayne Hussey, joined The Sisters of Mercy at the end of 1983, as we have already mentioned previously, replacing founder member Ben Gunn, who was unhappy with the band signing to the major label WEA. The struggle between Eldritch and Hussey will be covered in more detail in Chapter 6, as it forms part of the common goth memory of The Sisters of Mercy. For this overview of The Mission, it is sufficient to note that Hussey and bass player, Craig Adams, were in turn becoming exasperated by Eldritch in 1984 and 1985, especially when Gary Marx also left the band. Hussey wrote some new songs for the new album and took them to Eldritch, who rejected them; then, it appeared that the band was finished. This led Hussey and Adams for form a new band, The Sisterhood, towards the end of 1985, bringing in Mick Brown from Leeds band Red Lorry Yellow Lorry on drums, and Simon Hinkler on lead guitar. The Sisterhood had the same support crew that had worked for The Sisters of Mercy in 1985 and earlier. A tour was booked and the band hit the road in January 1986, as have mentioned, with The Cult in support. But, Eldritch saw what was happening and released the single 'Giving Ground' on 20 January 1986 (the date of the first gig of the tour) under the name of The Sisterhood. In a matter of days, Eldritch had secured rights to use the name and sue anyone who wanted to use it, or anything relating to The Sisters of Mercy.

So, The Mission were born in February 1986. Hussey and Adams were contractually tied to WEA from being in The Sisters of Mercy, but their management team found a way to release them. In the meantime, they released two EPs on an indie label run by the goth rock band Balaam and the Angel, which highlighted some of the rejected songs Hussey had written for The Sisters of Mercy. These songs – later collected in the album *First Chapter* – constitute what could be argued to be the most important evolution of goth rock in the period, because they combine the coldness of The Sisters of Mercy with the pop sensibility of Hussey, and his more direct appeal to emotions in his lyrics and arrangements. The immediate worldwide success of The Mission led to them signing to the major label Phonogram in July 1986. Although goth was now firmly rejected by the taste-makers of the press, there was still an enormous market for goth rock among people in the alternative scene, and there was still a huge mass-market for alternative music. The Mission's first album *God's Own Medicine* was released in November 1986, and took The Mission away from the cold aesthetic of The Sisters to embrace romance and lust. Hussey recruited Julianne Regan from All

About Eve as a backing vocalist to great effect on this album, and she featured on the hit single 'Severina'. Their rise was seemingly unstoppable even if Craig Adams had to drop out of one American tour for drinking too much.

For their next album, The Mission turned to John Paul Jones, who had been bass player and arranger for Led Zeppelin, one of the bands Hussey had adored in his childhood. Jones's long experience and knowledge of arrangements, and his keyboard skills, turned the 1988 album *Children* into a high point for the band, and the closest they got to mainstream acceptability, reaching number two in the UK Album Chart and selling across the world. 'Tower of Strength', The Mission's most-enduring single, was released off *Children*, and was itself a world hit at the time. The band toured the album to South America and the Far East, as well as Europe and North America, picking up support slots with Robert Plant. In 1989, they returned to Tim Palmer, the producer of *God's Own Medicine*, for yet another album. *Deliverance* came out in 1990, and was less immediately catchy as *Children*. The first single 'Butterfly on a Wheel' hit the charts, but it is not classic goth-rock pop song like 'Tower of Strength', or The Cult's 'She Sells Sanctuary'. The strain of constant touring and the excesses of drink and drugs were getting in the way of the band writing music as good as they had recorded in 1986 or 1987. Simon Hinkler quit in 1990 on the North American tour after much in fighting. They hired various stand-ins to cover headlining gigs at various festivals and continued into the nineties. But, the remaining band members wanted to explore different forms of music, and after the release of a very un-gothic *Masque* in 1992, Crag Adams also quit. The Mission drifted on another few years, dumped by Phonogram, and released two unremarkable albums before Hussey called time in 1996. But, he soon reformed the band, with various new line-ups, and has recorded albums that echo the goth-rock vibe of the original albums. The 2016 version of The Mission mentioned at the start of this chapter even includes Craig Adams and Simon Hinkler.

Fields of the Nephilim

Fields of the Nephilim are the final band that were crucial in the popularisation of goth rock in the 1980s, especially in Germany and northern Europe more generally (Brill, 2008). They formed in 1984 in Stevenage, a commuter town north of London with very little of interest then and now. The band's initial line-up included a saxophonist, which showed they were influenced by the ubiquity of the saxophone in early eighties pop music, and in post-punk bands (for example, Theatre of Hate). But, they were clearly set up to be a goth rock band. Their lead singer, Carl McCoy, had a deep, booming voice that sounded a lot like Andrew Eldritch. Their guitarist, Paul Wright, played a jangly guitar that sounded a lot like the one played by Wayne Hussey. Their drummer sounded like a drum machine, and their bass player replicated the goth-rock bass sound perfected by Craig Adams.

They had three things that made them more than just copyists. The saxophone was a novel addition to the goth rock template; however, it was not a well-thought-through addition, so they ditched the saxophonist for a second guitarist after the release of their debut EP in 1985. The other two things they had were more useful in launching their careers as goth-rock populists. They had incredible stage presence, and cultivated a 'death cowboy' look by wearing cowboy leathers sprinkled with flour. This stage presence was magnified by the commanding and awe-inspiring charisma of Carl McCoy: like a professional magician or any world-famous lead singer, McCoy was able to win over audiences just by how he clutched the microphone. Because this was gothic rock, his persona was dark, imperial and mystical, and fans truly believed he was channelling dark magic. In addition, McCoy's lyrics were the final thing that made them innovators: his lyrics were a combination of influences from H. P. Lovecraft through Sumerian mythology to the work of Aleister Crowley. In interviews, he maintained he was seriously interested in exploring this esoteric knowledge (Baddeley, 1999), and he has continued to maintain this persona to the present day.[10]

The band signed to the Situation Two label of the indie label Beggars Banquet, the home of The Cult, in 1985. Their first EP was not badly received by goth rock fans and music critics, but the saxophone was perceived as a sticking point. The second version of the band, minus the saxophonist with the additional guitarist, made the music more powerful, and allowed the band to be truly scary on record, and on stage. In 1986, they released two singles then, in 1987, their debut album *Dawnrazor*. The album reached the top of the indie charts and established the band in the United Kingdom and Europe. They returned with a second album, *The Nephilim* (1998), which explored McCoy's esoteric themes much further and on an epic musical scale. It reached number 12 in the UK Album Chart, and the lead single 'Moonchild' broke through into the mainstream UK Single Chart. This song captures everything that made the band a huge success in the goth rock scene in these years: it is firmly in the goth-rock sonic template, but it is a great pop song that can get people dancing; and the lyrics sound like Carl McCoy is actually summoning a moonchild (whatever one of those is). The next album, *Elizium* (1990), saw the band bring in Pink Floyd engineer, Andy Jackson, to produce, and the result was a masterpiece of progressive goth-rock, a magical journey that frightened then exalted as McCoy offered his goth listeners and fans a way through the afterlife towards some paradise.

Somehow, the creative energy used to create *The Nephilim* and *Elizium* faded away, and the band split up in 1991, with McCoy heading one way, and the rest of the band going another. But, their music and the memory of their live performances resonated through the nineties, in Germany, in Sweden and Norway, and in the goth scene in the United Kingdom.

Conclusion: Fuck the Tories[11]

As early as 1989, the arrival of goth rock in the United Kingdom earlier in the decade was being romanticised and mythologised, as a genuine, radical turn against the materialism of the age. In September 1989 in *Sounds* magazine, Cathi Unsworth reflected on the decline and fall of the Gothic Empire as follows:

> In the late '80s, elitism and imagination have long since fled The Passageway Of Goth. The Cult and The Mission both boast mass stadium gross-outs in their battle to become the Led Zeppelins of the '90s. The Neph, with their burgeoning army of followers, are not that far behind. Goth has become mainstream enough for the chainstores to exploit, and has (un)inspired as much of a sheep-like response from its followers as any standard fashion victims. But all is not quite lost. The Next Goth Mutation is already upon us, although all those involved can rightfully scream in anguish at being so unfairly labelled. It's just that all their followers wear black... Goth's rich escapism has been a necessary part of the austere, ten year Conservative reign. And despite its troughs – which, incidentally, have coincided with periods of dilution of mainstream pop and rock music – there is still a veritable army of people left who don't want to become part of the Me generation. The colours of darkness are still bewitching and beguiling.

For Unsworth, the communicative rationality of goth in the United Kingdom was in its ability to provide a space for a sub-cultural resistance against the Conservative government (Nehring, 2007). But, she also saw in goth a reaction against the wider selfishness and materialism of this period of economic decline and rampant individualism. This was the age when Margaret Thatcher served as the leader of a wide-reaching neo-liberal attack on the liberal consensus in the country. As the Conservative Prime Minister, elected in 1979 then again in 1983 and 1987, she saw her task to re-shape the British economy according to the theories of Milton Friedman (2009), so that markets would be free to generate wealth. She set out to roll back and privatise the public sector, and to reduce the power of the unions, while simultaneously preserving the rights of the privileged elites (Evans, 2013). Under Thatcher, there was no such thing as society, only individual agents who needed to be free to make money through their labour or their skills (or their inherited wealth or their luck). Local authorities responsible for schools, council housing, social services and youth services had their funding slashed. Funding was removed from big nationalised industries, before their sale. Factories, pits, and dockyards up and down the country closed as money was invested in the financial and service sector (Evans, 2013). This was a Britain exemplified by yuppies in the City of London, making money from deals in between binges of cocaine and champagne, when making money and showing off became the new social norm. When comedian Harry Enfield satirised the norm with his working-class builder Loadsamoney, the caricature and the catch-phrase were adopted proudly by many of the winners of the economic change.

Against the tide of Thatcherism and the 'Me generation', Unsworth positioned goth. She described the opportunity for rebellion and resistance in the phrase 'elitism and imagination'. This is not the elitism of Thatcher, but an elitism of young people rejecting the chains of neo-liberalism, using their imagination to make goth rock a space for communicative alternativity to be constructed. At the time she was writing, that communicative alternativity had been lost, as goth bands such as The Mission, The Cult and Fields of the Nephilim were becoming mainstream rock bands, and part of the music industry. Unsworth was critical of the fact that goth clothing was freely available in chain-stores, a mark of the instrumentality of the sub-culture, a mark of its commodification. But she believed that goth could survive on the fringes as part of the wider alternative scene, because she identified a new generation of young people who wished to rebel against neo-liberalism, the mainstream culture industry (Adorno, 1991), and the emptiness of the market.

There is no doubt at all that Thatcherism had an extremely negative impact on youth culture and on society in Britain in the 1980s. At the time, young people opposed her policies and her ideology through punk, especially the crust-punk movement around Crass (Dunn, 2014), as well as more widely in clubs and punk spaces (Nehring, 2007). Young people joined Greenpeace and the Campaign for Nuclear Disarmament (CND), alarmed at the global impact of Thatcherism (Bale, 2015). Young people found inspiration to be radical in the space of alternative comedy, a scene that led to a flourishing of new sitcoms and sketch shows on television, such as *The Young Ones*. People marched against her policies, organised to overturn her policies, and voted against her policies – although the right-wing press, and the right-wing shift in the public sphere of opinion, allowed Thatcher to win three elections in succession (Phillips, 1998). Thatcher, then, may have had just enough support to keep power, but she had an angry and significant section of the country that despised her (Evans, 2013). Some of those opposing Thatcher were against her for moral and ideological reasons, but many were against her because of the consequences of her policies on the social fabric of the country. In the north of England, her attack on the coal-mining communities and the National Union of Miners has not been forgotten to this day (Bale, 2015; Robinson 2016). Her economic policies limited life opportunities for generations of people living in working-class areas throughout the country, though the north of England – especially the industrial cities of Liverpool, Manchester and Leeds – suffered especial hardship due to the industrial decline that had already set in during the 1970s (Evans, 2013). When Andrew Eldritch arrived in Leeds as a university student, the city was already suffering seemingly irreversible urban decay. With Thatcher running the country, more mills, factories and businesses closed, and unemployment reached three million (Phillips, 1998) – in Leeds, the struggling industrial base pretty much collapsed (Spracklen, 2016; Spracklen, Henderson, & Procter, 2016; Spracklen, Richter, & Spracklen, 2013).

Goth in the 1980s can be seen as another significant space in which people rejected the instrumentality and ideology of Thatcherism, as Unsworth suggested. Goth emerged from post-punk and positive punk as space for communicative alternativity, as we have shown. Goth in the early eighties embraced the punk fear of selling out, of doing things underground or DIY. In the lyrics and early action of Andrew Eldritch and The Sisters of Mercy, there is an act of resistance against the industry, and against the spirit of the age. There is nothing essential that made Leeds – the city of urban decay and black stone – the crucial formative space in which goth rock was crystallised and popularised. Gothicness is not part of a northern English way of seeing the world, or part of Yorkshire's cultural heritage (Spracklen, 2016). Goth rock has nothing to do with *Wuthering Heights*. But, Leeds was a city in which resistance to Thatcherism could be found, because the impact was in plain sight. Our respondents all agree that the early goth rock scene was a continuation of the underground politics of punk, which transformed into a broader alternative scene typified by the political songs of New Model Army. Goths in the United Kingdom in the eighties saw the importance of the music sub-culture as a counter-cultural site. By being goth, that is, by dressing like a goth and listening to goth music, one marked oneself as an outsider.

But being a goth in 1989 had become, by Unsworth's reflection, something fashionable, something associated with the safe stadium-friendly goth rock of The Mission. This was goth rock shorn of the radical politics and the communicative ideology of alternativity. Put simply, if everybody was alternative, there was no alternative. To be alternative in the eighties was to stand against Thatcherism and neo-liberalism, to reject the fakeness of the culture industries and the mainstream. In that sense, goth had already become a mere sub-culture, or a fashion bought off the peg at TopShop. Its status as a fashion meant it was already doomed to be dismissed by the music press, who had already spent much of the late eighties mocking the big goth acts for their hubris and their fakery – stories about the excesses of The Mission were not celebrations of eighties decadence; rather, they were sarcastic put-downs of sell-outs who had watched Spinal Tap and failed to see the irony (Spracklen, 2017b). When Eldritch re-launched The Sisters of Mercy in 1987 with the album *Floodland*, it was preceded by the Jim Steinman-produced lead single 'This Corrosion'. This song has an eighties-rock lead guitar solo, a huge choir, and a ridiculous video channelling every bad copy of the *Mad Max* films. If this was the state of the art for gothic alternativity, there was no wonder the taste-makers of the music press turned against Eldritch, even as the song and the album made goth rock ever more popular around the world. Unsworth tells us she thinks the future of goth is assured because there is a new version of goth in the shadows. In the original piece, she identifies this new version of goth as the sixties-inspired indie shoe-gaze movement (though she does not call it shoe-gaze). In Chapter 7, we will show what actually happened was that goth continued to survive underground globally as an aesthetic and a music genre. Before that, we turn again to The Sisters of Mercy.

Notes

1. http://www.australianmusician.com.au/the-mission-return-to-australia-for-30th-anniversary-tour/, accessed on 22 September 2017.
2. The same logic applies to any two decades. Although we are discussing the fallacy of accepting stereotypes about decades, we need to also note that decades start in year one and end in year zero. That is, the eighties started in 1981, not 1980, and ended in 1990.

3. https://sisterswiki.org/Gigography, accessed on 05 March 2018.
4. https://sisterswiki.org/Radio_One_Sessions, accessed on 07 September 2017.
5. The historical county of Yorkshire was split into the three ridings: West Riding; North Riding and East Riding. The West Riding of Yorkshire was the industrial heartland. In 1974 Yorkshire was carved up into new counties: the metropolitan counties of West Yorkshire, South Yorkshire and Humberside (which included parts of Lincolnshire) as well as the new county of North Yorkshire. Parts of Yorkshire were given to other counties.
6. https://sisterswiki.org/Mon,_29-Mar-1982, accessed on 07 September 2017.
7. http://salvationhq.co.uk/biography/, accessed on 07 September 2017.
8. http://www.cvltnation.com/pink-turns-blue-interview-german-darkwave-pioneers, accessed on 07 September 2017.
9. https://www.youtube.com/watch?v=uAKnbKTmm2w, accessed on 07 September 2017.
10. Fields of the Nephilim have been a strong influence on black metal bands, and Carl McCoy contributed to a song on an album by the Swedish black-metal band Watain in 2013.
11. A slogan painted on the back of at least one leather jacket we remember from the early nineties.

Chapter 6

The Sisters of Mercy: A Case Study

Introduction

This is the first case study of the book. It discusses the band we have already established as the most important goth band in the 1980s: the Leeds band 'The Sisters of Mercy'. If The Sisters of Mercy were not the inventors of goth aesthetics and goth sounds, they are clearly the band that became famous worldwide for being the popularisers of goth. This band came to exemplify the goth look and the goth sound, and came out of a crucial local scene where goth was allegedly first used to describe the music. The band became hugely successful in the commercialisation of goth rock; but subsequently, the band's leader, Eldritch, publicly disowned the goth name. The band's history and its status in the collective memory of goths and those interested in eighties popular music more generally is still significant, even if Eldritch might argue otherwise. The band was *the* goth band; the band made the scene around the F-Club very important in goth memory; the band made Leeds the goth capital of England and arguably the world. This chapter will explore the band's story and liminal state through published interviews with band members, reviews and features by journalists, ethnography online and the interviews with our goth respondents undertaken by the authors.

All of our respondents accepted that The Sisters of Mercy were one of the most important bands in constructing and popularising goth. One of our respondents, too young to be around for the first years of the band, nevertheless told us that the song 'This Corrosion' played on radio acted as 'way in to goth'. All our respondents acknowledged that The Sisters of Mercy had continued to influence goth sub-culture through the years, even if the band's leader had disowned goth. The Sisters of Mercy continue to be associated with goth culture, with their songs played in nightclubs. Further, the band retains a status as important eighties goths in wider popular culture, with the music and band t-shirts often appearing in films and television to represent goth values and ideologies. In the film *The World's End* (2013), directed by Edgar Wright, for example, the lead character wears his Sisters t-shirt as it represents the lost freedoms of his teenage years, and the film's final scenes feature 'This Corrosion'. The Sisters of Mercy are clearly a crucial part of goth's genesis and evolution.

The Sisters of Mercy: A Short History

In the Chapters 4 and 5, we have already discussed the early career of The Sisters of Mercy. However, it is important to recap that so that we can show how the band evolved from the point we left them. Andrew Eldritch and Gary Marx founded the Sisters of Mercy in Leeds in 1980 as a way to make music inspired by the bands they had seen in the F-Club and heard on record. John Keenan of the F-Club and others who attended the club, including members of The Mekons, nurtured and supported the band. They played their first gig in 1981 and built up a strong local following in Yorkshire. The band went through a number of rapid line-up changes, recruiting Craig Adams on bass and Ben Gunn on guitar for the classic line-up. Eldritch abandoned drumming for a drum machine: this machine was used on record and live, and was given the name Doktor Avalanche. They established their own independent record label for their first release, and released a string of hugely important singles and EPs on it in 1982 and 1983. The music on these established a sonic aesthetic that was associated with goth rock. These releases also established a visual aesthetic for goth rock: from the font used (Caslon Antique) to the images, the logo of the band and the all-black backgrounds. On stage, The Sisters of Mercy perfected the goth rock look and attitude alongside the sound: they played behind large amounts of dry ice, wore black clothing, dyed their hair black, wore black sunglasses and experimented with black hats – all the while eschewing banter and informality. Their records in this period stormed the independent charts and received support from John Peel, and the band established a national and international following through extensive touring.

In May 1984, the band signed to the major label WEA. Before they signed, Ben Gunn had left the band to be replaced by Wayne Hussey. It has been suggested Gunn left because he did not like the idea of being on a major label, or did not like the idea of the band becoming so big (Thompson, 2007), turning something politically radical into something part of the culture industry (Adorno, 1991; Hebdige, 1979). Signing to WEA did not change the band's look or sound, but Wayne Hussey brought an appreciation of pop songwriting to the making of the debut album *First And Last And Always* (1985). However, there were continuing tensions over the direction of the band, and the strains caused by the touring cycle. Gary Marx quit soon after the debut album released. Then, the band fell to pieces altogether, as discussed in Chapter 5. With Hussey and Adams making a success of being goth rockers in The Mission, Andrew Eldritch released *Floodland* (1987). This album is a goth rock masterpiece. Away from the cheesiness of 'This Corrosion', the album is a cold classic of Eldritch at his best. The band had reduced to Eldritch and gothic beauty Patricia Morrison on bass, though she did not perform on the album. With hired hands and his own musical skills and beats, Eldritch created lyrics and vocals that still haunt every goth nightclub. The album spawned hundreds of electronic goth rock bands with hauntingly pretty young women playing instruments alongside the gravel-voiced male singer. A review (Sinclair, 1988) published in *Q* magazine in 1988 summed up the power of the album, and Eldritch's position in goth rock:

> While Andrew Eldritch has been away, all sorts of musical mice have been out to play. In the wake of the first and last Sisters Of Mercy album, 1985's *First And Last And Always*, the evil empires of Goth and Grebo have risen, and a new underworld fiefdom of boozed up, acid-spiked anti-heroes has emerged: Missions, Cults,

Mindwarped Doctors and Gaye Bykers all hell-bent on reviving an old-fashioned sense of irresponsible rockist hedonism. But, like the mysterious masked man who slips quietly away during the last reel of the picture, it was always a cert that Eldritch would be back for the next episode. Having recruited arch-vamp and ex-Gun Club bassist Patricia Morrison to the order, the pale emperor now returns to save the day with a rich, sepulchral set of songs as bible-black as his ever-present shades and leathers ... On 'Flood 1', with its references to the brooding, magisterial synth line of Led Zeppelin's 'Kashmir', and 'Neverland', where Doktor Avalanche (the drum machine) swallows and spits out John Bonham's drum sound whole, Eldritch treads a fine line between pomp-rock bombast and the gloomy, swirling atmospherics that are the trademark of the originator of Goth.

The author of the review, David Sinclair, welcomes the album as the re-establishment of goth rock by the person he identifies as its originator. He situates the album in the wider alternative scene (Goth and Grebo) and seems to indicate that the evolution of The Mission and The Cult at that point has been a rejection of the true values of goth. Andrew Eldritch is not the subject of mockery here: Eldritch has been recognised as the creator of goth, the man who shaped it and gave it to the world, and its saviour at a moment when The Mission and The Cult had watered down the sound and the aesthetic in pursuit of popular success. At this point in the history of The Sisters of Mercy, fans of the band waited excitedly for the next move. Would Eldritch tour with Patricia Morrison? Would the next album be even more coldly gothic? Was there any chance Eldritch would get Gary Marx back? Was there an even wilder chance that Wayne Hussey and Craig Adams would return? We ourselves remember having those conversations. No one really believed Hussey and Adams would come back, not after The Sisterhood, not after the song 'This Corrosion', which is a cruel if indirect attack on his former band-mates for being 'hired hands' seeking glory and fame. However, everybody waited and hoped that the band would play live again, and perhaps release another album to file neatly under goth rock.

In 1990, the band returned with another album, *Vision Thing*. By this point, Eldritch had ditched Morrison and recruited guitarist Andrea Bruhn – whom he had met in Germany – and bassist Tony James of shock-pop band Sigue Sigue Sputnik (Thompson, 2007). They then added Tim Bricheno from British goth-rock band All About Eve as a second guitarist, who had rather ironically just been working with The Mission as a live guitarist. All members of the band appeared on this new album. The album was – as always with the band – driven by the heavy beats of Doktor Avalanche, but the atmospheric reverbs and keyboards of *Floodland* had vanished. This version of the band feels like a send-up of a heavy rock or heavy metal band, with crushing riffs. There are guitar solos, for example, in the song 'Detonation Boulevard'. Eldritch had rejected his gothic persona and was trying to re-invent himself as a rock 'n' roll front man such as Lemmy. Despite these changes, the album still felt part of the goth rock genre, and displayed much of the sonic and visual aesthetics of goth, especially in the speed-driven 'Ribbons', and the mournful 'When You Don't See Me'. The album cover is an Eye of Horus, a mystical sign that was familiar on the goth scene (Baddeley, 1999; Mercer, 1997). Tim Bricheno's guitar riffs add gothic colour to the metal machine of Andreas Bruhn. Eldritch still sings in his rich, deep Leonard Cohen voice. The goth/rock/metal music combined with the maturity and political rage of Eldritch's lyrics was like nothing else at the time. Eldritch sends up the politics of the West, the emptiness of the culture industry, and the excess of rock. This version of the band toured extensively during 1990 and 1991, culminating in a headlining slot at Reading Festival. If this was a joke about the commodification of alternative music, it seemed to be one misunderstood by those who bought the album and the t-shirts.

In 1992 and 1993, the band continued to headline festivals and play other big gigs around the world. They re-recorded and re-released 'The Temple of Love' with Israeli singer, Ofra Haza (Regev, 1996) on backing vocals, a single that reached number three in the UK Singles Chart. They released their last single 'Under the Gun' with a re-recording of 'Alice'. Their label released two compilations – a greatest hits and a re-release of the independent singles and EPs first put out by Merciful Release. Everything seemed to be going well. However, behind the scenes in 1994, Eldritch was arguing with East West, the successor label to WEA. We can only speculate on the nature of the fallout. The *Vision Thing* version of the band had been a commercial success, and perhaps the label wanted more of the same. Or, possibly they wanted Eldritch to stop antagonising goths, his major fanbase, who he had been scornful of in the music press for some years (Mercer, 1991; Thompson, 2007). Perhaps, the fallout was due to some personal issues, or something as instrumental as financial percentages. What is known is Eldritch wanted to be released from his contract, and when the label insisted he had to give them another album before he could be free from their control, he gave them the hastily put together album *SSV* (*Screw Shareholder Value*) in 1997, which they accepted even though it is unlistenable and named as an insult.

With various shifts in line-up, The Sisters of Mercy continued to tour and play festivals through the rest of the 1990s and 2000s, without any contract to a label. They dropped the live bass for a bass synth controlled by the person running the drum machines and keyboards. Eldritch started to wear colourful tops. They wrote new songs but these are only available to listen to in unofficial live bootlegs. Adam Pearson, who had joined the band in 1993 and played on the 'Under the Gun' single, wrote the music for most of the new songs. When Pearson left the band in 2005, it seemed the chance that any new material would be officially released had vanished. The Sisters of Mercy continued into the 2010s with a stable line-up of guitarists – well-known Leeds alternative musician Christ Catalyst (joined 2005) and Ben Christo (2006) – and Eldritch started to claim that the band had no intention to ever release an album again, though he said they had loads of new material. He expressed his disdain of the whole music business, though he promised he would release an album if Donald Trump was elected (he has not so far).[1] A few new songs have emerged, but not the same number emerged under the guidance of Adam Pearson. Gigs continue to be performed, and fans turn out in good numbers to see them play. However, there is a bitter debate online over the current form of the songs and the vocals – fans complain that there is no bass, that the guitars are too metallic (as if they have not listened to *Vision Thing*), and that Eldritch's voice is now too weak (see Section 'How the Internet and Popular Culture See The Sisters of Mercy').

How the Internet and Popular Culture See the Sisters of Mercy

Once upon a time, independent music shops flourished in the United Kingdom, the United States of America and across most countries in the world. It was in these shops in the global North in the eighties, where, if they had a goth section separate from the alternative section, that was the place where you could buy records by The Sisters of Mercy. The Sisters of Mercy were explicitly filed as goth by shop owners. We both remember going into Jumbo Records in Leeds to dig through the goth section, searching for other 12-inches released by The Sisters of Mercy. The Sisters of Mercy records were filed next to all the other goth bands of the period. There are still a few record shops that fight against the tide of commodification heralded by digital leisure and commerce – and Jumbo Records continues to trade – but they are not where most people buy music. Most people buy music online, or they stream or steal it (Spracklen, 2015b). Apple's iTunes store is the contemporary legal space for buying music. This is what it says about The Sisters of Mercy (Huey, 2017):

> One of England's leading goth bands of the 1980s, the Sisters of Mercy play a slow, gloomy, ponderous hybrid of metal and psychedelia, often incorporating dance beats; the one constant in the band's career has been deep-voiced singer Andrew Eldritch … The Sisters of Mercy recorded their first full-length album, First and Last and Always, in 1985, but two years later, internal dissent had split them apart; Marx left to form Ghost Dance, and Adams and Hussey departed shortly thereafter. A legal dispute ensued over the rights to the name Sisters of Mercy; Adams and Hussey attempted to use the name Sisterhood, but Eldritch released an EP under the name to prevent its usage, and the two finally settled on the Mission. Eldritch… rebounded with his two biggest-selling American LPs, Floodland and Vision Thing. Despite ceasing studio recordings, Eldritch kept the band active as a performing entity through the first decade of the 2000s and beyond.

The sequence of events in 1985 and early 1986 has been incorrectly recorded, and the author has failed to include the capitalised definite article before Sisters in their name; however, essentially, this is an accurate summary of the rise and fall of The Sisters of Mercy. Apple have identified that The Sisters of Mercy had their greatest hits in *Floodland* and *Vision Thing*. They acknowledge that the band has continued to exist as a 'performing entity' into the twenty-first century without releasing any recordings – so iTunes users do not need to worry about missing something they cannot buy. In addition, they identify the band for what they were, and what they are: one of England's leading goth bands of the 1980s.

Apple use the label and this short history to definitively position the band. They have listened to the music, read articles and lurked in fan sites to try to capture what the essence of the band is – not what fans would prefer to think, not what the band themselves would label themselves as, but as consumers in the music market might hear it. Apple are telling their users: if you want the essence of eighties goth rock in the United Kingdom, you cannot go wrong by buying the work of The Sisters of Mercy. Apple's description of the band is their expert opinion, designed as a marketing gimmick. As we have said earlier in this book, Wikipedia is a sum of the knowledge of the people who choose to edit the site, and whose edits do the site's editorial groups accept. This is how Wikipedia reports on The Sisters of Mercy:[2]

> The Sisters of Mercy are an English gothic rock band, formed in 1980 in Leeds, United Kingdom (UK). After achieving early underground fame there, the band had their commercial break-through in mid-1980s and sustained it until the early 1990s, when they stopped releasing new recorded output in protest against their record company Time Warner. Currently, the band is a touring outfit only.

This is spot-on, if grammatically incorrect (there is a missing definite article before 'mid-1980s', a common error among the inhabitants of the internet). What is curious about the Wikipedia page is there seems to have been no attempt to edit out the goth in goth rock in this description. Wikipedia makes it easy for a musician or manager to edit a page so that a band is described in the way the band wants their music to be described. Has Andrew Eldritch tried to re-write this page, or does he see it as below him? Certainly, the wording is not one Eldritch would like. Towards the bottom of the page in a sub-section head 'Influence' is this discussion:[3]

> The band shares influences with other bands in the first wave of what is termed 'goth music'. Whilst the band enjoys a consider-able fan base with overlapping interests in so-called dark culture, the Sisters of Mercy consider themselves first and foremost a rock band. They have discouraged their association with 'goth' via reg-ular public statements in the press, and stipulations in their stand-ard contract riders. Nevertheless, this has not stopped them from regularly appearing at festivals where this music is featured, such as M'era Luna.

The editors of this Wikipedia page really know their stuff, although frus-tratingly they provide no supporting evidence or references of their claims about the riders. The band is a goth band, loved by goths since the eighties, and listened to by new generations of goths in nightclubs, on stage and at home. All our respondents have identified The Sisters of Mercy as an important band who brought them into the scene, or one they think is an important band in the history and evolution of goth culture. There is in this final discussion an ironic 'nevertheless' that refers to the band appearing at the goth festival M'era Luna. The Sisters of Mercy are a rock band that will turn goth for the right price, it seems.

Another way of exploring what music people think The Sisters of Mercy play is to explore the comments under videos on YouTube. For an unofficial post of the video for 'Lucretia (My Reflection)', one of the hits of the *Floodland* album, there had been 4,183 comments by the time we viewed it.[4] In the first 100 comments, only one person tries to make the argument that the bands that emerged out of post-punk never called themselves goths. For everyone else who says anything about the genre, it is clearly goth. When poster approves of the video and the song by saying 'Industrial Goth at it's [*sic.*] best', 11 people reply and agree. One does say 'except it's not goth lol' but the lol shows that poster is having a joke at Andrew Eldritch. Another replies that it is not industrial – that is, it is goth, plain and simple.

The fans who maintain the SistersWiki site are more respectful of the wishes of Andrew Eldritch. Their front page[5] has a summary that begins: 'The Sisters of Mercy are a rock band that came out of the British post punk scene in 1980–1981'. This is true but rather coy. Further down at the end of the potted history is a sentence that reflects on the tension:

> The Sisters of Mercy are one of the most popular and influential bands among the gothic rock scene, although since the late 1980s Eldritch has tried to disassociate both himself and the band from that scene.

These fans then recognise that The Sisters of Mercy were in the 'gothic rock' scene, that they were and are popular and influential in goth culture. However, Andrew Eldritch has rejected the label of goth, while at the same time maintaining a career in band that has this history of being the key band driving the evolution of goth. It is time to explore how Andrew Eldritch resolves that tension.

How Andrew Eldritch Sees the Sisters of Mercy

In his attempt to claim ownership of the history of The Sisters of Mercy, Andrew Eldritch maintains a website that deliberately avoids describing the band as a goth band.[6] We have made a thorough search of the site and there are only the few instances where goth is mentioned (see the following paragraphs) – and all are scornful of the culture. The front page is white, with red text and orange imagery. The front page[7] states: 'We are a rock'n'roll band. And a pop band. And an industrial groove machine'. They are indeed all of those things. All rock music owes its structure and sonic roots to rock and roll, whether it is prog, stadium rock, punk, post-punk, goth rock, heavy metal, thrash metal, death metal or black metal – all use the same core elements and instruments (Frith, 1998; Spracklen, 2017b). In addition, pop music can be used to describe all music that is not classical music or folk music, so goth is one sub-genre of contemporary pop music, even if many people use pop music to mean the manufactured hit-factory, disposable love song form of music (Hesmondhalgh, 2013). Goth was and is part of pop music even if it claimed to be alternative and constructed on the wider communicative alternativity of the eighties, and The Sisters of Mercy – despite the radical politics of the lyrics and the indie ethos of their post-punk roots – embraced the stupidity of the instrumentality of the culture industry (Adorno, 1991). Industrial groove machine is a good description of the current sound of the band. However, we argue that this could equally be used to define the more aggressive parts on *Floodland* and *Vision Thing* – this is industrial music with dance influences, also labelled as goth rock. Is Andrew Eldritch playing with his fans?

On the page titled 'Information, Interviews and BioMechanics', there are a number of links to pages that deal with the band's history, the gigs played and the discography. There is a page titled 'What We're Not', which leads to a black-and-white picture of Andrew Eldritch with then-band member Tony James. It is dated to 1991: James looks like a goth with his top hat and (seemingly) black boots and black hair; Eldritch seems to be wearing black jeans and black boots, and he has black hair. They are reading a headline on a newspaper that says 'Black Horizon'. The picture looks like it has been taken on tour somewhere sunny, as they are reclining on sun loungers on a hotel terrace. Eldritch asks us: 'What is wrong with this picture?' Now, this question could be answered by pointing out the sheer awfulness of trying to look dark and gothic on a sun lounger, and the cheesy 'Black Horizon' headline is clearly a fake constructed by someone in the media team surrounding the band at that time. Perhaps, then. Eldritch wants to distance the band as it now exists from this cheesiness – this, he seems to be saying, is not who we are anymore, and never really were even if we got caught up in the phenomenon. Nevertheless, the question can be answered in another way. This is a picture taken when The Sisters of Mercy were being labelled as goth, at the height of their popularity and at the height of the global goth rock bandwagon, even if Eldritch distanced himself from it. Is Eldritch asking visitors of the website to realise the way the band is dressed and set up by the headline as goths is something that he regrets? Is he asking us to forgive him for the lapse?

On the page 'Rationale & Rhyme & Reason', there is a long piece titled: 'Where and why the Sisters started in the first place', which is followed by text from the album compiling the early indie releases.[8] The long piece is evidently written by Eldritch, as it repeats memories from the text written for the album. This is how Eldritch sees the early history of the band (note we have removed some of the more rambling sentences to reach the essential narrative):

> They may have gone their own way since, but originally the Sisters were a product of their times. That doesn't mean that they typified

the times. Punk had mocked traditional rock bands, which is why the Sisters had so much fun referring to them, and the fashion victims had turned to bad funk... When the Sisters started, the times – then as now – were typified by bad disco music. The Sisters were fans of Gary Glitter, T Rex, Motörhead, The Stooges, Suicide, The Velvet Underground, Père Ubu and The Fall. The Sisters liked good disco music... but they couldn't understand why even the NME was assigning the future of popular music to the likes of Kid Creole And The Coconuts ... to the exclusion of intelligently savage fun.

The Sisters were to form part of an anomalous rebellion along the M62, a motorway that crosses northern England and joins Liverpool, Manchester and Leeds. In each city, the rebellion had a different dominant flavour. Leeds, as The Sisters knew it, was a speed town, charged with a broadly political kind of gang warfare. The sub-culture in Leeds was clearly divided at the time. The punks were almost exclusively left-wing (to varying degrees, but united in their contempt of the right-wing) and vaguely allied to the dub factions of Chapeltown and Harehills. On the other hand was a right-wing alliance of general Aryan types, skinheads, would-be mods and a few confused teds... The F-Club offered a relatively safe base for the punk contingent, and every visiting band would play there which was not big or mainstream enough for the university. It is where the first Sisters (and many of their lifelong friends) met each other. The Sisters were not part of the art-school scene, which threw up excellent bands like Gang Of Four, Mekons, Delta 5, and (indirectly) Scritti Politti. The Sisters belonged firmly to the non-student, city end of things... The counterparts in Liverpool were The Teardrop Explodes, Pink Military and Echo and the Bunnymen; Manchester was primarily represented by Joy Division and The Chameleons.

There is no mention of goth anywhere in this history, which is an absence of great significance. The band is situated correctly in punk and post-punk, and the bands named as influences are uncontroversial. The history writes the rise of The Sisters of Mercy and their brand of gothic rock as a consequence, or an accident, of their situation in Leeds and the north of England. This history situates the band as outsiders in the same provincial north that had already spawned Joy Division, the band we have seen who first deliberately tried to evoke a twentieth-century gothic sound to reflect the urban wastelands that existed in Manchester. This official history of The Sisters of Mercy touches on the failure of Leeds as an inclusive urban space at in the late seventies and early eighties. The problems caused by neo-liberalism – no jobs, no hope, reduced support and public spending – led to a violent city centre. This meant the F-Club was safe haven for punks, post-punks and anyone who wanted to be alternative (Spracklen, Henderson, & Procter, 2016). It was a place where students and townies could interact. The statement that The Sisters of Mercy did not belong to the 'art-school scene' around Gang of Four is contestable; though, Eldritch had come to Leeds to be a student (though he quit), they did hang around with members of those bands, and they lived in the student area of Leeds. Perhaps, this is a way of constructing and presenting the band as authentic working-class radicals and not middle-class flâneurs dabbling in working-class life (Hebdige, 1979; Savage, 2002).

In the text from the collection *Some Girls Wander by Mistake*, there is an interesting reflection of what Eldritch thinks about the band's impact and aim around their gigs, and their recordings. It states:[9]

> I like to think it was the songs that made this band. I know it wasn't. We used a lot of smoke, very few lights, stepped right back and just made a space where you could lose yourself (but more probably find yourself) in a tide of colour and noise. It sounds simple, but no-one that really wanted to be a rock'n'roll star could have done it. Apart from anything else, it took a long time and burned more than a few people out. The records were never supposed to reflect that experience... when we had the money (and often, when we didn't), we would drop in on Kenny Giles in Bridlington. He had an eight-track and he was the only person who would help us make records the way we wanted... They may not sound like anybody else's, they may not even sound like records, but we loved them.

From the beginning, then, Eldritch understood the success of the band was not him as a front man, or the content of his lyrics. The attraction of the live performances was the whole experience. The clouds of dry ice that obscured the band, and the subdued lighting, made watching the band unlike regular bands. The technical expertise of the band's sound engineer ensured they played louder, yet more clearly, than their rivals did, and the sound was propelled by the abnormally perfect beats of the drum machine. This was all achieved through persistence and planning. On recording, Kenny Giles's studio was a place where he could work to ensure the music was how he wanted it to sound on the independent releases. With total control, Eldritch and The Sisters of Mercy constructed music on those early records that he still loves. This is the sound in Andrew Eldritch's vision: goth rock. Nevertheless, it is the sound he dare not name.

Elsewhere in the information section of the website, there are a few pertinent places where Eldritch has posted material that shows his scorn of goths. The most infamous is an interview Eldritch gave to the now obsolete Internet Service Provider virgin.net, which was set up in 1996 by Virgin to tap into the (then) novel craze for internet browsing through modems connected to domestic telephone landlines. Virgin.net was very hip when Eldritch gave the interview, and included coverage of music on its own home pages – so, the interview shows us that in May 1997, when the interview took place, The Sisters of Mercy were still hip and fashionable. It also shows us that Andrew Eldritch was adopting to the new possibilities of digital leisure precisely when other goths were becoming 'net goth' (we will discuss them later in the book). The interview is very lengthy, but it is essential to our analysis of The Sisters of Mercy that we cite it at length. To begin with, the interviewer, Alexa Williamson, refers Eldritch to the official fanzine the band produced, *Underneath the Rock*, which was sold through Reptile House, the band's merchandising arm:[10]

In a UTR interview (Issue 13, title: Free State Declared – if this rings any bells) from late 94 or 95 (?), the Sisters are referred to as 'legendary techno rock gods', while many Goths consider the Sisters to be one of the original bands of the Gothic rock movement, and on the phone you referred to the Sisters as that 'Northern pop band.' How should people think of the Sisters? Should they classify them at all?

Williamson has not asked the crucial goth question, as a favour perhaps to a singer who has become dismissal of the goth scene. Nevertheless, her opening gambit is an excellent one. She has shown Eldritch she reads the fanzine, and understands he has been trying to re-define the band's history and place in goth culture. She also knows that goths consider The Sisters of Mercy to be one of their own goth bands, a crucial band from the 1980s, and that this is something that winds up the singer. Andrew Eldritch responds by thanking her for reading the fanzine and then turns to the crucial matter. Remember, this is the one interview that Eldritch lists in full on the website to this date, so this is the crucial argument that he still wants to make now. He continues:[11]

> I'm not interested in what g***s think. I gather Mick Mercer keeps revising his Book Of G*** to include ever-more-ascerbic comments about us because we still refuse to talk to him. Go figure.

The habit of masking goth with asterisks, as if it is a swear-word, is something that continues through the interview. His opening response is awful to read for many of the band's fans. Goths have been his biggest fans; they have bought singles, albums, clothing, gig tickets. They have supported The Sisters of Mercy even as goth started to become unfashionable. The goths have supported The Sisters of Mercy through the difficult days of 1985 and 1986. They turned out in huge numbers to support the all-conquering version of the band in 1991, even though Eldritch was already dismissing goth and goths in 1989 (Mercer, 1991; Thompson, 2007). Eldritch is not interested in what goths think; though, he is interested enough to keep track of how Mick Mercer is reporting on the band in his various books. Eldritch continues, clearly fired up by the very suggestion he was ever anything to do with goth:[12]

> I recently declined the opportunity to do guest vocals on a single for somebody (who shall remain nameless) because the lyrics were appalling – and very silly. I thought 'If I sang that rubbish, people would accuse me of being a g***!'. (The artist who shall remain nameless was not, of course, accused of any such thing.) Turns out the lyrics had been written for her by David Dorrell, a prime originator of the 'Sisters are g*** and therefore crap' smear. There's a nice irony for you. Pot calling kettle black, I'd say – except that we're a stainless-steel kettle and very shiny. He remains a dimwit, and he's scraping a living writing crappy g***

lyrics for mainstream pop artists. Better than the fat professional-retard who now does the annoying adverts for washing powder, I suppose, or the fat professional-retard who went off to write for the Sun. They didn't like us either. British music journalists never die, they waddle off to reveal their agenda for a derelict spiv nation in a media half-life more grotesque than anything I've ever been accused of. The Sisters are occupied by politics and philosophy but we lack a spiritual agenda. Apart from the fact that we're not very spiritually-minded and only ever use the idioms ironically (when we use them at all), it's disappointing that so many people have in all seriousness adopted just one of our many one-week-of-stupid-clothes benders, just like it's currently disappointing that the rest of the nation is in all seriousness wearing those crappy seventies clothes that we wore for a week in '84 because we'd taken enough medication to find it funny. Well, okay, we wore crappy seventies shirts for more than a week, but that's because we kept taking the medication. And it really was funny.

This long rant starts with Eldritch getting annoyed that someone has asked him to be a guest singer on a song for some woman singer more famous than him. Two years before this interview, the then world-famous pop star, Kylie Minogue, had sung with Nick Cave and the Bad Seeds on the gothic-tinged ballad 'Where the Wild Roses Grow'. The single was released in October 1995 and was a hit around the world. Is Eldritch suggesting this is the song he was asked to sing? The problem with that suggestion is that the song was written by Nick Cave, and Kylie was his guest, not the other way round. It sounds rather that the success of that pairing had led someone to try to duplicate the strange pairing with Eldritch as the Nick Cave type. Eldrich identifies the British journalist, David Dorrell, as the lyricist involved, which allows his anger to switch to him and the other music journalists in the British press who have supposedly invented goth, named the band as goth, and who have built up then brought down the band. Towards the end of the cited paragraph, he admits that the band wore 'crappy seventies clothes' for more than a week, but it was a brief moment that was brought about by being on 'medication' – speed and other drugs, and alcohol. He ends this part of the interview by saying:[13]

Anyway, I'm constantly confronted by representatives of popular culture who are far more g*** than we, yet I have only to wear black socks to be stigmatised as the demon overlord. Luckily, this is a particularly British misconception, so we don't usually have to deal with it much. Mainland journalists very rarely ask questions like the one above, and then only in reference to British media practices...

It is not clear who Eldritch thinks is the band or the musicians who are more goth than The Sisters of Mercy. It is somewhat disingenuous, anyway, as earlier in the interview he wants to attack people who followed the goth trend by dressing in the clothes worn by his band back in 1984. Eldritch here blames the British press for accusing him of being a goth, and he thinks it is unjust because being labelled goth brings with it the stereotypes about being the demonic overlord of goth, or the godfather of goth. He thinks the British press want to portray him as some stereotypically goth living in a gothic castle, drinking blood and writing his thoughts in a book of magick (with a k). What really angers him is the way goth has become a fashion – wearing black – and an aesthetic associated with bad poetry (and lyrics) about death and vampires. In that sense, we have some sympathy for him. Goth has become Eldritch's monster; and like Frankenstein, Eldritch is unable to stop his monster for going on the rampage. People want him to like a goth culture that is attracted to the romance of the night and the graveyard, which was never his goth rock – which was politically charged, clever and sardonic. For a moment, Eldritch was too excited by the fame and the attention to care that he had created this monster; but since *Floodland*, he has struggled to keep his contempt in check. Seeing the adulation accorded his ex-band mates in The Mission must have been particularly hard to take, especially in 1990 when they had a hit with the single 'Deliverance'. That song begins with the words 'believe in magic', then roams around the usual suspects of the New Age: fairy rings, stone circles, swords in lakes, healing hands, a fairy queen, Avalon and Beltane fires. This is all very far from the fight against capitalism, Thatcherism and the cruelty of modernity.

Another place on the information section that refers to Eldritch's view of goth is in the 'Frequently Asked Questions (of the Boring Kind)'. Under the inevitable question 'Do you always wear black?' is the following reply:[14]

> Not at all. Traditionally, we very often wear shirts of the most flamboyant colour and design. We certainly wear less black than all the other pop acts we can think of (and we can think of plenty). You shouldn't be that bothered anyway. What we wear is designed to be practical and/or entertain *us*, and we're far more interested in songs than fashion statements. Apart from anything else, if we'd made fashion statements we'd probably have had the same short career as every other bunch of fashion victims. If anything, it would be sensible to deliberately avoid being fashionable anywhere, although we're not sure what that would look like, and we couldn't be bothered anyway. You have to remember that we live and work in different countries with very differing ideas of fashion, and we think global. White, for example, is a funereal colour in Japan and certain other Asian countries... A TV station or a magazine or a citizen with a particularly desperate agenda might insist on parsing statements that we're not actually making, exaggerating the importance of the occasional black sock, or reviewing clothes that we're not actually wearing; you don't have to make the same mistake. If the songs are too difficult to concentrate on, or you're simply so sad that you have to draw substantive conclusions from what we wear, you should at least ignore those morons who need to discuss the kind of capes

we wear. Because we've never worn any. The best thing would be
to ignore us as well. Go find a band which is all about clothing.
There are plenty of them.

Eldritch has definitely stopped wearing black; he makes an effort to dress in
bright colours on stage. He dismisses anyone who wants to link The Sisters of
Mercy to bands that care about fashions, bands who wear capes and have built
any following based on their look as opposed to their music. It is a commend-
able point to make. However, all pop music is about how bands and artists look
(Frith, 1998; Hesmondhalgh, 2013), the clothes they choose to wear when on
stage – even bands like the new version of The Sisters of Mercy with their bright
shirts and football tops. Eldritch does not mention goths here but it is obvious
whom he is pointing at when he says there are 'plenty of them'. Further down in
the same list[15] is another telling question: 'Surely you actively dislike some of the
bands who end up on the same bill?' The answer is:

> 'Fraid so, but you play what you can get. You can't always play
> with bands you like and/or bands whose audiences will broaden
> your constituency. In the early days, obviously, we got no choice at
> all. Even now, if we want to play in a certain territory at a certain
> time, we often have to accept that the only willing promoters are
> incompetent or dim. Most promoters are indeed dim (except, of
> course, the ones who are reading this). We can't do their jobs for
> them, or we'd be the promoters. That's not our business. We don't
> always get the right of veto over the opening acts. Even when we're
> presenting a touring package to promoters, it has to be something
> they'll invest in. Most promoters want to invest in a line-up which
> they think is a marketing no-brainer, and we can't afford to be
> too bothered, especially at one-off concerts. We did, however, once
> turn down an offer of £200,000 (very approximately $300,000) to
> headline some g*** fest in Whitby. Go figure. While we're on the
> subject of dim promoters.... we provide promoters with current
> photographs and current artwork and a concise up-to-date biog-
> raphy. Most of them still prefer to dredge up ancient pictures and
> myths from the very bottom of the internet pond. Very few pro-
> moters can even be bothered to put The Sisters Of Mercy on the
> billing. Our concert contract clearly states that all these offences
> are Very Bad...

The Sisters of Mercy are not so anti-goth to refuse to be on a line-up that has
goth bands on it, or organised as a goth music festival. Nevertheless, they would
prefer not to be on that line-up, and claim to have refused to play Whitby Goth
Weekend, because either the money was too low, or the festival was just too gothic
for Eldritch. Moreover, finally, they would like promoters not to label The Sisters
of Mercy as goth, the 'myth' from the Internet, using old pictures that presumably show Eldritch looking like the gothic godfather he actually was.

Fans on the New Sisters' Sound and the Gothness of The Sisters of Mercy

One of the longest running fan-sites online is the Heartland Forum.[16] In its current iteration, it has been live since 2002, and it has roots in an older mailing list. The site's long-serving Administrator Quiff Boy has strong connections to the band, and is based in the north of England – the users of the forum themselves include people from around the world. There are 4,492 registered users at the time of writing, and 67 of those are active (12:31 p.m., 03 November 2017). On the site, fans of the band can post information, ask questions and answer other people's questions. Like all chat forums, the site is not as popular as it once was, as people in the 2010s use social media to get news and information (Spracklen, 2015b). However, it remains an important source for information for the fans who use it, so it is a useful subject for a semiotic analysis of what fans think about the band sand about goth culture. There are sub-forums specifically about The Sisters of Mercy (Sisters Chat, various sub-forums for tours and gigs, resources and interviews), and more generic sub-forums (General Chat, Trading, Jokes).

In the General Chat on 03 November 2017, posters seem comfortable mentioning goth bands. There is a discussion about Bauhaus at the top of the listings. However, more tellingly, there is two-page discussion about the 'Goth World Cup', a best goth song competition organised by BBC Radio.[17] The competition organisers asked listeners to submit nominations, and then had the nominated songs playing off against one another in cup-like rounds. The Sisters of Mercy's 'Lucretia (My Reflection)' is one of the winners of the first round, and the posters are elated. It loses closely to Bauhaus's 'Bela Lugosi's Dead' in the second round, and one fans notes that 'general consensus seems to be The Sisters would win if it was a song from FALAA [*First And Last And Always*]'. At no point has anyone chastised the BBC for putting the band into the goth category. Instead, they are pleased that the band is in the running, and are encouraging each other to vote to try to get Lucretia voted the winner as the best goth song. Everybody knows The Sisters of Mercy were and are a goth band, and everybody is able to situate the band among other goth bands such as The Cult.

In the Sisters Chat sub-forum and our experience of lurking there every day in order to see what may or may not be happening, there are regular posters who question the current version of the band's line-up – given the age of Eldritch, issues with his voice in the mix, the style and competence of the two guitarists, and the absence of a live bass guitar. There are others who deny there is anything wrong, and claim The Sisters of Mercy as they have performed this year (2017) are actually better than they were in 2007, or earlier. Typical of the type is 'How long can the Sisters continue...?'.[18] The first post was made on 01 September 2017 and is a complaint about the lack of a new album, but it soon descends into a question about how the band can keep going when some people think the band sounds poor on stage. There are 49 additional comments – the best one in our opinion is the person who answers the question by saying 'for as long as they continue to sell tickets'. The band has lost some of its fans, *some* of whom continue to post on the forum complaining about the various changes they do not like, but they still have enough fans willing to pay to watch them. For the fans who do not like the latest version of the band, there is always the tribute act The Sisters of Murphy who do the songs exactly like the original band played them; or there are the video clips and bootlegs from the days when it was okay for Andrew Eldritch to consider himself part of goth rock – that week in 1984 he mentioned. Our respondents are divided in whether they will go to see The Sisters of Mercy when they next tour. For some, it is worth it to see Eldritch standing on stage and singing the old songs again; for others, the band have changed so much, and Eldritch has become so objectionable, that they would rather spend their money on the above-mentioned Murphies.

Conclusion

The Sisters of Mercy were the most important band in the genesis and evolution of goth. They perfected the sound and the look, and made goth a truly alternative sub-culture even as they sold records, concert tickets and merchandise. Whatever Eldritch might claim, they were goths from at least 1982 all the way to the last recordings in 1993, shaping and influencing the careers of dozens of other goth bands. However, we sympathise with Eldritch's unhappiness at the takeover of goth's alternative space, its commodification and its reduction to instrumentality and Gothic folly. He has spent his career since the end of the eighties trying to reject and resist this takeover, and we appreciate his desire to distance himself from it. However, we also believe that he needs to realise that most of his fans are goths, and his band's songs are goth songs, and sooner or later goths will stop buying tickets for his gigs if he continues to behave like he does.

Notes

1. All statement from Eldritch can be found in the forums at www.myheartland. co.uk, where interviews in various places are carefully analysed for any sign of anything new or interesting.
2. https://en.wikipedia.org/wiki/The_Sisters_of_Mercy, accessed on 31 October 2017.
3. https://en.wikipedia.org/wiki/The_Sisters_of_Mercy, accessed on 31 October 2017.
4. https://www.youtube.com/watch?v=IuezNswtRfo, accessed on 31 October 2017.
5. https://sisterswiki.org/Main_Page, accessed on 31 October 2017.
6. It is not entirely clear whether it is actually Andrew Eldritch writing the content, it may be someone who does the work for him – but it sounds like Eldritch. We will assume that it is Andrew Eldritch because we know he was an early adopter of the internet, and he has the skills and knowledge to maintain his own website.
7. http://www.thesistersofmercy.com/, accessed on 31 October 2017.
8. http://www.the-sisters-of-mercy.com/gen/rrr1.htm, accessed on 02 November 2017.
9. http://www.the-sisters-of-mercy.com/gen/rrr1.htm, accessed on 02 November 2017.
10. http://www.the-sisters-of-mercy.com/gen/vnettext/vnettext.htm, accessed on 01 November 2017.

11. http://www.the-sisters-of-mercy.com/gen/vnettext/vnettext.htm, accessed on 01 November 2017.
12. http://www.the-sisters-of-mercy.com/gen/vnettext/vnettext.htm, accessed on 01 November 2017.
13. http://www.the-sisters-of-mercy.com/gen/vnettext/vnettext.htm, accessed on 01 November 2017.
14. http://www.the-sisters-of-mercy.com/gen/faqdim/faqdim.htm, accessed on 01 November 2017.
15. http://www.the-sisters-of-mercy.com/gen/faqdim/faqdim.htm, accessed on 01 November 2017.
16. https://www.myheartland.co.uk/.
17. https://www.myheartland.co.uk/viewtopic.php?t=26488, accessed on 03 November 2017.
18. https://www.myheartland.co.uk/viewtopic.php?t=26379, accessed on 03 November 2017.

Chapter 7

The Goths and the Globalisation of Popular Culture

Introduction

What happened to goth in the 1990s? Did it die out? Why did Marilyn Manson call goth a metal band? This chapter explores the trends that made goth music, culture and aesthetics cross from the post-punk scene in the United Kingdom into Europe, America and then the rest of the world. In this chapter, then, the globalisation of goth sub-culture is reconstructed. We will explore how goth initially spread as a form of alternative culture in the 1980s, and continued to maintain its alternative status once its moment of fashionability had passed in the early nineties. By using our multiple data sources, we will explore how goth was transformed in the process of globalisation, becoming an identifiable form of popular culture, from the nineties onwards, seen as both an alternative space operating underground and far from the mainstream – while at the same time, being an alternative space that embraced mainstream cultural practices and habits, and one that became increasingly defined by the stereotypes imposed on it by mainstream cultural commentators. In this chapter, we will explore the connections between goth and metal, and how metal started to claim some practices and forms from goth, from wearing black to transgressing everyday cultural norms.

The Received Standard Version: Mainstream Goth Died in the Nineties

It has become a myth retold with certainty that goth died out in the mainstream in the 1990s, surviving only through the emergence of an underground goth sub-culture focussed around small independent labels, fanzines and clubs. We call this the Received Standard Version (RSV) of what happened to goth in the nineties.[1] This is the goth sub-culture reflected in Hodkinson's (2002) book, for example, which shows the resilience and communicative action of goths in action, as they defend their sub-culture through maintaining loyalties inside the scene, and by developing alternative commercial activity. It is the goth sub-culture of the underground club scene seen in the work of Brill (2008), and in the history of goth as dance music in the recent book by van Elferen and Weinstock (2016). In this narrative, the underground of goth culture was formed across the world in this period, with strengths in mainland Europe and North America. In this narrative, goth was very underground in the United Kingdom, but still survived as a functioning sub-culture even if the mainstream music industry and media had decided that goth had died in the 1990s. This is the narrative found in the popular book by Scharf (2011), and the later work of Mercer (2002). Our respondents all say the same thing in their interviews – goth survived the nineties outside of the mainstream, and through the rise of goth music as dance music, played by Disk Jockeys or DJs in clubs, not bands on stage. A quick search of the Internet finds the RSV still forming the collective memory of goth in the period:[2]

> By the mid-1990s, however, the gothic culture had seemingly used up its time in the media and commercial spotlight and all but disappeared from public view. The intense attachment of many participants to the style of the goth subculture, though, ensured its small-scale survival. From across and beyond Britain there emerged a new generation of bands who were reliant upon small-scale specialist labels, media and clubs, and who were motivated more by their own enthusiasm than by any realistic hope of breaking into public view or making significant money.

The RSV as seen in this iteration is essentially correct. But it is missing a crucial context and element, which we will come to shortly. The date is an approximate one, because there is no moment when we can identify the mainstream music media and the music industry abandoning goth. New bands and new scenes emerge all the time in the mainstream music industry, from three distinct but interconnected sources: young musicians and fans, the media, and the music industry itself. Some scenes are the products of younger people rejecting the music that is in the mainstream (which is where punk, post-punk and goth all emerged), though they do so in a way that is informed and constrained by the mainstream (Frith, 1998; Hebdige, 1979; Hesmondhalgh, 2013). Other scenes are constructed or validated by the media seeking to label something new and trendy (possibly goth again), or the media seeking to pigeonhole something that has already become a residual part of popular culture (Savage, 2002). Finally, scenes and genres can be constructed deliberately by the music industry to make money, to greater or lesser success, such as nu metal (Brown, 2008). As early as 1989, as we saw in Chapter 5, some journalists had declared goth to be dead, which is why Unsworth (1989) wrote her piece saying it was still alive, albeit in a changed form. We could take 1993, the year The Sisters of Mercy released their last single, as an endpoint for goth in the mainstream, but that is an arbitrary date. A similarly arbitrary date might be 1991, when The Cult's difficult album *Sanctuary* came out at the same time as Nirvana's *Nevermind*, signifying the passing of the alternative torch from old goth to young grunge. What is true is that all the big British goth rock bands stalled or broke up in the early nineties. Between the late eighties and early nineties, it is also true to note that dance culture and dance-infused indie bands became popular as alternative music and sub-culture, fuelled by the friend-making drug ecstasy (Nehring, 2007; Redhead, 1997; Thornton, 1995); perhaps, the shift in underground goth to dancing in clubs reflected that wider sub-cultural trend (Brill, 2008).

By the middle of the 1990s, then, is true to say that the mainstream culture industry had dismissed goth rock – the music of The Cult, The Sisters of Mercy, The Mission and Fields of the Nephilim – and consigned it to the past. Bands that adopted the eighties goth rock sonic template were dismissed as copyists by journalists and key musicians associated with the eighties goth rock scene such as Andrew Eldritch of The Sisters of Mercy, as we saw in the last chapter (Thompson, 2007). Moreover, alongside that, goths actively developed a sub-culture based on a communicative alternativity because they were rejected by the mainstream, and because they rejected the mainstream in turn (Hodkinson, 2002). Miranda Yardley (2010) writes a reflection and justification of the vibrancy of the nineties goth scene and its bands for the *Dominion* section of *Terrorizer* magazine that defended the legitimacy of the 1990s, while repeating the RSV:

> With a recent reawakening of the mainstream's interest in all things dark, a new generation of music fans are discovering classic 80's Goth. What is less well documented for those to that have started to develop their interest in music in the last 10 years is what came after. Was Goth a musical dead end that stopped in its tracks in 1991 (as the NME have often proclaimed)? Of course not. Those that grew up with Gothic music throughout the 80's and 90's will inevitably find the contents of this article to be at best old news and at worst, hopelessly romanticised. But the fact remains that unless you were around at the time, it's unlikely that a music fan in this day and age is going to be exposed to the musical wealth of the 90's underground in anything like the same volumes as that of the 80's. Many of the 'great' Goth bands of the 80's resented the tag that was placed upon them and it's arguable that the early 90s was the first time that a whole generation of bands actually took up the mantle of being 'Gothic' willingly. Even at the time, there were many that saw these bands as being derivative and lacking the integrity of their predecessors, but with hindsight it's plain to see that the era had a unique sound and charm of its very own.

Yardley wants the bands from the nineties to be respected by people in the new century, and when she was writing in 2010 wanted them to be heard and recognised in the same way as the goth rock bands from the eighties. We will discuss some of those key bands later in this chapter. What Yardley's argument shows is she believes that the bands from the nineties were dismissed because they were not the founders or popularisers of goth. Yardley mentions the myth that goth had died in 1991 was just that – a fable put about by the mainstream music press bored with goth and looking for the next new thing. However, what she goes on to say does not contradict that myth. She writes about the bands as a next generation overlooked because she knows they did not receive the same attention back in the nineties, and they do not receive the same attention today compared with the eighties bands. She is correct to say that these bands and the people in the sub-culture were the ones who fully embraced goth; these were the people who had Mercer's (1997) *Goth Bible* to hand, as one of our respondents has suggested to us.

The context and element missing in the RSV is metal – the extreme metal underground, and the mainstream metal scene. Both of these influenced the evolution of goth in the nineties, shaping it, and being shaped by it in turn. Simpson (2006) comes close to the significance of metal in his reflection on the history and evolution of goth published on the website of *The Guardian*, but he only touches upon half of the metal influence, and sticks mainly to the well-worn narrative:

> [Wayne Hussey of The Mission] began the 80s quietly reading Rimbaud and ended them fronting the Mission, whose wine-spilling, cartoon image was almost Carry On Goth. 'We made buffoons of ourselves in public', he says, 'but it was endearing for a lot of people'. It didn't last. Hussey vividly remembers standing on a railway station platform and seeing two girls in Stone Roses T-shirts. 'I knew something else was coming'. In the 90s, goths all but disappeared as dance music became the dominant youth cult. The movement went underground and fractured into cyber goth, Christian goth, industrial goth, medieval goth and the latest sub-genre, zombie goth. Around the world, however, goth hit the mainstream. Goth crossbred with electronica and heavy metal in the form of Nine Inch Nails and Marilyn Manson. While the music of Nine Inch Nails owed more to the industrial-influenced music of Throbbing Gristle and Ministry, their subect matter (murder and trauma) and style (head-to-toe black leather) were unmistakably goth. Marilyn Manson, meanwhile, fused Alien Sex Fiend's electro-goth with Alice Cooper's theatrics and went to the arena circuit. In Germany, the industrial-techno-metal sextet Rammstein took much from gothic horror, and Hussey says his mother often tells him how much the cult Finnish band HIM sound like the Mission.

Hussey is right to say that The Mission had become a caricature of everything that had gone wrong with eighties goth rock in the first place. His memory of the two women in the t-shirts may well be genuine, but it does not mean much without context. The Stone Roses were huge in 1989 when they released their debut album, when The Mission, slightly older, were working on their third album. This memory may be a personal gripe that the attention lavished on The Mission was being lavished on The Stone Roses. Simpson takes this as evidence that dance-based indie music, and dance music itself, had won the battle for the wider alternative sub-culture's attention – he claims dance music became 'dominant' in the nineties and forced goth into the underground, where it splintered into a number of sub-genres. This is still the RSV, and Simpson's words can be found cited and referenced on Wikipedia.[3]

Where Simpson adds metal to the evolution, he is, as we have said, half correct. Goth music did not go underground in the nineties. Goth music and the goth aesthetics were adopted by mainstream metal bands. He mentions, correctly, Marilyn Manson, HIM and Rammstein as metal bands, which found the audiences that had been created by The Sisters of Mercy and the eighties bands. In turn, they found new audiences around the world. But he does not mention the extreme metal underground that took goth rock's aesthetics and sound: the gothic melodrama of My Dying Bride and the Peaceville trio (Yavuz, 2017): the misery of doom metal more generally; goth metal; and the misanthropy, anti-modernity and elitism of black metal (Spracklen, 2006, 2013a, 2014). In the Section 'Extreme Metal, Mainstream Metal and Goth: The Nineties Connections', we will explore the relation between goth and metal in this crucial period in the evolution of both genres and sub-cultures globally. We will then discuss specifically some formative underground goth bands and spaces that ensured goth as a communicative alternativity survived.

Extreme Metal, Mainstream Metal and Goth: The Nineties Connections

The origins of heavy metal are as strongly debated as the history of goth (Brown, 2015a). There is agreement among scholars and fans that heavy metal became hugely popular across the global North in the 1980s, especially among working-class white men (Walser, 1993; Weinstein, 1991). It appealed to young people disaffected by the condition of modernity, and cynical of the music industry's manufactured pop. In other words, heavy metal appealed to individuals seeking the same rebellion and resistance – the same communicative alternativity – that had made punk transform into post-punk and goth. In 1982, when The Sisters of Mercy released the single version of 'Alice', heavy metal was already triumphant in the charts in the United Kingdom. In March of that year, Iron Maiden released *The Number of the Beast*, arguably their most important album, the first one to reach number one in the UK Album Chart, and the first one to feature Bruce Dickinson as lead singer. The album included the song 'The Number of the Beast', which caused controversy for its references to Satan, devil worship and the Book of Revelation, and which helped associate the occult and darkness with heavy metal (Baddeley, 1999). In July 1982, Judas Priest were in the charts with their album *Screaming for Vengeance*. The band were led by Rob Halford who wore black leather and bondage gear, which were adopted from punk and the S&M scene. This look had already become part of heavy metal's look, and it became part of goth's look. These two bands typify the status of heavy metal in the period. It appealed to people who did not want to buy pop records or listen to Radio One. It allowed its fans to feel alternative, as the songs and imagery evoked the outcast, the rebel, Satanism and horror films, the outlaw bikers or fantasy warriors fighting (Weinstein, 1991). At the same time, heavy metal was most definitely a profitable part of the music industry. Similar to the rock bands of the seventies, heavy metal bands in the eighties sold out arena tours, sold millions of records, and had huge numbers of loyal fans who bought patches, badges, fanzines and t-shirts. Iron Maiden and Judas Priest were on major labels, and despite the flirtation with evil and danger, they stayed on the right side of censors, editors and shareholders. Music critics generally rejected heavy metal for its lack of ideological purpose, its lack of clever lyricism and its lack of a good tune; or they dismissed it as sexist, stupid music for stupid people (Walser, 1993). Post-punk and goth were supposedly against everything 'rockist' about bands like Iron Maiden and Judas Priest. However, the Satanism and darkness of the former, and the black leather of the latter, were formative influences on the goth aesthetic.

Extreme metal emerged in the eighties as a reaction in the scene against the dominance of bands such as Iron Maiden – considered too safe or too commercial. Extreme metal also rejected thrash metal as party music. Taking their cues from then-unfashionable bands such as Venom, bands started to experiment with the sounds that became death metal in the eighties, and then later black metal (Kahn-Harris, 2007). Death metal is loud, fast and brutal, and the death-growl vocals are a million miles from goth rock. However, death metal defined an underground alternative to goth. Bands who played death metal tended to focus on lyrics associated with horror or politics, but some such as Deicide embraced Satanic lyrics and imagery (Phillipov, 2012). This extreme metal scene had become global by the end of the eighties; however, it was tiny, and almost completely underground in most places, with the United States of America and Sweden two of the countries where death metal bands received coverage in the metal and rock press. In the underground scene, fans became aware of bands through reading reviews of demos and mix-tapes in fanzines, and these tapes were traded with those fanzines through the post by writing off to strange people who paid for classified ads in the metal magazines (Kahn-Harris, 2007). From this underground network came the so-called 'second wave' of black metal, centred on the Helvete record shop in Oslo (Reyes, 2013; Spracklen, 2006). This second wave rejected death metal for being a sell-out, a way to make money and a betrayal of the supposedly authentic Satanism and elitism of Venom and Bathory.[4] What became the definitive black metal sound and ideology was perfected by a string of Norwegian bands – Darkthrone, Burzum, Mayhem, Immortal and Emperor – who developed black metal vocals as demonic screeches, and who introduced spooky dissonances, intervals and minor chords over death metal's blastbeats (Spracklen, 2006, 2013, 2014).

The circle around Helvete started to gain notoriety in the underground extreme metal scene in 1992, as key figures expressed strong views about elitism and Satanism in fanzine interviews (Spracklen, 2006). This was the time when the first Norwegian church was burned down, and others followed. In January 1993, the Norwegian press investigated the scene and linked it to the church burnings. The bands received attention around the world in various music magazines and newspapers. Then, the murder of Helvete's and Mayhem's Euronymous by Burzum's Varg Vikernes ensured black metal was known around the world, as Varg was tried and imprisoned in 1994, and others were arrested and found guilty of offences from the church burnings to murder. In this period, many death metal bands became black metal bands, and many black metal bands were formed, as people wanted to be associated with the anti-Christian, anti-Establishment ideology of the Norwegian bands. Many of those musicians and fans were already fans of goth rock, and saw in black metal's occultism a natural evolution of the themes of Fields of the Nephilim, and in black metal's elitism the communicative alternativity of post-punk and goth rock (Baddeley, 1999; Spracklen, 2006, 2014).

The interconnection between goth and black metal is seen in the British band Cradle of Filth (Baddeley, 1996, 2006). They were formed in 1991 as an extreme metal band, and then they adopted the black metal style as they toured and released demos. However, they were influenced lyrically and visually by gothic literature, horror films, vampires, preferring a refined Satanism to the violent anti-Christianity of their Norwegian pen-friends. Their debut album *The Principle of Evil Made Flesh* begins with a two-minute intro 'Darkness Our Bride (Jugular Wedding)' that uses keyboards that are inspired by goth. The song titles hover between those that could only be black meal ('Iscariot') and those that are more ambiguous ('The Forest Whispers My Name'), and others that are gothic in inspiration ('A Crescendo of Passion Bleeding'). Although the music is mainly black metal once the intro has played out, the opening part of 'A Dream of Wolves in the Snow' is inspired by the romanticism of death/doom (see the following paragraphs), and sounds gothic lyrically and goth musically. Cradle of Filth started to build a dedicated fan-base of goths and metal fans, and sealed the connection with goth with the release of their second album, *Dusk... And Her Embrace*, in 1996. This album was released on the big indie label Music for Nations, who had the expertise and the money to push the band into the press and onto stages around the world. The album had Sara Jezebel Diva on backing vocals, and her vocals inspired numerous bands to include operatic female voices – which later came to be associated with gothic metal. More importantly, *Dusk... And Her Embrace* included two songs with titles designed to appeal to the goth part of their audience: an instrumental called 'The Graveyard by Moonlight', and the egregiously named 'A Gothic Romance (Red Roses for the Devil's Whore)'. Cradle of Filth continued to be associated with both black metal and gothic aesthetics through the nineties and into this century. Their song 'Ghost in the Fog' released at the end of the nineties on the 2000 album *Midian* is the best example of the genius of the band. The song combines the operatic drama of gothic metal, goth-club friendly keyboards and beats, with furious black metal passages to which dancers can mosh along. The video shows the band dressed in stage costumes that are taken from nineties cyber-goth – and even the black-metal corpsepaint is essentially the same white make-up adopted by many goths since it was still known as post-punk (Brill, 2008).

Death-doom is (not surprisingly) a sub-genre of extreme metal that combines death metal with doom metal (Kahn-Harris, 2006; Yavuz, 2017). In the nineties, it became associated with the British independent label Peaceville Records, who for a moment in time had three bands signed to them who were selling records and making a name for themselves internationally. The first band was Paradise Lost, who Peaceville signed in 1990. Their debut album was a huge success and Paradise Lost soon themselves back in the studio working on a follow-up. This second album, released in 1991, was called *Gothic*, and incorporated goth keyboards and female vocals, but they still sounded like a death/doom band. The success of the album led to the band signing with Music for Nations, who gave them access to bigger markets globally. Over next few albums, the band slowly changed their style: the death-growl was abandoned, more gothic elements were used; eventually in 1997, the band became a goth-club favourite in Germany and Sweden with the album *One Second*, an album where the band embraced electronica and pop-synths. Paradise Lost, then, started out by being an extreme metal band curious enough about goth culture to call their album *Gothic*, before embracing nineties goth-club sub-culture to the extent they changed their style altogether.[5]

The second band of the Peaceville Trio was My Dying Bride.[6] Their name itself is a work of gothic genius, and it has inspired a clutch of doom metal, emo rock and goth bands to find similarly doomed and romantic names. My Dying Bride were formed in Bradford in 1990, and soon attracted the attention of Peaceville Records, who were based down the road in Cleckheaton. My Dying Bride's first album *As the Flower Withers* featured Matrin Powell as a session musician playing violin. By the time of their second album, 1993's *Turn Loose the Swans*, he had joined the band as a permanent member, playing violin and keyboards. Unlike the first album, *Turn Loose the Swans* is slow and majestic, and clean singing and spoken-word passages complement the death growls of singer Aaron Stainthorpe. Stainthorpe sings his clean-voiced lyrics with pain and heartbreak in his voice, a mournful cry that channels Elvis, Leonard Cohen and Andrew Eldritch. Like Eldritch, he sings and writes with a Yorkshire accent[7]. The album cover is very gothic, and it is rightly considered a classic of gothic metal, and death-doom. This album received strong critical acclaim for the band, as did their next two albums. After that album (*Like Gods of the Sun*) Martin Powell left the band, and the next album experimented with post-rock sonics, but they came back to their familiar sonic landscape in the follow-up. They chose to remain with Peaceville Records, and became headliners at metal festivals and goth music festivals in this century, with thousands of devoted fans around the world, and a sonic template that does not veer far from the one established in the nineties (Yavuz, 2017). Around the world, they are described as death/doom, doom metal, extreme metal or goth metal. They are not identified as goth or goth rock; but, they are appreciated by goths, including some of the people we interviewed – in 2016, they were the headliners of the Bram Stoker Festival in Whitby, a short-lived rival alternative/goth festival to Whitby Goth Weekend (see Chapter 10).

Another channel of underground, communicative alternativity to spring from extreme metal was doom metal. Doom metal is heavy metal played slowly, and its sonic and lyrical template comes from the first Black Sabbath album (Cope, 2016; Kahn-Harris, 2006). In the early eighties, doom metal bands such as Pentagram and Saint Vitus perfected the template, and Candlemass were the first doom metal band to be known widely in the underground scene with the release of their debut album in 1986. Doom metal, like aspects of goth rock at the time, was mournful, inspired by romanticism and death. At the end of the eighties, it offered a way for death-metal musicians and fans, and punks from the hardcore scene, to escape the race to increase tempos and impose hyper-fast blastbeats over everything (Kahn-Harris, 2006). Doom metal bands were formed at this time that looked back to the founding sonic template, and took with them ideas about singing, lyrics and imagery from goth. British band Solstice, formed in Dewsbury in 1990 by former hardcore musician Rich Walker, are the best example of this – their debut album released in 1994 even has the name *Lamentations*. Electric Wizard, formed in 1993 by Jus Oborn, became popular enough to break through into the mainstream music press in this century. Their lyrical themes draw heavily on horror genre stereotypes, the stories of H. P. Lovecraft and the occult more generally – the same sources that informed Fields of the Nephilim.

Black metal, death/doom and doom metal, then, are the untold connections between goth and metal in the eighties and nineties. The extreme metal underground was influenced by the goth rock aesthetic and template. So, when the big goth rock bands faltered or went on strike in the early nineties, their fans found new music that sated their desire for blackness, alternativity and belonging. These new bands and sub-genres tweaked their sound and aesthetic in turn, consciously or not, so that by the end of the nineties people outside of the alternative underground would find it hard to tell the difference between goth and metal – especially goth and black metal (Scharf, 2011). Around half of our respondents admitted an interest in metal and black metal, though they did not see metal as being part of goth; rather, it existed in a different sonic space, even if there were crossovers such as goth metal and industrial.

One metal band in the nineties captured goth's audience more than any other, and brought goth to the mainstream of American popular culture: Marilyn Manson, already identified in the history of goth in Simpson (2006), even if Gunn (1999) shows that goths resisted this takeover of the goth name by Marilyn Manson and their fans. Marilyn Manson the band have been labelled goth rock and industrial metal; but over the years, their frontman Marilyn Manson has been reluctant to allow his band to be pigeonholed as goth or metal (Baddeley, 2000, 2002). As Wikipedia records it under a section labelled 'Musical Style' on the band's page, with a multitude of scholarly footnotes to interviews and reviews:[8]

> Although the band's music has often been labeled as shock rock by mainstream media, Manson disputes the use of the label, preferring instead to identify their music as rock and roll. Over the course of their career, the band has produced music which has been ascribed to many genres, including industrial metal, industrial rock, industrial dance, post-industrial, alternative metal, progressive metal, hard rock, electronic music, glam rock, gothic rock, death metal, blues rock and pop.

They have been reluctant to self-identify as goth because the style that made the band famous (on 1996 album *Antichrist Superstar*) is a hybrid of nu metal and the industrial metal of Nine Inch Nails, whose frontman, Trent Reznor, was their producer and key supporter. He was sent their demo when he set up his own label Nothing Records as a subsidiary of the major label to which Nine Inch Nails were signed, Interscope. Presumably, he could see their potential to be bigger than his own band – they had already built a cult local following when they were called Marilyn Manson and the Spooky Kids, because Manson was a show-man and entertainer in the style of Alice Cooper or Gene Simmons from Kiss (Wright, 2000). Presumably, he could see how the band would appeal to every disaffected goth and metal kid, drawn to the band because of the pop grooves combined with metal riffs, and sing-along choruses with swearwords. Marilyn Manson and guitarist, Twiggy Ramirez, mainly wrote the songs in the band from *Antichrist Superstar*. The combination of Manson's clever lyrics and eye for the shocking effect, and the stomping glam-rock tunes of Ramirez, is already present in that first album with the two of them writing together. Ramirez took over from Gidget Gein, who wrote half of the first album *Portrait of an American Family*, when Gein was thrown out after becoming a heroin addict. Gein's writing and playing were good enough for the band to be noticed and build up their profile, but replacing him with Ramirez allowed the band to hit the music charts. *Antichrist Superstar* became a global hit, and the video to the single Beautiful People remains a classic of the period. Global tours and two other strong albums followed through the nineties, though the band was followed by moral panic and hysteria, especially after the shootings at Columbine (see Chapter 8). In 2001, when the band were at the height of their popularity, they recorded their version of 'Tainted Love', the northern soul track by Gloria Jones covered by Leeds F-Club attendees Soft Cell. It was officially released in 2002 and became their biggest hit, charting across Europe and in the United States of America, and remains a goth-club regular.

Marilyn Manson continue as a band, although much changed in line-up (Ramirez left the band twice, most recently in 2017). Marilyn Manson continues as one of the most well known and immediately recognisable figures in alterna-tive culture. The band can still headline festivals, and have toured albums around the world, playing mainly to metal festivals but reaching rock and pop festivals. They were booked to headline an alternative/goth music festival in the United Kingdom that unfortunately went bust in its first year. Marilyn Manson, the man, still generates headlines, and is still interviewed by journalists who work in main-stream media, and who are not music journalists. His relationships – especially that with burlesque dancer Dita von Teese – have been dissected by tabloid news-papers, gossip blogs and lifestyle magazines. For people who are not alternative, or goth or metal, who are unaware that he is not goth, he is the living embodiment of goth – and his fans are goths too (Baddeley, 2000). So he is goth, whether he likes it or not, and whether we like it or not. However, if he is not goth, he has certainly attracted the goth-shaped place in the mainstream that The Sisters of Mercy filled, and taken advantage of being alternative while having the culture industry's instrumentality working to sell his alternativity to those who wanted to resist by watching his videos on MTV. As Cadwalladr (2015) puts it, looking back over Marilyn Manson's career as a musician a symbol of the alternative in the mainstream:

> The Marilyn Manson who emerges from the cuttings I read is
> a confusing, hard-to-pin-down figure. On the one hand he's an
> American icon, a heavy metal rock'n'roll star who's sold more

than 50m albums. On the other he's a middle-aged man who still hasn't got over his goth stage. He's an interesting and intelligent commentator on America's twin obsessions of violence and celebrity (he was born Brian Warner; his name is a blend of Marilyn Monroe and the serial killer Charles Manson). And yet he's also prone to writing the kind of songs you might expect from a narcissistic teenager with antisocial behaviour issues.

Marilyn Manson as a character for the frontman of an industrial metal band was always going to be a caricature. Now that caricature has become a myth in the history and evolution of goth culture, his songs can be simply dismissed as juvenile poetry complaining about being un-liked and un-loved. This, we think, is rather unfair and untrue. While some of his lyrics and songs might be simple complaints, the classic albums of the nineties are filled with intelligent critical discussion of the role of religion and authority in late modernity. Unfortunately, the 'middle-aged man who still hasn't got over the goth stage' has become the defining feature of Marilyn Manson in the public sphere, and all critics know they need not bother to engage with anything beyond that crude image.

Type O Negative called themselves a goth metal band, though they wrote songs and had a visual aesthetic that mocked goths. This band was formed in 1990 – at the end of the eighties, and when *Vision Thing* has just been released by The Sisters of Mercy – by Peter Steele and Sal Abruscato, two members of a New York thrash metal band fed-up with the thrash sound, and enthralled by the possibilities of combining goth rock with doomy, down-tuned metal guitars. Steele was the frontman, singer and bassist, and wrote most of the lyrics as well as designing their look on stage and on record covers. Seeing tribes of goths wearing black in the nightclubs and venues in New York, Steele and the band decided to wear all-green clothing, and use green as a primary colour for their records. Not looking like their audience did not harm their career. The songs they wrote were inspired by the hybrid goth rock of *Vision Thing*, but the riffs were heavier. The slow doom metal style of some of their songs made them almost like ballads, and with Steele's strikingly good looks and deep voice, they were soon attracting the notice of labels and the media. They signed to Roadrunner Records and released their first album in 1991. But their breakthrough moment came with the second album, 1993's *Bloody Kisses*. This was released in the same year that The Sisters of Mercy released their last single and started their strike. Steele sounded a lot like Eldritch, but had more range in his voice. Like Eldritch, he loathed the goth scene around him, and his songs play with the stereotypes of goth: being depressed, being different. But unlike Eldritch, Steele was comfortable being a part of the crazy scene he mocked. *Bloody Kisses* was their moment when they became big around the world, and this was mainly due to the single 'Black No. 1 (Little Miss Scare-All)'. Its video is suitably black-and-white and gothic, the song has many catchy hooks, and the lyrics are the best lyrics anyone could write about the stupidity of goth. The song addresses an ex-girlfriend of Steele's who is 'in love with herself/ She likes the dark/On her milk white neck/The Devil's mark'. She is into the occult and witchcraft and smokes cigarettes. She looks like Liy Munster. But they cannot go out tonight 'because her roots are showing'. 'Black No. 1' refers to hair-dye, the vanity of spending time and effort to look suitably gothic. The song ends with Steele twisting his cruel knife even more, by claiming 'loving you was like loving the dead'. Type O Negative continued to be successful through the decade and into the new century, serving as the archetype of goth metal and attracting attention in the metal media.

Rammstein were formed in 1994 in Berlin as an attempt to create a new form of industrial metal that was German, with lyrics in German. They combine nu metal with hard electronica, making music to dance to as well as music to mosh to. Their music is dark, groovy and very heavy, with live drums triggered and looped to ensure a machine-like sound. The vocals are reminiscent of Andrew Eldritch, though colder and more scornful. They were part of the industrial goth scene popular in the country at the time, and from which a number of other bands emerged (Brill, 2008; Scharf, 2011; van Elferen & Weinstock, 2016). The band play with foreign stereotypes of German culture, masculinity and martial-ism, evoking the propaganda of the Nazis while simultaneously poking fun at it, and people who think they are fascist in any way (Burns, 2008; Kahnke, 2013). Their first album was a huge hit in Germany, and led to them being invited to play in London for MTV. Trent Reznor of Nine Inch Nails heard them around this time and chose two Rammstein songs for the soundtrack of David Lynch's *Lost Highway*. When their second album *Sehnsucht* was released in 1997, they were headlining shows across Europe; at the end of that year, they toured America. Although the band never called themselves goth, and goth is not used in any publicity material or reviews, the band was considered part of goth metal, or industrial goth, by some of our respondents. Their songs were played in alternative clubs alongside Marilyn Manson, Type O Negative and Paradise Lost. In 2001, they released the album *Mutter*, which is the closest they came to the sonic template of goth, and the album that gave them a huge audience in the rest of the world.

Two bands who became huge in the 2000s emerged in the nineties. HIM from Finland were formed in 1995, although they existed under a different line-up and the name His Infernal Majesty between 1991 and 1993. Led by Ville Valo, singing darkly romantic songs in a goth rock style, they were signed up by major label BMG very swiftly after their (re)formation. Their first album, *Greatest Lovesongs Vol. 666* released in 1996 hit the charts in Finland. Their second album *Razorblade Romance* released in 2000 hit the charts in Finland, Germany and Austria. At this stage of their career, HIM were goth enough to appear at goth festivals and events. But they were increasingly playing to metal fans. In 2003, they released an album called *Love Metal*. This was a name the band chose to describe their style of music, but it cleverly played to the instincts of metal fans who embraced them around the world in the first decade of the new century.

The second band formed in the nineties that became huge in the 2000s was Eva-nesence. They were formed in 1995 by singer Amy Lee and guitarist Ben Moody, and struggled through the nineties playing in their hometown in the United States of America. They defined gothic metal with their album *Fallen* in 2003 – pop metal with a good-looking woman singing plaintively – which was released on the big American indie label Wind-up Records. Other bands had been using a woman as the lead singer in front of simply structured pop metal, but Evanescence were the most successful – and their breakthrough created innumerable copycat acts. Gothic metal as female-fronted goth metal became a huge sub-genre of metal for the rest of that decade and into the 2010s, as if Paradise Lost or Type O Negative had ever existed.

It was in the nineties that the goth tag started to be used for metalheads, because metal had taken goth's place in the alternative part of the mainstream. Some of this labelling was obviously just people in the mainstream not understanding the difference. But people started to appear who embraced the name of goth and the darkness of goth, who were actually fans of metal bands: bands such as the ones we have described here (Gunn, 1999). If they thought they were goths, then they were entitled to call themselves that name. But this mainstream, global appropriation of the name of goth meant other goths went further underground, further alternative, to express their gothness as communicative alternativity.

Goth Bands and Spaces in the Nineties as Communicative Alternativity

Goth continued to thrive in its underground spaces through the nineties, even as metal started to resemble goth. Goth clubs, or goth nights in night clubs or other venues such as universities, flourished through this period, and goth fashions started to become variegated in the way Brill (2008) shows. In any large goth club, one could find people dressed as cybergoths, wearing clothing and accessories that borrowed from cyberpunk comics and films, generally dancing to Electronic Beat Music (EBM). This is a loose phrase that captures fast electronic, rave-style goth dance music, which spread from Germany into the rest of Europe and North America as music with which one can dance infectiously. As van Elferen and Weinstock (2016) demonstrate, dance music was a key part of the goth scene and sonic aesthetic in the ninety-nineties, and DJs, fanzines and early internet sites were important curators of taste. Even people who did not dress as cybergoths danced to EBM and the electronica-based music of contemporaneous goth bands. The non-cybergoths included many people who stuck with the black lace and leather of the eighties, as well as people who started to dress up as vampires, or as Victorian brides, or medieval princesses. As Brill (2008) and Hodkinson (2002) show, in the underground goth scene, there was much experimentation around transgression, as well as much experimentation around sex and sexuality; however, all within two limits: the limits of hegemonic masculinity, which still expected women to look sexy; and the limits of the gothic aesthetic, which worked to discourage entry and participation by people who did not look 'dark' or transgressive, such as townies in shell-suits and football tops. That is, the sexual freedoms and exploration reported in the American research of Wilkins (2004) seems to be an outlier: in clubs in the underground in Europe, dance spaces, while more open to transgression and tolerant of difference of any kind, remained spaces where sex and sexuality were constrained.

As well as EBM, people listened to a wide range of goth sub-genres, from 'classic' or 'trad' eighties goth all the way to Wiccan goth, Mittelalter and neo-folk. Wiccan goth tapped into the pagan revival of the time (Spracklen & Spracklen, 2012), and its most important exponent in Britain were Inkubus Sukkubus. Mittelalter was medieval folk music, which was popular in the goth scene in Germany, best exemplified by Corvus Corax. Neo-folk had a more liminal status in the underground goth scene because it was associated with some musicians accused of being fascists and neo-Nazis (Shekhovtsov, 2009) – such as Tony Wakeford of Sol Invictus[9] – but the music and the bands remained on goth festival line-ups and reviewed in goth magazines (Spracklen, 2013a; Spracklen & Spracklen, 2012).

The underground goth scene survived and spread globally in this period through the production and selling of fanzines (Hodkinson, 2002), and also through the emergence of the Internet (see Chapter 9). Fanzines allowed local goths to read news and features about new goth bands from a different country, and they allowed local goths to look at pictures showing what men and women were wearing at goth festivals and other goth events. Readers of the fanzines could write to independent labels advertising in them to buy the records that received good reviews. Fanzines also offered people in places where goth was non-existent to see goths flourishing in counties such as Germany, which was the real heart of goth in the nineties, and in the United States of America, where so many of the important underground bands emerged from in the decade: London After Midnight, for example; or Faith and the Muse. Finally, fanzines allowed their readers to find out about events happening close to where they lived, or shops in the nearest major city. All our respondents acknowledge that this was a key function of how goth sustained itself in the nineties, and in their own experience of being goths or coming to goth in the period. We ourselves used to catch the train into Leeds to buy whichever fanzines we could find in Jumbo Records, or in one of the few alternative clothing shops that had stayed open after the goth rock boom of the eighties.

Independent record labels, distributors and record shops were also crucial in maintaining the goth underground, from labels with global deals and profiles such as Mute Records to labels essentially run as DIY labours of love by musicians and fans. Nightbreed Recordings from Nottingham was set up by Trevor Bamford of the band Every New Dead Ghost in 1990 to release a compilation album. It soon grew into a label with bands signed to it from around the world, and a mail-order shop. As he recalls on the label's website (Bamford, 2017):

> Orders for demos, LPs and singles started coming in every day...
> All of this was happening at the very same time as the scene was
> being 'killed off' by the music press. There was no Gothic music
> being played on the radio, nothing in the music press and defi-
> nitely nothing on TV! I suppose it could be said that the Gothic
> scene suffered a cultural clampdown in this country tantamount
> to a kind of racism! Anyway, in this atmosphere it seemed a lit-
> tle foolish, to put it mildly, to start an underground Gothic-based
> company! However, I quickly discovered that the 'scene' had a

great heart, despite the attitude of the music press, and that significant numbers within the scene were up for supporting the rapidly developing underground.

Bamford's exasperation with the mainstream media is understandable, but it is clear from his story that goths continued to be interested enough in new music and new sub-genres of goth that they supplied his label and mail-order service with a steady source of customers. That is, if the media had decided goth was dead and of no interest to it, goths would and could work around it by using their own communicative alternativity and agency. Of course, that meant that goth culture started to replicate the instrumentality of the mainstream, by constructing its own logic of production and consumption. This is the period, then, in which goth entrepreneurs appeared selling their wares and persuading goths to spend huge amounts of money to consume: this was the period when people started to buy expensive costumes, instead of reusing old clothes or making their own clothes, and it was the period in which enormous shoes such as New Rocks became fashionable.

We will end this reflection on the underground goth culture of the nineties by concentrating our attention on Faith and the Muse, a band we think captures the power and meaning of its communicative alternativity than any other. The band was set up by Monica Richards and William Faith, and their first album *Elyria* was released in 1994 by the tiny American underground goth label Tess Records, which was also the home at the time for Clan of Xymox. As Wikipedia explains on the origins of the band:[10]

> Monica Richards, a native of Washington, D.C., is a musician/artist/poet/scholar. She met William Faith in 1992 when her band, Strange Boutique, opened for Shadow Project in Norfolk, VA. Before starting Faith and the Muse, both had had experience in the gothic rock and post-punk culture of the 1980s. Richards had sung for the band Strange Boutique, while Faith had performed with gothic/death rock icons Shadow Project, Christian Death, Mephisto Walz, and Sex Gang Children. Faith and the Muse was started in 1993 with Richards and Faith exchanging tapes while Richards was still living on the east coast. Shortly thereafter she moved to Los Angeles where the duo was based.

Faith was a product of the eighties goth rock scene with professional experience working with some of the well-established bands, while Richards had been in a goth band with a small profile. Together, they embraced the new pagan, magical turn, while retaining the boundaries of what constituted gothic rock. The song 'Sparks' from *Elyria* is arguably the best goth song of the nineties. The guitar tone is present and correct, but Faith extends the sonic template by adding psychedelic, fuzzy effects. Richards's singing is ritualistic, frightening, but restrained – there is no operatic tone in her voice, this is not egregious gothic metal. The rest of the album is the same, interspersed with acoustic interludes, tribal drumming and sound effects. The lyrical themes are taken from Shakespeare and classical Greek literature, and are radically feminist and spiritually pagan. In their second album *Annwyn*, the musical themes continue, but the lyrics are drawn from Welsh mythology, and specifically the stories in *The Mabinogion*. Again, Richards uses the songs to situate women as powerful agents. Both Elyria and Annwyn were highly regarded in the underground goth scene, and Faith and the Muse were invited to tour in Europe and in North America. They released a third album then signed to Metropolis Records for their 2003 release *The Burning Season*. This album was even more pagan in feel than the other albums, and included a cover of 'Willow's Song' from the 1973 film *The Wicker Man*. Through the end of the nineties and into the next decade, they were on the bill at Whitby Goth Weekend (a number of times) and Wave-Gotik-Trefen.

Conclusion

It is incorrect to say that goth died in the nineties. What happened was that goth became unfashionable in the music press and the culture industry (Adorno, 1991). Our respondents report a healthy sub-culture operating out of sight of the mainstream, surviving through a sense of community and belonging, and through the application of communicative rationality and action to construct a communicative alternativity. However, what also happened was that goth influenced a new generation of musicians in the metal scene, providing them with the themes of darkness and transgression. For black metal elitists, goth showed a way to be truly evil and against the modern world. For Marilyn Manson the frontman, goth showed a way to find new audiences seeking a chance to be transgressive and to annoy the authorities. Goth in this crucial period, then, existed underground and in plain sight in the mainstream as metal-derived goth, although that version in the mainstream was rejected by some goths in the underground because of its embrace of the logic of instrumental rationality. As we will show in Chapter 8, the centrality of goths in popular culture in the nineties – and the conflation of goths with metallers – would also lead to moral panics about them.

Notes

1. As we discussed earlier in the book, we use decades very cautiously as frames of historical analysis, and recognise that the nineties is a social construct that comes with stereotypes about the essence of the decade.
2. http://subcultureslist.com/gothic-culture/. Accessed on November 6, 2017.
3. https://en.wikipedia.org/wiki/Goth_subculture. Accessed on November 7, 2017.
4. We are aware that none of those bands were either of those things.
5. Since then, they have returned to their original sound.
6. The third was Anathema, who did not borrow from goth or influence goth in turn. Their death/doom period was brief, and they transformed into a progressive rock band (REF).
7. Like Eldritch, Stainthorpe was not born in Yorkshire. But he spent his childhood in Halifax and still lives nearby, so had a Yorkshire accent imposed upon him. Eldritch's Yorkshire accent was either a deliberate choice or an accidental

acquisition. Given his political views about the north and working-class Leeds – and his student interest in languages – we suspect the answer is the former.

8. https://en.wikipedia.org/wiki/Marilyn_Manson_(band). Accessed on November 8, 2017.

9. Wakeford has admitted he was involved with the National Front in the early eighties, but regrets it and now disowns the far right (REF).

10. https://en.wikipedia.org/wiki/Faith_and_the_Muse. Accessed on November 10, 2017.

Chapter 8

Goths as Harbingers of Doom, and Moral Panics about Them

Introduction

Women of Grace[1] is a website run by, and for, female Roman Catholics in the United States of America. The website has an active blog and news feed, updated daily (or near-enough daily), which offers Catholic interpretations of the news, as well as news from the Catholic church. The website promotes a conservative form of gender politics called Authentic Femininity, and an inspection of the blog posts suggests the website is strongly pro-life and anti-liberal. The phrase Authentic Femininity is trademarked; Women of Grace is a registered trademark, and the site has many products to sell to Catholic women who are uncertain of what is right or wrong in the modern world. Thus, it is a good example of the marketed Christianity that dominates the United States of America (Moberg, 2017) – fundamentalist[2] when it comes to preaching about tackling poverty and immorality; conservative in its view of the moral vacuum in contemporary America; and professional in its use of instrumental logic to get people to sign up and pay up (Habermas, 2008). Like other conservative Christians, the women on this website are grappling to make sense of the limits of their theological beliefs with the things they see around them in contemporary America. Like many other Christians, they believe in the real power of Evil – Satan – in the world (Giroux, 2004). In a blog post on 07 May 2014, goth sub-culture is tackled:[3]

> DB writes: '*There is a young girl who I think is under the impression that Gothic dress is no big deal, it has no dealings with the occult. I beg to differ, because the evil one will use anything to move in on a person*'.

The girl you mention sounds as though she might be a tad naive about the full scope of the Goth subculture. It's not just about fashion. It might start out that way, but will it stay there? Probably not. For those who are unfamiliar with this subculture, Goths tend to be into dark and morbid imagery and have a fascination with death. Their style of dress reflects these tendencies and is composed of mostly black attire, heavy dark makeup, black lipstick and nails, dyed black hair, bondage accessories and multiple piercings and/or tattoos. The grim look originated in England in the 1980s with the advent of the gothic rock scene and prevails today in their penchant for heavy metal bands. The problem is that there is no specific ideology associated with Goths. Some are very non-violent and espouse tolerance for all, but others are definitely into the darker arts.

For instance, two of the most famous American Goths are Eric Harris and Dylan Klebold – the shooters in the Columbine massacre in Littleton, Colorado in 1999. The two high school seniors were outcasts and considered themselves to be members of the Goth subculture, enjoying satanic rock band Marilyn Manson, guns, bomb-making and violent video games. Although they were later found not to be genuine members of the subculture, by then it was too late and the damage was done. Their association with Goth instantly scarred the public's perception of the subculture which many came to believe was associated with satanism, violence, white supremacy and intolerance, which is really not true for the vast majority of adherents.

The reputation is not altogether unfounded, however. As this story relates, eight Gothic satanists were arrested for murdering and dismembering four people in a Satanic ritual in Russia. That there is a connection between Goths and Satan is undeniable. As this article by Sandro Magister describes, Goths are frequently found among those who practice 'low satanism', the kind the doesn't have an organized church and generally lives among the internet, discos, drug users and, in particular, those who cherish Dark Wave music, the kind that spawned the Gothic subculture four decades ago. Bands such as *Alice Cooper* and *Black Sabbath* were the headliners in the beginning and grew into a subculture 'dripping with blood, death, and the macabre, with its own slang, its own style of dressing all in black, its magazines like *Propaganda* and *Ghastly*, its horror fiction, like that of Anne Rice, its music groups'.

Magister quotes the lyrics from one of the most successful bands, *Venom*, found in a song called *Welcome to Hell*... Not exactly dance music, is it? I find it hard to believe that anyone can listen to lyrics like this and not be affected by them in a not-so-pleasant way. However, that's not to say that all Goths are Satanists. Many will have nothing to do with Satan or the occult and have themselves been victims of crimes, such as the brutal slaying of Sophie Lancaster in 2008 who was killed just because she dressed in Goth style.

The bottom line DB, is that you are right to say that the devil will use anything to get his claws into a person's soul. Goths, who are already flirting with the darker side of life, are prime targets for the evil one who can easily inspire in these adherents a larger appetite for the kind of evil that lurks in the darkness they find so fascinating.

We will return to an analysis of this blog post in the following paragraphs. However, it serves as an ideal introduction to this chapter and the content in it. In this chapter, then, we explore the ways in which goths have been stereotyped as dangerous outsiders. This has come as goth expanded into the realm of mainstream popular culture, as something alternative and transgressive but paradoxically in the full view of the culture industries. This occurred in the nineties, when goth became a shorthand for *anything* deviant, as we have discussed in Chapter 7. In that chapter, we showed that the communicative alternativity of goth went underground in the spaces of clubs, fanzines and independent music labels. This underground associated itself with transgression, deviance, paganism and Satanism. At the same time, metal and rock bands and scenes adopted some of goth's ideology and aesthetic, so goth retained a space in the mainstream. In this chapter, then, the reception of the globalisation of goth culture in hegemonic, mainstream public discourse and spheres is explored and critically analysed using the theory of communicative alternativity. We will examine how goths came to be seen as dangerous outsiders by moral majorities in different nations around the world. Much of the data for this chapter will be found from online sources such as news sites and conservative religious campaigns against goths – both Christians in the West and Muslims in the East. We will explore how Muslims can be goths, and how Christian goth has emerged as a key sub-genre of goth in part as a reaction against the reactionary attacks on goth by Christians. We will discuss how these two religions have sought to brand all forms of popular music as deviant and immoral because they encourage young people to question authority, take drugs and have sex. In doing all this, we will explore how some of the stereotyping about goths has operated in a general way to stigmatise all those considered alternative, transgressive or deviant – and consequently, goth has come to mean anyone in black, with emos and metallers being lumped together under the goth category.

The Liminal Status of Goth in the Christian West

The blog post from Women of Grace confirms a number of things about the accepted knowledge and status about goths among conservative, fundamentalist Christians in the United States of America, and beyond into the rest of the West. First, goth has entered the mainstream of popular culture, and entered up to such an extent that Christians are fearful of their children becoming goth. The blogger and the person posing the question are both familiar with goth culture, and know it is associated with a range of symbols, fashions and musical genres. The fact that goth has become a moral problem to be solved on the blog, inserted alongside warnings about New Age mysticism and political correctness, shows that goths are visible across the United States of America, from big cities to small towns. The initial question even shows us that goth is seen by some people as another fashion choice, a way to stand out or be cool. The blog might not be a representative sample of what conservative Christians in the West think about goth;

however, it is an indicator of some of the awareness of goth, and some of the concerns and moral panics that exists around goth. That is, there is no sustained movement against goths in any way comparable to the campaigns against abortion (Swank & Fahs, 2006). There are not millions of dollars raised by believers to condemn goths and try to remove them from the public sphere, as there is against abortion clinics and their users. But the blog shows that goths are in the mainstream enough for conservative Christians to be uncomfortable about their presence, and questioning about how to deal with goths.

Second, goth has become to encompass a wide range of alternative music and fashion, and has become confused with heavy metal. The blogger tells us correctly that goth started out in the eighties in England as a 'dark look' associated with goth rock, but then she conflates the movement with heavy metal. She tells us that the Columbine school killers were fans of Marilyn Manson, who she describes as a 'satanic rock' band, and that they are two of America's most famous goths – but then tells us that they were never 'genuine' goths. The blogger seems to confuse goth and metal music, and has possibly heard people argue that the killers were not goths after all (Mears, Moon, & Thielo, 2017). But she keeps Marilyn Manson in the list of goth influences on the killers. She also takes the killers' political views to suggest there is a link between goth and white supremacy, a link that might be found with heavy metal, especially in America (Futrell, Simi, & Gottschalk, 2006), perhaps, but probably not so clearly for goth sub-culture at any time of its history and evolution (Griffiths, 2010). She goes even further in confusing goth with metal when she says that some forms of goth are Satanic. The story she refers to from Russia could equally be about black metallers – what it shows is how murder is sensationalised by the local media then the Satanic goth meme is spread around the world (Griffiths, 2010). She then mentioned Black Sabbath and Alice Cooper. These bands have no connection with Satanism, or indeed goth, though the latter put on a baroque performance designed to shock the morals of middle America. And Black Sabbath could be thought of being Satanic because of the name and some of their early musical and lyrical themes; however, this was only ever a way of connecting to horror films and cross-selling to horror fans (Cope, 2016). The most egregious conflation with metal in the blog is the way she uses the English metal band Venom as proof of Satanism: they might have had a song called 'Welcome to Hell', but Venom were working-class men from Newcastle using Satanism – again – to shock people and sell records (Kahn-Harris, 2007).

Third, the blogger clearly understands that there are differences among the goth sub-culture over their adherence to fashions, ideologies and religions. In the nineties, as we have discussed in Chapter 7, goth had a pagan turn, as its communicatively alternative space went underground. Many goths around the world embraced various forms of paganism, from serious Wiccan beliefs to paganism as a form of performative pantheism. Some goths did find Satanism, of the kind informed by the work of Crowley and his rivals and followers (Spracklen & Spracklen, 2012). But as the blogger says, not all goths are (pagans or) Satanists just as not all goths are taking drugs and drinking alcohol. The blogger accepts that some goths are just goths interested in the idea of darkness, and the idea of being alternative and performing alternativity. The blogger does acknowledge that goths can be victims of hate crimes, by telling the tragic story of the murder of Sophie Lancaster (Garland, 2010). There is no necessary connection in the blogger's mind between being a goth and being a Satanist, or being tempted to sin. It is perfectly possible, she suggests, being a goth and being free from Satanism, and it is of course perfectly possible, she suggests, that being a goth will not make you a bad, amoral or immoral person.

But the blogger sums up like Yoda warning Luke Skywalker in *The Empire Strikes Back* about the seductive power of evil: the allure of the dark side, and the malign presence of the evil one. Goths are not Satanists, but goth culture is a lure the Devil has used – and will use – to trap young people. In this Catholic woman's opinion, the Devil has the agency and ability to use goth to inspire a bigger 'appetite' for evil among its followers. The blogger's simple answer is not to panic – her questioner's young friend is not doomed – but be aware that goth is a step towards evil, because it is already very Satanic. Wearing a black dress and painting fingernails might appear harmless, but for this blogger they are the first signs of the danger to that young person's soul.

If the Women of Grace represents a considered conservative Christian response to the rise of goth into the mainstream, the website of Protestant evangelist David J. Stewart[4] reflects a real moral panic that goth will undermine America and American culture. The front page of the website is filled with links to conspiracy theories, from ones familiar on the alt-right around 9/11 being a set-up to more unusual ones such as Donald Trump is a Jew working for the Illuminati, so we might question Stewart's sincerity.[5] But most of the content is religious, fixing Stewart as anti-Catholic and an old-time nonconformist. He believes that the only true Bible is the King James Bible, and rejects the use of modern versions of the Bible because he claims that people linked to Freemasonry have corrupted them in their translation.[6] He has an extensive list of things wrong with America (what he calls 'Evils in America'), and a list of things that he thinks need to be done to make it a true (Protestant) Christian nation again. He has no time for any rock or pop music, sees the entire industry as immoral and even finds Christian rock and pop music misguided and immoral. Goth, then, is just one of the many things Stewart finds wrong with his country and his society, and he only dedicates a few interconnected pages to it. This is how he begins his account, on a page headed 'Goth Death Subculture Will Destroy Your Teen' on a suitably gothic all-black background:[7]

> Goth is a deplorable type of heathen culture that glorifies everything that is vile and unholy. The dictionary defines 'Goth' as: A crude uncouth ill-bred person lacking culture or refinement. This pretty much sums up the Goth culture today. I didn't invent that definition, it's in the dictionary. Goth glorifies things that are sick,

> nasty, improper, freakish, and downright demonic. Goth is NOT
> just the music. In fact, not all Goths listen to Goth music...

Stewart begins by confusing the old goths with the new goths. He uses the dictionary definition at Vocabulary.com, where it is a phrase synonymous a barbarian or boor.[8] This website's definition of goth does not include the goths who belong to the goth sub-culture, unlike the Oxford English Dictionary (OED), so it is not a helpful dictionary definition for Stewart to cite. Even if the modern goths are lacking culture and refinement, it does not follow that this lack leads to anything demonic. He then proceeds to use the Wikipedia page for goth sub-culture (or an undated version of it) to explain the origins and evolution of goth, using that (or his version of it) to show that there are different types of goth music, different types of goth and different types of goth fashion. But, he proceeds to use the diversity of goth in its evolution to equate goth with heavy metal, and black metal and Marilyn Manson in particular:[9]

> The term 'Goth' refers to all categories of Gothics, from Emo
> 'Goths' to black metal 'Goths' to vampire 'Goths; from thrasher
> 'Goths' to punk 'Goths' to industrial 'Goths.' 'Goth' is just a word
> the media uses to group a certain type of people together. The
> Goth culture includes Emos/ punks/ Wiccan witches/ self-abusers/
> thrashers/ grungers/ heavy metallers, et cetera. This includes the
> Marilyn Manson, AC/DC, Smashing Pumpkins, Van Halen and
> Ozzy Osbourne crowd as well. Notice from the preceding Wikipe-
> dia information that Goth is often associated with sexual bondage,
> domination, sadism and masochism (BDSM). Nothing good ever
> comes from Goth! Even more creepy is that teen girls in particu-
> lar gravitate toward Goth, because in Goth, witchcraft and satan-
> ism, no one is turned away. Teens that have difficulties fitting in
> and being accepted often find comfort in associating with outcast
> groups, such as Goth. That's what Goth is really about about, that
> is, a club for social rejects. I do not say that to be unkind or judg-
> mental; but rather, to be honest. Teens who dress in Goth cloth-
> ing seek attention, and they get it! Seeing youth dressed in Goth
> definitely causes people to turn their head twice... 'What in the
> world?' they say. Goth look like something the cat dragged in off
> the street.

Stewart is way off the mark in making so many things fall under the goth label. Smashing Pumpkins and Val Halen are as far from goth as any band could possibly be. He includes all forms of punk and metal – including thrash metal! – into this evil, Satanic cult. Note how he elides self-abusers and witches with emos and punks and metallers – everybody alternative in his view is goth, and every goth is evil. He is right to point out that some people in the goth sub-culture transgress sexual norms and values, but that is a strength of the communicative alternativity expressed in the sub-culture. Most goths are tolerant of difference, and open to people with different world-views, so long as that tolerance is returned by others (Brill, 2008; Hodkinson, 2002). This includes some people exploring transgression and darkness by being Wiccan, or even following various forms of Satanism (Spracklen & Spracklen, 2012). This is the strength of the goth sub-culture as it emerged in the 2000s. So, it is something Stewart deplores, as his last sentence implies.

He seems to equate goth straight away with Marilyn Manson and black metal. The Norwegian black metal circle was definitely involved with burning churches and murders, and the circle was undoubtedly anti-Christian and Satanic, following the anti-Christian ideology of much extreme metal from the eighties (Kahn-Harris, 2006). But, it is important to note that they were not worshipping a real Antichrist, a real Satan. They were young people who lost all sense of their own personal ethics, and they were arrested and jailed for their mistakes. And as we have said, although there is a relationship between goth and black metal, the black metallers in Norway did not identify as goths.

Marilyn Manson the singer is a key bogeyman on Stewart's page. He was not a goth but as we have said, he became a goth by being called a goth by everyone else, and by adopting goth's transgression and resistance. Stewart goes on to reveal Marilyn Manson's real name, as if it some kind of occult secret and then tells us that Manson regularly blasphemes and rips up Bibles on stage. Stewart's fear of Marilyn Manson dates this part of the page to the second half of the nineties. At that time, the band and the front man were creating headlines all over the United States of America. They were at the peak of their popularity; as such, they were attracting the attention of the moral majority. Fundamentalist Christians, who were angry at what they saw as actual Satan-worship and blasphemy, carried out various demonstrations and campaigns against the band performing on stage (Baddeley, 2000). Marilyn Manson responded by becoming more provocative, selling more tickets, selling more records and annoying the moral majority who wanted to be annoyed. He wanted to show his audience that religion, and Christianity in particular, was irrational and oppressive (Baddeley, 2000). So, the album art of *Antichrist Superstar* shows Marilyn Manson standing like Jesus placing his hands on the head of his acolytes, but the acolytes are drinking urine from a device linked to his penis. It is actually very funny, but Stewart cites the picture as evidence of Manson's Satanic evil. Like the Catholic blogger, he goes on to link goth to the Columbine shootings, which were also linked to Marilyn Manson (Griffiths, 2010), and continues to rant as follows:[10]

> Goth influences teenage girls to become whores, depresses kids to the point of cutting themselves, and turns otherwise normal kids into Columbine shooters. The Goth culture is obsessed with death and the darker side of life, which is clearly evidenced in Goth music. Goth is of the Devil. I do not say this to be unkind. God loves everyone, including Goth. God loves the down and out. But God hates evil, and commands Christians to hate evil as well (Psalms, 97:10). Goth is evil. If you are into Goth, God loves you!

> Jesus Christ paid your debt of sin, and mine! My goal is not to
> upset or hurt anyone's feelings; but rather, to take a Biblical stand
> against every form of evil. Black lip stick, tattoos, pierced body
> parts, gothic clothing, freakish behavior – these are all worldly
> amusements.

Stewart displays little charity in this passage. If you are a goth, you are going
to hell, unless you reject all aspects of goth culture. Goth is the Devil's work. If
you are a goth, you are going to be a whore or a killer, or both. There is no room
at all for Christian goth in Stewart's moral panic. It seems like Stewart has read
Stanley Cohen's classic monograph *Folk Devils and Moral Panics* (Cohen, 2002)
not as a critique but as a 'how to' guide, because these Biblical commands raise
the stakes: to be a goth is to be not only a folk devil, but of the Devil Himself.
Stewart wants all Christians to reject any and all aspects of goth. To prove the
point about folk devils, he produces a long list of murders undertaken by goths.
He then rounds up by saying:[11]

> These are but a few of thousands of recorded mainstream news
> events involving Goth killers. To say that the Goth subculture
> isn't dangerous is to be very ignorant indeed. Goth is of the Devil.
> Convincing the world that the Devil doesn't exist is man's great-
> est weakness, and Satan's greatest strength. Parents must discour-
> age their teens from becoming involved in the Gothic subculture
> of death, rebellion, blackness of heart, heavy-metal and suicide.
> Don't send your kids to church…Take them

Stewart has a list of 29 events, but they are not all murders. One event is the
suicide of black metal singer Dead. Another is a suicide pact with three people involved. The Norwegian black metal murders are double counted, and he
includes the church burnings in Norway. As we have said, the Norwegian black
metal circle was not goth; so, the church burning in the United States of America
by American black metal fans does not count either. Stewart also includes the
attacks on 9/11 because he claims they came from a plan drawn up by one of the
Columbine killers. He includes some other cases where metal fans have killed,
others where it is not clear what kind of person the killer was. Even if we accept
all 20 or so murders are real and undertaken by people who called themselves
goths, it is a small number for 15 years, and says nothing about goth as a bad
influence, because those people were obviously mentally disturbed in some way.
We admire Stewart for his bullish insistence there are 'thousands' of news stories
just like the ones he listed.

Towards the bottom of the page – after expressing his fears about a rap-metal
band that was huge in America and was the subject of a separate moral panic in
the first decade of this century (Insane Clown Posse, great name, bad songs) – he
attacks all rock music as weakening the bodies and minds of those who choose
to listen to it. He also claims that goth music has lyrics that endorse killing and

paedophilia, something that has not come up in our exploration of the genesis and evolution of goth. He tells us:[12]

> Over 30 years ago a woman named Dorothy Retallack conducted experiments using music, plants and their combined environment. The results became, and still to this day, remain famous. Taking two identical sets of plants in two separated but identical rooms, she exposed them to music. The first set of plants were played quiet placid subdued devotional 'religious' classical music, while the other set were subjected to loud aggressive rock music played at full deafening volume 24 hours a day. The plants exposed to rock grew away from the music source, withered and died, while the plants that were played religious music grew towards the music source and thrived. The lesson? If rock music attacks and kills plants, what does it do to people? I think it's rather obvious – it does the exact same thing! Rock music attacks the nervous system, affecting one's emotional state. Is it any wonder why Americans, now more than ever before, are blowing-up in anger, flying off the handle, committing suicide, and losing their minds? Goth is particularly dangerous because the lyrics to the music often glamorize killing, brutality, sadism, masochism, pedophilia, torture, freakism and all sorts of heathendom. The music is often characterized by relentless yelling and screaming, freakish embellishments of the voice, evil sounding backgrounds, etc.

Retallack's 'experiments' were published in 1973 in a popular press not an academic one (Retallack, 1973), and is a classic example of pseudoscience (Pigliucci & Boudry, 2013). No one has replicated the research but conservative Christians repeat it as truth because it suits their world-view about the evils of rock music, and the importance of prayer and devotion. In the foreword of her book, Retallack (1973, p. 7) even says:

> The amazing way in which all of this came to me, and the subsequent interest and worldwide recognition of the phenomenon through the news media, without any effort on my part seemed to point to a larger God-given idea. So it is with awe and reverence for the Creator of all life that these words come from my pen.

Stewart believes rock music is bad and seems to have found a God-given bit of science to help him make the claim. The argument is then extended to goth because it especially hurts Stewart's sensibility – although the music Stewart is listening to cannot be goth aesthetically or sonically (the only band he has named are metal bands, and they probably are yelling and screaming and making a racket). As a conservative Christian the darkness, sexual agency and anti-Establishment freedom of goth sub-culture is just too much for him to bear.

Goth in Islamic Countries

On 21 August 2012, Diloram Ibrahimova reported for the BBC mews website on increased persecution of goths in Uzbekistan. The report featured a photograph of some of the young goths who were interviewed for the article, who are clearly goths. The article is headlined 'The Last Goths of Tashkent', and reports on the goth scene's persecution and slow decline under a government intent on imposing its will, and its version of correct Muslim behaviour (Hanks, 2016). The article (Ibrahimova, 2012) begins:

> The desecration of a cemetery in Tashkent has been blamed on goths, and two have been arrested. But members of this dwindling community say this is the kind of persecution that is forcing many of them to leave the country. With their pale painted faces, carefully sculpted dyed-black hair and heavy eyeliner, goths are not a common sight in the predominantly Muslim central Asian nation of Uzbekistan. The youth subculture has had a small presence on the streets of the capital, Tashkent, since the 1990s. A fascination with gothic horror, Victoriana and pagan-inspired flouncy fashion in dark moody colours is not normally a sign of political dissent. But goths here believe they are increasingly being targeted by the authorities who, they say, show little tolerance for alternative lifestyles.

Accusing the goths of desecrating a cemetery feels like an echo of the conservative Christian response to the church burnings in Norway (Spracklen, 2006). The goths interviewed reject any idea that they could have done it. They sound like goths anywhere in the world in the twenty-first century: intelligent, liberal and progressive. They have themselves embraced the form of goth that is broad enough to include heavy metal and bands like Marilyn Manson. They mourn the loss of the multi-cultural, multi-ethnic and tolerant world of Tashkent under the Communist Soviet Union (Khalid, 2015). Once upon a time, religion was banned, or at least pushed out of the public sphere, in the city and in the former Soviet Union. With the fall of Communism and the independence of the country, Islam and Russian Orthodox Christianity – the religion of the Russians who remain in the country – have been supported. While the government has tried to limit the growth of Islamist ideology and politics, it pays attention to and respects the aims of Islam: the transformation of the public sphere into a place where Muslims can live following the orthopraxy of Sunni Islam (Hanks, 2016). As some of the more conservative Islamist schools reject all forms of music (Osman, 2016), goth music has no chance of being accepted by the adherents of those schools. But, even the relatively liberal Islam supported by the government in Uzbekistan has little space for something that questions authority, family and tradition like goth music. As the article continues (Ibrahimova, 2012):

> Youths dressed in gothic fashion are likely to be harassed in public. A number are arrested and then released without charge, they

contend. They claim that the government, by arresting the goths accused of vandalising the cemetery, is looking for an excuse to ban alternative youth groups altogether. But the pressure is even greater for girls from a Muslim background who turn to the goth aesthetic and start wearing accessories like crosses and skulls. This creates significant public consternation and local media have even been at the vanguard of a backlash against alternative cultures. There has been a campaign in Uzbek media denouncing Western mass culture for encouraging 'immorality' among the youth and for 'damaging the country's national values and traditions'. Rap, rock and heavy metal have been labelled 'alien music' and some genres have been subsequently banned.

The attack on goth in Uzbekistan extends to many other forms of Western popular music, but goth is particularly problematic because of some of its aesthetic: dyeing hair black, crossing genders, wearing revealing clothes, and having tattoos, piercings, skulls and crosses as symbols and jewellery. All these things can be argued to be un-Islamic, and many of them might be labelled *haram*, not allowed for Muslims at all – such as women dressing immodestly (Osman, 2016). Looking like a goth might be enough to be accused of drinking, having casual sex, being gay or being a non-believer or apostate. The radical feminism of goth, and the progressive liberalism of goth, pose challenges to traditional, conservative Muslim norms and values about gender, sex and sexuality (Meriwether, 2018). Being a goth might also be seen as getting in the way of the Muslim submission to Allah. On the many Internet forums where what it takes to be a Muslim goth, and whether it is allowed to be a goth and a Muslim, one comment from a pious Muslim stands as a testimony about the problem:[13]

As a muslim convert I would say no, we always try to make excuses to make the transition to islam easier. But I found out that being a muslim is submitting the will of one self 100% to Allah. Being a Goth doesn't make sense in islam just like I was a 'Pseudo gangsta'. But Masha Allah! I let my false pride get crushed by the strength of submission to God(Allah) Alone. Just make the intension in your heart. If you take one step towards Allah he will run towards you :) If you close one door Allah opens another this always helped me. Just look into Islam with an open heart and forget these labels like goth it is only a trend. But the belief in God has been here since Adam and Eve and will exist to the end of times.

For this Muslim, as for many others, goth is a distraction from God and the Muslim's role in worshipping him. He calls goth a trend that gets in the way of the true relationship he thinks we should have with God. Returning to the story from Uzbekistan, we can see a real problem about what it means to be a Muslim. In this mainly Muslim public sphere, goths with crosses are seen as crossing the line between problematic youth with unconventional fashion sense to apostates from Islam. People accused of leaving Islam for Christianity, or denying Islam and becoming an atheist, remain at severe threat in Muslim countries; in wider Muslim society, it is still problematic. Being found out as apostate can and does lead to death in many Muslim countries, as Islamic jurisprudence makes it clear that such apostates are a danger to society (Saeed, 2017). Far wider than the legal status of apostates is the social one. People who reject Islam and become atheists or followers of another religion are often held to have betrayed the honour of their families and communities, and face being shunned or attacked by their loved ones and their close friends, just as they may be in fundamentalist Christian circles in America. Becoming a goth, then, brings with it the real danger of being disowned, rejected or accused under various legal codes based on Sharia of being an apostate.

Despite the fear about goths among conservative Muslim societies, and despite crackdowns on goths in countries like Uzbekistan, goths and goth culture manage to exist within Muslim societies, especially when goth is used in its broad, contemporary sense of everyone from punks through emos to metal fans. There are huge metal and punk scenes in Malaysia and Indonesia, which attract mainstream Muslims to them in large numbers (Ferrarese, 2014). Although police and conservative Islamists have attacked these scenes, the latter are now well established and supported by the media and the government in both countries. In these countries, it is usual to see women in hijabs dressing in black clothes and adopting some of the goth aesthetic while attending gigs (Donaghey, 2017). In Saudi Arabia, despite the harsh Wahabbi doctrines of the royal family and the clerics, there is evidence that university students have found alternative sub-culture, listen to alternative music and identify as emos and goths, even if they have to be careful about what they wear and how they look when they are in public spaces (Ashaalan, Alsukah, & Algadheeb, 2013).

Christian Goth

In the nineties, with the transformation of goth into its underground communicative alternativity, Christians started to be attracted into the scene as a space to explore their faith – and some goths who were exploring faith and religion, turned from humanism or paganism to Christianity. This phenomenon happened around the world, but was obviously more visible in the goth scene in the United States of America. This was partly because of there being a significant number of goths in youth culture at that time in that country (Siegel, 2005); it was partly a consequence of the popular culture of the country, in which Christianity has a unique place. As we said above, atheists and people who abandon Christianity are not threatened with laws of apostasy; however, they face social disgrace and stigma, especially among the small towns of middle America. Almost every politician seeking election to a national office has to show they have a religion and they take their faith seriously, and that tends to mean Christianity in a country founded by Christian white men. So being Christian was and is the norm (Giroux, 2004), and the American goth scene was soon adapting to demonstrate it was part of American culture by embracing the Christian goth identity. Like all sub-genres of a sub-culture, Christian goth was driven by bands aligning themselves to each other by including Christian themes in their lyrics and imagery (Whittaker, 2007). Individual Christian goths started to adapt their clothing and rejecting anything that had a pagan or Satanic origin (such as pentagrams) in favour of more obviously Christian-friendly devices: rosary beads, veils and crosses. With the rise of the Internet in the late nineties (as we shall discuss in Chapter 9), goths were able to share their ideas over what was goth across the world – and Christian goth spread largely because of newsgroups, websites and forums that articulated Christian goth as truly goth, and truly Christian (Latham, 2014; Whittaker, 2007).

The tension at the heart of Christian goth identity still remains unresolved. There are many goths – such as one of our respondents – who do not like the idea of Christian goth, especially because the Christianity in question is often American, born-again and evangelical. At one stage in late nineties, as we can recall ourselves, Christians seemed to be everywhere in goth, threatening to push out the pagans and deviants for a form of goth sub-culture that concentrated on the after-life and obedience to the teachings of Christ. Most goths argue that goth is about tolerating difference; so, Christian goths are just as welcome as anyone else is, as long as they obey the unwritten rules about tolerance. Goths claim they do not have any rules about clothing or ideology or musical sub-genres or faith, but they are suspicious of people who want to close down any part of the communicative alternativity: people in the goth spaces must be allowed to explore sex and sexuality, take drugs and drink alcohol and explore their own identity and agency. So, Christian goths have to work hard to prove they are proper goths because some of them want to reject some of that communicative alternativity – goths do not mind Christian goths rejecting sex before marriage, for example, but do not want that morality imposed on the wider goth scene. Having said all that, Christian goth is seen by other goths as a legitimate expression of goth, and a legitimate part of goth music and goth aesthetics, unlike the white metal or un-black metal that uses black metal to make Christian music (Moberg, 2015).

The other tension at the heat of Christian goth is the Christian identity. As we have seen, there are some people in the Christian world that think goths are dangerous, deviant or the work of the Devil. Christian goths have a hard time reaching out to their fellow Christians to accept them as Christians into their churches. They make hard work of writing blogs, FAQs and articles that are aimed at Christians who think goth is wrong or un-Christian. In one of them, the author tries to show how the story of Jesus in the New Testament has many parallels with goth culture and goths rejected as outsiders in the mainstream. The author begins by suggesting Jesus was rejected by those around him and that he was interested in the strange, the shocking, the artistic and the dark. The author then shows that Jesus believed in tolerance, like goths, before coming to the most important parallel:[14]

> Goths are like Jesus in that Christ based His opinions of people on
> who they were, not on how they looked or appeared. While many

churches would call the police on a dirty, scraggly homeless person
or a hardcore metal Goth if they were to walk into the sanctuary
during the Sunday service, Christ looked at people for who they
truly were. He saw that many of those who were dressed in the fin-
est clothes and who were the cleanest on the outside, were actually
the most corrupt on the inside. And He saw that many of those
who were considered the lowest scum of the earth, were actually
some of the most righteous people on the inside. The story of the
rich man and the beggar in Luke 16:19-23 is a perfect example of
this. Jesus could see that the luxurious man dressed in fine linen
was actually one of the worst people, as opposed to the dirty beggar whose sores were licked by dogs. While most would be irritated
by a mass of people following them around, Christ looked on the
masses that followed Him as a flock of sheep in need of a shepherd
(Matthew 9:36). In His parables, Christ honored the repentant pub-
lican. To Him, the humbled sinner who turned from His ways was
a better person than the righteous man who looked down on everyone else (Luke 18:9-14). Christ, without drawing judgments on
people He didn't truly know, accepted and loved the prostitute who
repented and yet was rejected by everyone else (Luke 7:38-39,50)
and the repentant thief on the cross (Luke 23:40-43). In like manner, Christian Goths are known for their accepting personalities.
Gothic Christians are the modern social equivalents of Christ,
who 'eat with sinners'. We do not shun those that society shuns.
We do not accept rumors or hearsay. We base our opinions of
people on what we know about them personally. Christ was very
Gothic in this respect.

For this Christian goth, Jesus was 'very Gothic' because the New Testament
shows him acting and behaving like modern goths. This Christian goths show
their knowledge of the Bible by citing crucial parts of the New Testament to
make the case that Jesus is with the outsiders, and is a radical in his politics.
This is not an argument aimed at other goths; it is an argument aimed at other
Christians.

Conclusion

In the three major world religions with their roots in Abrahamic theology (Judaism,
Christianity and Islam), there are clear rules about what is allowed and what is forbidden, in terms of sex and sexuality (Lindsey, 2015). Men have power over women, even
over the choice of having sex. In this Abrahamic morality, sex is something that should
only happen in marriage between a man and his wife. Homosexuality is wrong, and sex
outside of the sacred bonds of marriage is wrong. In the sacred laws and commands
associated with these three religions – and especially in their modern, fundamentalist variants – there is an uncompromising fear of sex and sexuality as leisure
activities that are sinful, or evil (Runkel, 1998). Goth music and its sub-culture

encourage young people to feel free about sexuality, as with much of popular music and alternative counter culture. People use pop music and dance music to socialise and find sexual partners. So, this leads to a reaction against pop music and its goth form as evil, the work of the evil forces of the Devil, because it is linked to sex and sexual freedom. Goth is worse than pop music, because as well as encouraging young people to explore their sexuality it encourages and shelters other acts of transgression. It is radical in its politics; it is committed to difference and tolerance and plays with dark ideas and imagery. In the Christian West, this action against pop music has taken the form of campaigns by conservative Christian groups against rock and roll from the 1950s through to today (Frith, 1998; Wright, 2000). In the Islamic world, hard-line Sunni and Shia theologians make similar arguments to their Christian counterparts to ban pop music where they have power (Roy & Boubekeur, 2012). Goth music and the people in goth culture have just been one other form of pop scene condemned by religious fundamentalists for their sexual and political freedoms.

Goth culture has also been seen as dangerous because it is seen to be a space where young people can transgress laws and religious edicts around the use of drugs and alcohol. Psychoactive substances such as cannabis and alcohol have been used by humans for thousands of years as a way of altering the mind, bonding and having some pleasurable moments of leisurely respite (Goodman, Lovejoy, & Sherratt, 2007). These substances have been – and continue to be – problematic for religious leaders and secular law-makers. If the pre-modern use of such substances suggests some ritualistic function, in historical times the legal and moral status of using these substances has been carefully constrained, if the substances have not been banned altogether (Goodman, Lovejoy, & Sherratt, 2007). So in the Christian West, alcohol has been privileged as a legal psychoactive substance, part of the popular culture of the West, but a drink that has been banned on numerous occasions by Christians concerned about the morality of drinking and the harm that goes with heavy drinking (Yeomans, 2014). In contrast, in most Islamic countries and in Islamic theology, alcohol is strictly forbidden (Matthee, 2014). In most countries that follow the guidelines of the World Health Organization, recreational drugs such as heroin, cocaine and LSD are banned because they are perceived to be addictive, threatening to life and threatening to social order. Excessive drinking is also discouraged, and there are warnings about the effects of cannabis that make it remain illegal in many countries (Goodman, Lovejoy, & Sherratt, 2007). Of course, the banning of recreational drugs such as heroin and cocaine may come as a surprise to anyone who was born in the age of high modernity in the middle of the nineteenth century, when these modern drugs were sold legally as health-restorers. This fear of the use of psychoactive substances among religious leaders and politicians keen to impose moral order is one final way in which goth is seen as evil and dark. In the eighties, goth was closely associated with the use of speed. Then, in the nineties, goth's tolerance as well as its communicative alternativity saw other substances become common on the scene. When Wayne Hussey returned with a new line-up of The Mission in the 2000s, he ensured he stood on stage holding the latest substance in his hands as proof of his romantic, dark and transgressive heart: red wine. Goths, then, have embraced these transgressions precisely because they transgress religious and societal norms and values. And the leaders of the moral majority – in the United States of America and every other country where religion is important – have responded by condemning goth as being too immoral for their young people.

Notes

1. http://www.womenofgrace.com/en-us/default.aspx.
2. Fundamentalism used to refer purely to elements of Protestant Christianity in the United States of America. We use the term here to define a religious belief that the laws of sacred texts are the word of the god (or the gods), and need to be obeyed without any compromise or the world will suffer the consequences of the judgement and wrath of the god (or gods) (Giroux, 2004; Moberg, 2017).
3. http://www.womenofgrace.com/blog/?p=29887, accessed on November 27, 2017.
4. http://www.jesus-is-savior.com. Accessed on November 30, 2017.
5. http://www.jesusisprecious.org/wolves/donald_trump.htm. Accessed on November 30, 2017.
6. http://www.jesusisprecious.org/bible/easy_to_read_lie.htm. Accessed on November 30, 2017.
7. https://www.jesus-is-savior.com/Evils%20in%20America/goth.htm. Accessed on November 30, 2017.
8. https://www.vocabulary.com/dictionary/Goth. Accessed on November 30, 2017.
9. https://www.jesus-is-savior.com/Evils%20in%20America/goth.htm. Accessed on November 30, 2017.
10. https://www.jesus-is-savior.com/Evils%20in%20America/goth.htm. Accessed on November 30, 2017.
11. https://www.jesus-is-savior.com/Evils%20in%20America/goth.htm. accessed on November 30, 2017.
12. https://www.jesus-is-savior.com/Evils%20in%20America/goth.htm. Accessed on November 30, 2017.
13. https://answers.yahoo.com/question/index?qid=20130710093434AAhQUVl. Accessed on December 19, 2017.
14. http://www.angelfire.com/scary/g4j/articles/thegothicjesus.html. Accessed on November 30, 2017.

Chapter 9

Goth as Virtual Identity and Virtual Culture Online

Introduction

Technology played a key role in the definition of the goth rock sound in the early eighties. As we showed earlier in this book, The Sisters of Mercy's sonic template was underpinned by the new technology of drum machines. The band adopted drum machines after an early attempt by Eldritch to play the drums himself. They were part of the local Leeds post-punk scene embracing drum machines and keyboards for their quality and their utility. Not every goth rock band used drum machines in the eighties; however, they shaped the sound of other bands that had real drummers. In the nineties, goth culture was fortunate to take advantage of another technology: the Internet. We have already discussed the importance of the Internet in earlier chapters, but we need to return to it because it explains why goth globalised and continues to survive into the current age. In this chapter, then, we argue that goth survived through the nineties and into the new century partly due to the rise of digital leisure and digital culture – but the Internet, by its nature as a globalising, homogenising force, has changed goth identity and culture. We will explore the rise of so-called 'alt.' culture more generally on the Internet in the 1990s through to the 2000s, and the ways in which goth culture has been continually reconstructed and its core identity reproduced. Using online ethnography, we will show how goths struggled to define gothness that was both inclusive of others seeking belonging, while being exclusive in the forms and myths associated with being a goth. We will show that goth has essentially changed from being a music sub-culture into one defined by some loose idea of darkness and transgression found online. Before we explore the history and evolution of goth in this period, it is necessary to situate the Internet in our theory of communicative alternativity. But before we discuss how the Internet works as a leisure space, let us first give a brief historical overview of the Internet.

The Internet as a distributed network emerged out of the American military's desire to build fail-safe telecommunication connections between its computers and build fail-safe duplications, so that wars with the Soviet Union could be fought even if some computers were destroyed (Mahoney & Haigh, 2011). Engineers and scientists were naturally more interested in communicating with one another through electronic messaging, and allowing other researchers to access their data. A number of American universities and research groups used the military network, ARPANET, in the seventies, and organisations in other countries joined it in this period. In 1981, ARPANET was opened up to the computer science departments across America; for many computer scientists, it became a crucial tool of work and an everyday tool for leisure. Throughout the eighties e-mail spread across this network, and the first commercial Internet service providers appeared. It was also a period when other networks such as Usenet with its newsgroups were available commercially in the United States of America and other Western countries (Hill & Hughes, 1997; Kayany, 1998). Newsgroups allowed individuals to share news and information with others in the group, and soon became places where people could debate – albeit at the speed of a dial-up connection. This was the space and moment in which netiquette was developed, the rules of engaging politely with others and respecting different opinions (Spracklen, 2015b). Newsgroups soon became repositories of pornographic material, as well as sub-cultural information from *Star Trek* fandom onwards. All of this activity remained niche leisure undertaken by scientists, engineers and early computing enthusiasts caught up in the development of the home computer by Apple and IBM (Mahoney & Haigh, 2011). At the end of the eighties, just after a new link had been made between the CERN laboratory in Europe and the United States of America, Tim Berners-Lee at CERN developed the software and naming system for the World Wide Web. In doing so, he paved the way for the launch of a number of Internet service providers targeting domestic markets across the world, as home users were able to use dial-up modems and web browsers without necessarily having technological awareness of how the Internet worked (Castells, 1996). Crucially, commercial Internet service providers were able to win equal access to the Internet's physical infrastructure in the United States of America through a series of protocols, agreements and court cases that established the Internet as something analogous to a public commons (Mahoney & Haigh, 2011). These early commercial Internet service providers for domestic users sometimes limited the access to a part of the Internet controlled by them, but this model did not last very long, and most users wanted easy access to every part of the World Wide Web. Domestic user numbers grew exponentially in the 'dial-up' age, but still remained relatively small compared to the browsing habits of others. Dialling-up to the Internet at home was slow, and often failed, and many people could not afford a home computer; even if they did, they could afford the cost of a modem and a monthly variable-rate subscription. In the nineties, then, the stereotypical user was still someone accessing the Internet via their place of work, or the place in which they were being educated (Spracklen, 2015b).

As the second decade of the World Wide Web appeared at the beginning of this century, costs for domestic Internet connections and subscriptions fell as dial-up speeds increased. Internet use grew across the world, and the transnational corporations that dominate the Internet in the 2010s were becoming well-established: Amazon was becoming the only place to buy anything by ruthless cost-cutting and undermining rivals; Google had already taken over the search function for most users of the net and was beginning its takeover of everything else it could monetise; and Facebook was becoming the social media platform of choice for young hipsters and university students. These corporations worked closely with the wider telecommunications and computing industry to develop new generations of hardware and software. They worked with governments to ensure networks were upgraded, developing broadband (Mahoney &

Haigh, 2011). Mobile phones became the easiest way for many people to access the Internet, especially with the craze for smartphones with built-in or downloaded apps, and these phones, apps and Internet connections allow users seemingly limitless access.[1] They do actually offer convenience and ease of access, although that ease of access to the entire internet is mediated by the Scylla and Charybdis of social media.

In the nineties, many of its users claimed the Internet as a utopian space, free from control, free from copyright and corporate privilege (Castells, 1996). Many users of the early Internet created and shared free software such as Linux. Others copied and shared music and other files (Spracklen, 2015b). These utopians also believed that the Internet had a liberating, emancipatory potential. For people living in totalitarian countries, the Internet could be used as a source of knowledge about democracy, and a space where campaigns to promote democracy and human rights in those countries could take place. For people living in the West, the Internet was heralded as a space for other forms of liberation and social justice: the Internet would promote gender rights, educate about racism and other forms of oppression, and would allow progressive social movements to campaign for greater rights and equality (Castells, 1996). Less dramatically, the Internet was seen as a leisure space where people could find people with whom they shared something in common, where people could find belonging, identity and community. For anyone alternative living away from major cities, then, such as goths, the Internet, it was argued, could be a space where they would find belonging and others like them (Castells, 1996).

In other words, the utopia of the Internet was seen a space for Habermasian communicative rationality to be preserved, nurtured and grown (Habermas, 1984, 1987; Spracklen, 2009, 2014, 2015b). Using our theory of communicative alternativity, we might argue that the Internet offered a space to resist the instrumentality of mainstream culture (the culture industry, hegemonic culture associated with hegemonic power), a counter-hegemonic space to enable being alternative and thinking alternative. We will argue, however, that for goth at least his communicative alternativity has been dissipated online. Our theory of digital leisure is that adopted in Spracklen (2015b). Digital leisure is just like any other form of leisure. It can be communicative and freely chosen, but is always at this point in modernity in danger of being colonised by instrumental rationality and converted into instrumental leisure. But, digital leisure spaces are unique because of the way in which the technology has shrunk the world, and made it possible to feel part of a global community. Again, that may be something that allows communicative rationality and communicative alternativity to be shaped; however, the loss of distance potentially serves to make us less aware of anyone other than people who like our taste in music. As Habermas (2006, p. 423) himself says, responding to utopians who claim the Internet is one of his communicative, public spheres:

> Allow me in passing a remark on the Internet that counterbalances the seeming deficits that stem from the impersonal and asymmetrical character of broadcasting by reintroducing deliberative elements in electronic communication. The Internet has certainly

reactivated the grassroots of an egalitarian public of writers and readers. However, computer-mediated communication in the web can claim unequivocal democratic merits only for a special context: It can undermine the censorship of authoritarian regimes that try to control and repress public opinion. In the context of liberal regimes, the rise of millions of fragmented chat rooms across the world tend instead to lead to the fragmentation of large but politically focused mass audiences into a huge number of isolated issue publics. Within established national public spheres, the online debates of web users only promote political communication, when news groups crystallize around the focal points of the quality press, for example, national newspapers and political magazines.

For Habermas, the Internet has some communicative potential, but only in the instance of helping undermine totalitarian regimes. Beyond that, Habermas sees the Internet as a space where millions of special interest groups talk to themselves in chat rooms. That is, the Internet is not a truly communicative public sphere because it does not bring different citizens together in a collective space to undertake collective action against the interests of their governments and corporations. At its worst, Habermas believes the Internet is a diversionary tool, used to remove the communicative, counter-hegemonic 'heat' from the lifeworld of the public sphere (Spracklen, 2014). In the conclusions of his book, Spracklen (2015b) endorses this view of the Internet and digital leisure and culture. There is enormous emancipatory potential in these new technologies, but what happens in the future, he argues, is far from certain. If governments and corporations continue to use their instrumentality to shape the Internet and digital culture, the Internet will become as instrumental and constraining as modern sports have become: the Internet will be about consumption, not active participation; and collaborative works such as Wikipedia will be replaced by carefully controlled and curated repositories of pay-to-view knowledge. With this theoretical framework in mind, we now turn to a history of how goth found a space online.

Goth Joins the Internet: The Nineties

Paul Hodkinson's (2002) book has an excellent chapter on goth on the Internet in the nineties. His participants tell him of finding the Internet as an extension of the fanzines, flyers and conversations that were already shaping the communicative alternativity of the goth underground. One participant describes excitedly finding free Internet access at university, and using it to search for goth rather than academic subjects (Hodkinson, 2002, p. 178). Our own respondents remember their own moments when they joined the Internet for the first time. They were all net-savvy users at work and university in this period, though their use of domestic Internet connections was less prevalent – only one of our respondents remembered buying a personal internet subscription in the nineties. However, for this person, that personal access to the Internet allowed him to devote his leisure time to be actively involved in goth websites.

Hodkinson's book shows us the extent of goth on the nineties Internet. There were a number of important local and national websites that were set up around the world that listed club nights and gigs, but not so much global browsing and interaction. There were hundreds if not thousands of personal websites set up by goths who wanted to share their aesthetics and their opinions with others. Some of the bigger websites had message boards or chat forums, where individuals could interact with other goths from around the world. But, as domestic Internet access was not prevalent, and connection and download rates were very slow even when people had such access, chat forums were not the most popular way people talked to other goths (Dahlberg, 2001; Spracklen, 2014).

As Hodkinson (2002) demonstrates, goths in the nineties were users of newsgroups, which often came via email, but which could be accessed through dial-up accounts and through the Internet at work (Mahoney & Haigh, 2011; Spracklen 2015b). Newsgroups had their origins in the eighties, and allowed people to find out the latest news, find out the history of something, and to talk to other users about whatever was permissible in the confines of the newsgroup. Newsgroups were organised by a logical naming system. In the United States of America, this led to the creation of the newsgroup alt.gothic, where alt. was already used to identify other newsgroups that were deemed to be part of alternative culture. From the first newsgroup, it was possible to create more specialised sub-newsgroups, focussing on specific sub-elements of the subculture, such as cyber-goth or vampires. Although alt. had been used before it was prefixed to goth, its use to signify alt.goth led to everything in alt. newsgroups becoming associated with goth, and alternative culture merging with goth in the perception of many people inside and outside the goth scene in the nineties. Reading through the alt. newsgroups in the nineties, one might easily think goth was obsessed with transgression and sex, and not a music scene. We suspect this is the reason why Siegel (2005) is so confused about what the essence of goth is – she must have read the alt. newsgroups and assumed what was in them was the only thing that mattered. Of course, goths are interested in transgression and sex (Brill, 2008; Wilkins, 2004), but those two things are not the only two things that matter to goths in their own identities as goths. Alt.gothic and other alt. newsgroups were also essentially American. In the United Kingdom and in Europe, goths could subscribe to domestic newsgroups and mailing lists, such as uk.people.gothic (Hodkinson, 2002, p. 179).

One American website set-up in the nineties (goth.net) has published its own history of the site's development, which is a perfect source. It can serve as a narrative for the rise of goth online in this period, so we cite the first part here, before we cite from it again when move onto the later history of goths online:[2]

> GOTH.NET was originally started June 1997 by Raven in Dallas, TX, USA. This was run from his home systems, on a 64k ISDN line. GOTH.NET was a largely unused domain with only pictures of Raven himself on the website, and the rest of the box sitting idle. This is the way it stayed for a long time, mainly due to the fact Raven had little time on his hands to do anything with it. Not

long after, PreZ emailed Raven asking him, of all things, to sell
the domain. Raven of course refused, however he allowed PreZ an
account on it, and PreZ became the first GOTH.NET user. Within
weeks Raven decided to let PreZ run the system, and stipluated
only one thing - that the domain should not become an unused
domain, and he wanted goths around the world to make use of
it. With this being said and done, PreZ started giving out email
accounts and webspace, and the first members signed on. It didnt
take long before GOTH.NET outgrew its current connection to
the net, and had to be moved. Raven then co-located the box at his
work at the time, NKN (National Knowledge Network), which
increased its bandwidth to a full 10mbit. Things went fine for a
while, and then it started running out of resources. GOTH.NET
at the time was a Sun SPARC LX, and had only 16mb ram and an
800mb hard disk. So Raven once again lent a hand and moved it
to a box with a Dual PPro/200, 64mb ram and 4gb of hard disk.
At the same time, GOTH.NET was moved to a 100mbit network.
This gave GOTH.NET a new lease on life, and it stayed this way
up until early 2000, when it seemingly got a little too popular,
and the CEO of the co-location host for GOTH.NET pulled its
plug. After months of being down, GOTH.NET finally came back
online in November of 2000. It had moved physical locations from
Dallas, TX, USA to Sydney, NSW Australia in the meantime, and
went from a 90mbit uplink up to a 155mbit one. The physical box
was upgraded too, to become a Dual P3/800 with 128mb ram
and 20gb of hard disk. The website itself was re-designed by the
new webmistress, and several functions were also streamlined and
automated. A Privacy and Content policy, and some Terms and
Conditions for usage of GOTH.NET were implemented, along
with lots of new content and features.

The site was originally a personal website for its creator, Raven, using very
limited technology at his home. The domain name shows how early this is in the
history of the World Wide Web: no one else had registered the name and Raven
was able to own it. The site was set up so that Raven could show off pictures
of himself, dressed in his gothic finery.[3] Then, it was a matter of weeks before
someone else wanted to buy the domain name, seeing the potential of goth.net
to attract many users at a time when search engines were not very reliable. This
someone, PreZ, then got involved with Raven to run the website as a space to
host other people's personal pages. The number of users grew so much that it
became necessary to physically move the site to Raven's office, where he could
take advantage of better bandwidth to access and use the Internet. We do not
hear about what his bosses thought about this, but the data and the number of
users kept on growing, and they had to upgrade the hardware and the network
connection. The history then says that the site was 'too popular' and they were
forced off the Internet by their host server, presumably because they were using

more bandwidth and storage than they had paid for. By this time, the end of the nineties, they had grown so big that they could go global, shifting physical location to Australia, where they had new hardware and a much faster Internet connection. They also hired someone to re-design and look after the website professionally, and became respectable by developing formal Terms and Conditions and various other policies.

Goths were seemingly early adopters of the Internet, and quick to take advantage of it as a space for the construction of goth identity, community and culture. A more systematic, quantitative analysis remains to be done to see is goths were earlier online than metal fans, or the average young person on the street in the West in the nineties. Goths were associated with higher levels of education – Hodkinson (2002) notes this in his book; and we have seen that in our own interactions with the goth scene in the nineties onwards, and in the experiences of our goth respondents. In our own experience and collective memory, goths in the underground shaped by communicative rationality were apparently more bourgeois, and whiter, in America and Europe at this moment in time. Being a goth in the underground in the nineties required a certain level of independent, critical thought, the skill developed most of all in universities. Being in the underground required maintaining an identification with goth and its liberal, progressive ideology. It required being a goth when goth had become unfashionable and seemingly invisible, and required a commitment to uphold goth even as it transformed. We suggest that goths probably were more educated in the nineties than metal fans, or the average young person listening to chart music. And, it was a university education that exposed them to the Internet so early in the history of the Internet. They found it as university students, and moved into jobs in the creative arts, science and the public sector, where access to the Internet remained free and easy in the crucial few years at the end of the nineties. Furthermore, we believe that the large number of goths involved in the early years of the Internet as website creators shows that goths were computer-literate and able to understand and use hardware and software at a moment in time when people needed to read books to make sense of programming and the Internet (Mahoney & Haigh, 2013). In other words, many early net.goths[4] were either hobbyist programmers and developers, or professionals working in IT or in universities (Hodkinson, 2002; Mercer, 2001). As goth moved underground, the ubiquity of the net.goth seems to have an impact on the fashions and music of goth. For example, cybergoth aesthetics borrowed from the cyberpunk of William Gibson and other science-fiction tropes (especially the Borg from *Star Trek: The Next Generation*), but the concept reflects the idea that goth was a hybrid subculture, with one foot in virtual space, and the other in the physical space of the nightclub. The technophilia expressed in net.goth also made electronic sounds and instrumentation of EBM even more prominent in the play-lists of nightclubs.

The advance of net.goth culture also ironically led to the creation of vampire goths and then Victorian goths. We saw in the previous chapter how the Internet allowed Christians to shape their own identity as goths within the scene in this period. Other goths used the Internet to develop and perform identity as vampire goths in the nineties. Siegel (2005) is at last correct about something:

for some goths in the nineties, Anne Rice's vampire novels were a template for how they constructed their identity as goths. As we have said, Rice's novels were especially popular in the nineties, in popular culture as well as the goth culture. The novels and the films are mainly terrible, but they are easy to read and watch – Rice's vampires are deeply sexual, deeply romantic and possessors of ancient magical lore. It is easy to see how the tropes from her novels became popular when re-constructed among goths already aligning with darkness and transgression. Online, vampire goths could dress up, perform and talk to each other about drinking blood. They could contribute to the evolution of the aesthetic. And, this was the way that Victorian goth emerged. As early as Bauhaus's song 'Bela Lugosi's Dead', there had been an element of post-punk and goth interested in horror films and horror tropes. Goths interested in vampires could not help but be drawn towards *Dracula*, the most famous vampire story, and the one that defined the romantic ideas of vampirism in the collective memory of the West (Luckhurst, 2017). *Dracula* was a very modern story in its day, but it is celebrated as a historical text revealing something of Victorian culture and society: the trains and telegrams, the fog of London, and the bourgeois young women waiting to find a man suitable to be a husband (Prescott & Giorgio, 2005). Count Dracula in the book, and especially in the 1992 film adaptation by Francis Ford Coppola, is portrayed as a tragic, doomed figure. In that film, he is revealed to be in love with Mina Harker, who he believes is the reincarnation of the woman he lost when, believing him dead, she threw herself off the walls of the castle. To be a vampire goth soon evolved into being a Victorian vampire goth, a goth woman inspired by the faux-Victorian dresses worn by uber-goth Winona Ryder, or a goth man wearing the stiff suits, hats and red-tinted glasses of Gary Oldman's Count.

The Internet craze for dressing up and being photographed as a vampire or a Victorian vampire goth soon found an outlet in goth clubs. As Dracula first arrived in the United Kingdom in the town of Whitby, and the town was where Bram Stoker had written parts of it, the town became an obvious choice of a site for the first Whitby Goth Weekend (as we discuss in Chapter 10). The vampire Victorian goth craze rapidly mutated into a Victorian goth fashion, the precursor of steampunk, as people started to become interested in trying to dress more authentically Victorian. People became confused over the real historical movement of Victorian Gothic with goth because some goths were dressing as Victorian brides (Spracklen & Spracklen, 2014). This then fed back through the Internet into goth culture, which started to draw on Victorian Gothic even more to construct an identifiably goth form of Victorian fashions: black top hats and mourning suits; canes and black gloves; jet jewellery; and black velvet dresses. This look continues to be prominent in goth culture in the 2000s.

Goth on the Internet: The Twenty-Hundreds

In the 2000s, social media sites started to appear, where people could have a home page in which they received news feeds, and in which users could acquire friends, likes, follows and fans. For goth bands, especially those in the underground, this new generation of websites proved particularly useful. Myspace allowed existing fans to find out about new songs and albums, new gigs and merchandise, in a way that was easier to navigate than a clumsy, rarely updated web page. Myspace also allowed bands to find new fans by using the site's algorithms to ensure they appeared in recommended lists. The site was particularly important for new bands trying to find an audience: they did not need a local following; all they needed were enough followers on Myspace to build up an interest in their songs. For a moment in the 2000s, Myspace was dominated by band and music fans of all genres, all trying to reach out to each other. An entire gothic underground survived by fans around the world finding the artists and bands they had only read about in fanzines, or who they did not even know existed – band such as Zeitgeist Zero, or Rhombus or Grooving in Green. As well as Myspace, Facebook and Twitter appeared in this decade, and grew beyond their initial media and university audience to consume Internet-browsing time in the 2010s (Spracklen, 2015b). All our respondents reported early adoption of social media, and continued to be actively engaged in it as a way of sharing and refining their goth sense and taste. YouTube appeared in this decade as somewhere that allowed video content to be shared, but it did not have much of an impact as other big sites at this time, as the technology of smartphones was not yet widespread, so sharing and streaming videos remained a niche activity.

Most of the big goth bands had fancy, professional-looking websites by this point, where merchandise could be bought. Better search engines and cheaper and faster Internet connections allowed fans to easily find and use band websites. Bands of any size could take advantage of curating their identity, history and music unmediated by critics and other music journalists. Independent goth labels could use the Internet much easier as a space to sell the music of their bands, and the better technology in the 2000s allowed these labels to run audio and even video clips. At the same time, goth shops flourished as goth fashions spread around the world, although the Internet started to have a negative impact on goth shops in towns and cities: as we have seen in Leeds, where none of the original clothing shops have remained. In addition, the Internet rapidly became a space where it was possible to copy and share music files uploaded illegally. While none of our respondents said they had downloaded goth music files illegally, and we have never done it ourselves, goths caught up in the utopianism of the early Internet will have seen no ethical problem in sharing music for free. The argument that one is too poor to pay is a common one for users of illegal file-sharing sites (Lindgren, 2013), and while that may be true for some goths (especially those from the global South), the middle-class university-educated profile of goths suggests poverty is no excuse. Goths who remained attached to the anarchist or radial-left form of communicative alternativity will have seen copyright as a tool of capitalism, so illegal file sharing was a requirement in the struggle against capitalist hegemony.

The Internet for goths in this period, then, remained a space where they would construct their own personal websites, on which they shared photos, stories, histories and likes and dislikes. This was the period in which many older goths started to argue online and on their personal dislikes that Marilyn Manson or was not goth, that metal was not goth, and when some goths started to argue that goth was defined by a narrow range of musical styles. We remember ourselves reading these rants and lists by people who were mocked off-line as trad goths, fundamentalist types who argued that the only true goth was that played by a goth-rock band from England in the eighties. The Internet was also a space where they would use chat forums and message boards to debate goth identity and the symbolic boundaries of goth, as well as learn about goth history and goth bands.

The huge numbers using individual websites in this period is evidence by the continuing rise of membership and content on goth.net. In their history, they describe the challenges and successes they had as the Internet became more commercial, and more easily available to users around the world:[5]

> In January of 2001 our co-location once more pulled the plug on us, this time for about 5 weeks due to DoS (Denial of Service) attacks and the like. The issues were resolved and at the end of February we were back in business. Then in mid-August our co-location pulled the plug on us once more, 1 or 2 days into the 3 weeks notice we'd been given to find an alternate home for the box after the person that had arranged the co-location ended his working contract there. Initially we tried to find another co-location in Australia but there were no offers forthcoming, and we decided to have the box shipped to us in the US to house it on our own high-speed link. Even though it was sent overnight courier, it took about 2 and a half months for the box to get here due to the human factor involved. November 3, 2001 we finally received it and it was up and running within hours.

The team struggled with where to physically host the box that contained the files that constituted the website because of hackers trying to bring the system down. The attempt to bring the site down through Denial of Service attacks was a crude way of forcing something to crash. It shows the dangers in the murky dark leisure world of the Internet, when individuals and groups use their programming skills to disrupt sites – for fun, or for financial gain (Spracklen, 2015b). Goth.net may well have been targeted because of its popularity, as the large number of members could have been the target for the hackers. Or, the site may have been threatened because goth culture was perceived as deserving of attack, just as high school bullies typically attacked goths in class for being different (Griffiths, 2010; Wright, 2000). It is impossible to say what caused the attack. It is clear, though, that the host organisation were unhappy with the website being the subject of such attacks, and this was probably a factor in the co-location hosts 'pulling the plug'. So, the box ended up being sent back to the United States of America, and connected to the Internet through a new 'high-speed' link – at one of their homes through a domestic account, as we find out below. The history continues:[6]

After arriving in the US GOTH.NET was updated quite extensively and some of the HTML code was re-written and the site
received a slightly different look. Since then the server has been
online and stable. In 2002 we opened the forums, which are now
the most popular and visited part of GOTH.NET. In May 2004,
the server once again relocated to a paid hosting facility. We found
residential internet too unstable and restricting to be able to continue hosting the server in our home. GOTH.NET has been phyi-
cally located at that colocation facility ever since. In 2006 it had
some major hardware upgrades, making the site able to handle
much more traffic, as at the time it was becoming rather slow as
the server began to show signs of age. This process was relatively
smooth given that PreZ was more than 3000 miles away from
where the physical server was being hosted.

The biggest change in the 2000s was the opening of the chat forum. These were
hugely popular right from the beginning. As we have discussed earlier, and in the
chapter on The Sisters of Mercy, chat forums were a crucial resource for goths in
this decade. The personal websites started to be used less, and users focussed their
time and resources on asking and answering questions. The forum was divided
up into a number of sub-forums, some about goth.net itself, others of a general
nature. Under the general sub-forum category were forums on General Discussion (normally about anything not necessarily goth-related), and Gothic (*sic.*), in
which anything goth-related was directed. There were other sub-forums over the
years, public and member-only. As of 6 December 2017, we can see the following
sub-forums in the public chat forum: Politics and Related; Fashion and Crafts;
GothGeeks; Domesticated; Trading Post; Music; Users Submissions and Feed-
back; Movies/TV; Print and Art; Clubs/Events; The Net; Humour; and Archives
(http://goth.net/forums/). These helped define what goth is – they also allowed
users to shape goth identity and perform identity. While discussing politics, goths
showed that goth was progressive, green, tolerant and willing to accept difference
and outsiders. In discussions of fashion, goths helped define what they considered to be the proper goth aesthetic: dark, transgressive, but showing a willingness to experiment and be playful. In discussing literature, films and television
the goth on the forum could decide what was part of the goth canon, what was
definitely not in the canon, and what remained debatable. Interestingly, the music
sub-forum included all forms of music, not just goth, so goth music was buried
away in a different place to the sub-forum titled Gothic. The huge number of
users and posts on the forums led to the goth.net founders return to paying for
a professional, commercial hosting facility, abandoning the domestic connection
established just a few years previously.

Goth on the Internet: The Twenty-Tens

The last section of the history of goth.net discusses the latest upgrade, which
happened in 2015:[7]

In 2015, once more it was time for an upgrade, the site was re-designed, and moved from a static and manually updated HTML website to using a real CMS (Content Management System). This allowed for much more user interaction and user input into the main website itself. Submitting artwork, web links, or creating groups for posting material for people interested in that group's subject became a less manual process. No longer was an email required, and then manual changing of the website, now content could just be submitted directly and approved with a few clicks from the site's content moderators. At the same time the hardware the system was running on (and indeed, much of the software) was upgraded drastically.

The founders and owners of the site have been determined to re-design the site to make it appealing to users. They have made it easier for pictures and links to be shared. They have abandoned clunky html web-design for a fancy CMS. They have tried to make the user interaction as easy as possible. They have invested in new hardware and software that makes the site load faster, and allows users to take full advantage of the broadband speeds that have been introduced around the world in the 2010s (Spracklen, 2015b). They are clearly concerned about falling user numbers. A simple search around the public part of their website's chat forum on 6 December 2017 shows that the last post was on 21 October 2017, in response to a thread started on 25 August 2014 under the sub-forum Gothic entitled 'Pet peeves concerning people not understanding Goth culture?'. Before this post in October, the previous post in the thread was as long ago as 15 January 2017. The person who posted the most recent post was also responsible for the second most recent post on 13 September 2017, again responding to a thread in the Gothic sub-forum. The next most recent post happened on 15 February 2017, in the General Discussion sub-forum. In the three sub-forums labelled GothGeeks, Fashion and Crafts, and Music, no post has been made since January 2017; in Clubs/Events, nothing has been posted since 2016; and in Trading Post, 2015.

In other words, the changes made have not brought in additional users and posts. In fact, the chat forum has become a ghost of its former self, despite the work put in by the founders. This seems to be something that has happened to chat forums around the world (Barnes, 2018; Spracklen, 2014, 2015b). Our respondents are all aware of this in their own browsing habits. We ourselves have felt this shift happening. People do not spend precious seconds signing into a chat forum when they are attached instantly to social media through updates to their email, and apps on their smartphones. In this new decade, this new technology and Internet use has become the new norm around the world, with smartphone usage reaching saturation levels and costs reducing hugely.

All of our respondents use social media. They all use Facebook to keep up with news and events in the UK goth scene. Some use Instagram to post goth pictures. One uses Twitter to promote his blog; another uses Twitter to promote his events. They all agree that the Internet has enabled goth culture to survive, and all suggest that social media has just become the most convenient way to keep track of all matters related to goth culture. A couple of our respondents still use chat forums (not goth.net, but band related ones). A cursory search for 'goths' on Facebook on 11 December 2017 brings up dozens of open groups and pages for goths, goth bands, goth culture, eighties goth, goth and post-punk, nineties goth, alternative goth, cybergoth, goth fashion, Whitby Goth Weekend, goth nights such as Leeds' very own Carpe Noctem. A page called 'Goth's Not Dead' has 69,515 people liking it, a group called 'Goths' has 18,804 members. We are not ourselves on Twitter or Instagram or any other form of social media other than Facebook, so we cannot say, for certain, that those kind of numbers are replicated on those sites – but we suspect they are. Going on these pages and groups we can see that they are incredibly active. 'Goth's Not dead', for example, posts pictures of bands and scenesters on an almost daily basis, getting dozens and sometimes hundreds of responses, which often include discussions about the subjects in the picture. On the 'Goths' group page, we are informed that there have been 199 posts today, and 1,404 in the last 30 days. Beyond goth itself, there are significant pages and groups for goth bands. The official page for The Sisters of Mercy has 250,958 likes, and its users regularly comment and interact on it. Then there are half a dozen unofficial groups, including one devoted to the 1980–1985 version of the band, which has 6,613 members and 208 posts in the last 30 days. What these numbers show is the market hegemony of social media compared to the rest of the Internet, and the changing habits of all users, not just goths. Where in the early years of the Internet net.goths made a show of being tech-savvy and willing to code and create, and in the second decade they signed up in huge numbers to have personal websites and accounts on chat forums, now they simply click like and move on to the next funny photograph like everyone else.

Our goths still browse beyond the social media sites. They continue to be committed to the communicative alternativity of the underground by buying clothes from independent goth shops, and music and merchandise from independent goth labels. They will read blogs made by goths, or by non-goths about goth culture and goth music. They will read websites that have information about club nights, gigs, and festivals. But, much of that browsing is mediated through social media.

Conclusion

Goth sub-culture spread around the world with the arrival of the Internet. Goth had managed to spread from its original home in the United Kingdom in the eighties, as punks, post-punks and other alternative types in Europe and North America saw the first stage of goth as something that met their own choice to be alternative. These radical taste-makers looked to the United Kingdom because the country was the source of music deemed to be alternative and radical, or authentic: all of which crystallised with the advent of punk (Frith, 1998). Then, as the music industry and music media promoted goth rock bands and goth fashions in new markets, what was a DIY, post-punk, radical phenomenon became something well-known among the wider music-consuming public in Europe and North America. That is, globalisation was already at work in the eighties helping goth become a movement in the West, and beyond. Goth survived through the nineties and into the new century partly due to the rise of digital leisure and digital culture. The Internet allowed goths to escape the attention of the mainstream media and reproduce the scene as a form of communicative alternativity, with its own rules and boundaries. The Internet allowed new goths to find out about the first generation of goth bands, and goth fashions. The Internet also allowed goths to construct a sense of community and belonging, and an identity as goths, while free from the controls and constraints of the culture industry (Adorno, 1991). This communicative space allowed goths who lived in towns and villages hundreds of miles away from big cities to be goths and speak with other goths through the medium of chat forums. It allowed goths in countries with no goth scenes to reach out to find goths in the goth heartlands. As such, it provided a space for goths facing bullying, oppression or even imprisonment to find a space to share their woes and find solace and sympathy. But, the Internet, by its nature as a globalising, homogenising force, has changed goth identity and culture. We have shown the rise of so-called 'alt.' culture more generally on the Internet in the nineties through to the 2000s fixed particular ideas about what goth music and goth fashions should be. Goth became something associated more with a dark aesthetic rather than a sonic template. Goth was assumed to be associated with S&M, with tattoos and piercings, and with vampires and Victorian Gothic. Goth culture, then, has been reconstructed and its core identity reproduced on the Internet. And, even though that construction is always open-ended, and identity is fluid, the Internet has fixed certain ideas about goth. Goths struggled online to define gothness that was both inclusive of others seeking belonging, while being exclusive in the forms and myths associated with being a goth. Goth has essentially changed from being a music sub-culture into one defined by some loose idea of darkness and transgression found online. We will return to these ideas in the final two chapters of this book. Before we get to them, we turn to our next case study: Whitby Goth Weekend.

Notes

1. At a price, and at a cost to one's privacy.
2. http://goth.net/aboutus. Accessed on December 5, 2017.
3. We know Raven is a man, because he tells us elsewhere on the site.
4. As they called themselves: Hodkinson (2002).
5. http://goth.net/aboutus. Accessed on December 5, 2017.
6. http://goth.net/aboutus. Accessed on December 5, 2017.
7. http://goth.net/aboutus, accessed on 05 December 2017.

Chapter 10

Whitby Goth Weekend: A Case Study

Introduction

Sykes Cottages is a well-known national holiday rental agency in the United Kingdom, competing with others to get owners of cottages to sign up to their agency – and to get holiday-makers to choose their agency as their first choice.[1] For people who own the properties, these agencies promise professional marketing and a good chance of hiring the property out to holiday-makers. For holiday-makers, these agencies represent a sufficiently high-quality standard and a one-stop shop to compare properties and check prices and availability. Ahead of the Whitby Goth Weekend in October 2017, Matthew Bridson wrote this piece titled 'Getting to Grips with Whitby Goth Weekend' on the Sykes Cottages website (Bridson, 2017):

> Black attire, eyeliner, and fangs galore. Think Whitby is all fish & chips and scenic views? Think again. Twice a year, this little seaside town is transformed into a marvellously macabre mecca, as thousands of Goths and other self-styled creatures of the night gather to celebrate Whitby Goth Weekend. What started as a meet-up between pen pals back in 1994 has grown to become one of the world's key events in the Goth calendar. Taking place in spring and October (as close to Halloween as possible, obviously) Whitby Goth Weekend is a two-day music festival at Whitby Spa Pavillion. It also features a Bizarre Bazaar of alternative wares for sale at venues right across town. Don't miss out on all the brilliant Fringe events taking place around Whitby too, including band meet-and-greets and the famous the Goth Football Match. Given Whitby's close ties to the novel Dracula, there's no more fitting a place in the UK to celebrate all things Goth. Over the years, the festival has become more and more diversified, and, as well as purist Goth attire, you'll also see plenty of attendees sporting a wealth of steampunk and Victoriana outfits. Don't miss a chance to escape the crowds, with a visit to Whitby Museum, one of Yorkshire's hidden gems and home to all manner of Victorian engineering and gruesome artefacts... There's a fantastic variety of music on offer at WGW, including Goth, new romance, and metal. To find out line-up for the next event, click here. There's always an eclectic mix of talented bands on offer, so make sure you give them all a chance. You might just find a new favourite!

This chapter tackles a topic we have touched upon in our previously published research (Spracklen & Spracklen, 2014). In that paper, we discussed some of the themes we turn to here, but all the research is new unless we are citing that paper directly. This second case study will be the history of the Whitby Goth Weekend, its status in British popular culture and the attitude towards it from goths. Whitby Goth Weekend is one of the most important events on the goth calendar; historically, it has appealed to goths across the country and the globe. Whitby Goth Weekend takes place in the town of Whitby on the coast of Yorkshire, England, famous for its ruined Abbey, its seaside resort delights and its key role in Bram Stoker's *Dracula*. In that book, it is the place where Dracula first appears on British soil, when the ship that is carrying him is caught in a storm. Unfortunately, it is also the place where Lucy Westenra is convalescing, and she is soon under Dracula's control. Bram Stoker also stayed at Whitby when he was writing the book. The chapter will explore how the weekend has become both a way of creating a 'Gothic' status for Whitby, and a way for everyday individuals to play as goths for the weekend. We will argue that while the Weekend is seen as important in the memory of our goth respondents and other goths online, they question its continued relevance and fear it has been taken over by people who want to be steampunks, or people who just want to listen to eighties rock bands. Before we look at the Weekend in more detail, it is necessary to put the festival in its context: Whitby.

Whitby

Whitby was a whaling town on the eastern coast of Yorkshire made rich on the back of that trade, and although it retains a fishing fleet until date, that is much reduced in number. Before whaling, the town had a long history stretching back to the Romans and then the early English. An abbey was built on the headland above the harbour as early as the seventh century, and was the place where the Church in Northumbria accepted the Roman dating of Easter as opposed to that adopted by the Irish Church (Rix, 2012). That abbey disappeared but another one was built in the later medieval period – and the ruins of that medieval abbey dominate the skyline above the town, the harbour and the beach. The town served as an important trading port through the middle ages and into the modern period, with fishing another vital part of the economy. But, it is the whaling industry on which modern Whitby, and Whitby's heritage tourism industry, is based. The wealth of the whaling industry led to the construction of fine Georgian cottages and terraced houses that still dominate and shape the old town and the harbour side (Jackson, 2017). A whalebone arch stands across the harbour on the headland looking at the abbey, and the local museum is dominated by material about whaling, or collected by whalers.

As whaling collapsed in the nineteenth century, another industry arose: tourism. The perfect sand of the beach and the clear sea was sold to the bourgeoisie as a perfect antidote to the stresses of city life. The arrival of the railways led to a boom in tourism, and an expansion of Whitby on the West Cliff, where terraces were built solely as guesthouses and hotels. Whaling was sold to these first tourists as an authentic part of Whitby's heritage. The first tourists were also shown the strange fossils and rocks that could be found around the town, and came back to their cities with jewellery carved from black jet. This stone became a fashion in Victorian times, as a black jewel suitable for mourning, when the Queen herself wore it (Hunter, 1993). More working-class tourists started to arrive after holidays became cheaper, and when they had weekends off legislated for by progressives in the Parliament (Walton, 2000). Whitby became a tourist town for all classes, though it preferred the bourgeois ones that stayed many days and behaved respectfully. In the twentieth century, Whitby's economy grew more reliant on tourism, as fishing and trading shrank. In the first half of the century that worked well enough, but from the sixties onwards British tourists were looking overseas for their summer holidays (Walton, 2000). The numbers of people coming to Whitby fell in the eighties, at the same time as the fishing industry almost collapsed, and the British economy was attacked by Thatcher's neo-liberalism. In the nineties, Whitby was struggling to find a role for itself and jobs for its people: unemployment and social exclusion rose, and the town felt like a ghost town outside the summer season. At the same time, however, speculators and holiday rental companies were buying cottages in the old town, as the older people who had lived in them all their lives moved out to council houses, sheltered homes, or passed away.

One of the ways Whitby re-invented itself in this period was to tap into the mythology of Dracula (Reijnders, 2011; Spracklen & Spracklen, 2014). As we have already discussed in the preceding paragraphs, Bram Stoker uses Whitby in the novel, and almost certainly wrote a good portion of the manuscript in Whitby, as he spent his summer holidays there (Hopkins, 2007). The presence of Bram Stoker holidaying on the West Cliff created a literary tourist trail that could include Lewis Carroll, who had also stayed in the town in the period. But, the most important tourism associated with Dracula became the places in Whitby in the book itself: the seat where Lucy sees the Count; the beach in the harbour where Dracula arrives on the wreck of a ship; and the graveyard and church across the harbour that act as focus and backdrop to the seduction of Lucy. People started to come to Whitby to visit these spaces and to walk in them, taking pictures while imagining that the work of fiction was actually a true story. In the nineties, vampirism was a fashion in goth and in popular culture (Khair & Höglund, 2013; Spracklen & Spracklen, 2012, 2014; Wegner, 2009), so many people came to Whitby to imagine themselves as the handsome Count, or helpless Lucy. And Whitby responded by selling itself as a destination for fans of Bram Stoker, vampires and the wider Victorian Gothic culture. Jet, and Victorian formal wear, became worn by would-be vampires and their human prey at goth clubs, and shops opened in Whitby catering for people who came to the town searching for Stoker and Dracula (Reijnders, 2011): goth clothing shops, Victorian clothing shops, with jet re-constructed as alternative and transgressive, as opposed to something worn by old women. These shops all existed before the Whitby Goth Weekend was established.[2]

The nadir of the vampire tourist industry came with the establishment of *Bram Stoker's Dracula Experience* on the harbour side. The name of the experience might seem odd – why not just *The Dracula Experience*? Do the owners think that visitors are too stupid to know that Bram Stoker wrote Dracula? In fact, Bram Stoker's Dracula is the title of the film made in 1992, and the Experience has copied that name, as well as the font design for the letters of the word Dracula. Furthermore, they have taken the stone gargoyle of the film's poster and marketing campaign and copied that too, along with the film's cheesy strap line: Love Never Dies.[3] This is the nineties Dracula, and nineties vampire goth: constructed from confusing goth with Gothic, as we have said, but channelling Anne Rice as well as Winona Ryder. Flashing red lights and spooky noises entice people to pay money to come in to see the sights of the Experience, to see displays about the book. In truth, the displays are animatronic props that deliver cheap horror frights, combined with the live-action delight of a bored teenager dressed in a Scream mask chasing you down the stairs. The effect of the gaudy lights and the black-painted spooky castle fake frontage is to put Dracula at the heart of Whitby's tourist industry, and its story as fictive history of Victorian Whitby. From the graveyard path, it is the first thing that grabs your attention, and it is impossible to walk past it without a crowd of schoolchildren looking inside.

The confusion between goth, Gothic, Victorian and Bram Stoker's Dracula can be seen in the blog with which we started this chapter. Bridson (2017) begins by using the dramatic phrase 'Black attire, eyeliner, and fangs galore'. Yes, there are some people who are still vampire goths, even though this has become unfashionable among goths, and no doubt, some people will be wearing fake fangs. A few of those may well have had dental cosmetic surgery so that they permanently have fangs, but most will be temporary embodiments of vampirism. More people will be dressed as vampires – possibly with fangs – because they have turned up at the festival thinking it is a fancy dress party, or a Halloween party: these are not goths. Bridson continues to describe the town as a space where goths and other 'creatures if the night' come for Whitby Goth Weekend. He is clever enough to know that there are all sorts of people attending the festival for all sorts of reasons, but he cannot help himself using a description made famous by the 1992 film. Further on, he points out the 'close ties' the town has with the novel, so that demonstrates for him that there is no better place to 'celebrate all things Goth'. We have already argued that the link between Dracula and goth is weak, and the link between Dracula and Whitby is not very strong, so his claim is erroneous. If there is a fitting place for a goth festival, it could be argued to be Leeds, where the F-Club shaped the scene that codified goth rock. He then goes on to note that the festival is more 'diversified', putting prospective holiday-makers at ease: anyone can join in; you do not need to be a 'purist'. He tells us the music includes new romance and metal as well as goth; and the look is no longer all black because you can wear lovely made-up fake imperial steampunk and 'Victoriana' fancy dress if you want. He suggests that a perfect holiday to the Weekend might be combined with a trip to the Whitby Museum we have mentioned, which he has to sell to the reader by mentioning 'Victorian engineering', possibly good for steampunks and Victorian Gothic types, and 'gruesome artefacts' that sound very exciting and horrible at the same time.[4]

This blog demonstrates, however, that Whitby Goth Weekend and Dracula have become key elements in the growth of Whitby as a tourist destination. Sykes

Cottages are competing with other holiday rental agents, hotels and bed-and-breakfast establishments to capture the increasing number of people wanting to come on holiday to Whitby. More holiday accommodation has appeared in new housing developments, and locals feel squeezed out of the housing market by rich out-of-towners buying second homes or homes for holiday rental. Goths and other such 'creatures of the night' are generally well-behaved and spend money generously in restaurants and shops, so like Bram Stoker and other Victorian bourgeoisie, they are welcomed and desired by Whitby's tourist trade. They visit the town outside of the dates of the festival, as likely to go there in winter as summer (if not more likely, as the high season remains a time for families with young children).

Whitby Goth Weekend

Whitby Goth Weekend plays an important role as a sub-cultural space in Paul Hodkinson's (2002) book. His ethnographic participant-observation of the festival and its participants was undertaken when goth had transformed into what we have called its underground, communicatively alternative state. His account of the festival and the people in it, as we have discussed earlier in the book, is essentially positive – his goths want to be at the festival, and get pleasure and community from going to it. Hodkinson thinks it is a meaningful space where sub-cultural capital is constructed, even if he raises questions about commodification and constraints of power around identity construction. Since its creation, though, the festival has evolved and faced a number of challenges and criticisms. As most readers of this book will be unfamiliar with the festival, its history and evolution, let us begin with an account from the festival's website, which states:[5]

> The Whitby Goth Weekend® (WGW®) is an alternative music festival. It was founded in 1994 by Jo Hampshire of Top Mum Promotions and has grown to become one of the world's premier Goth events. Alongside the music as part of the official event there is also the Bizarre Bazaar Alternative Market which features over 100 stalls across multiple venues.

This does not tell us much, though the fact that the official website stresses that the name and even the initials are registered trademarks, which suggests founder Jo Hampshire feels the need to claim the festival as her own intellectual property. In recent years, there have been attempts to run other goth festivals in Whitby. In 2011, rival promoters staged Whitby Alt Fest in some of the same spaces as Whitby Goth Weekend, only on a different two weekends timed around the same time of the year as Whitby Goth Weekend.[6] This rival festival drew some goths and traders away from attending the Whitby Goth Weekend that year, as people complained about the Weekend not being goth enough.[7] There were all kinds of unsubstantiated rumours at that time about the reasons for the emergence of Whitby Alt Fest, and people like our respondents remember wondering about the future fate of the Weekend at the time, tied up as closely as it was to the hard work of Hampshire and her close circle. If she quit because of the competition and the complaints about it not been proper goth any more, then what? The Weekend survived that attempt to move in on the Whitby goth pound, but more recently the Bram Stoker International Film Festival based in Whitby started to put on bands and other events as well as films, and in 2016 booked the Pavilion on the Halloween weekend – though this festival did not re-appear in 2017.[8]

Wikipedia offers a more informative account of the genesis and evolution of Whitby Goth Weekend. The entry begins:[9]

> The origins of WGW are in a meeting of around forty of Hampshire's pen-pals in 1994. The first meeting was held in the Elsinore, public house in Whitby which with the Little Angel continues to be a meeting point during the weekend. Hampshire said Whitby was chosen for its Dracula connections, although probably more so because the connection had already fostered a sense of acceptance on the part of locals and businesses rather than any inherent romanticism regarding the location. The festival was held yearly until 1997, when it became twice-yearly in April and October. It has grown into one of the world's most popular goth music events attracting around 1,500+ attendees from across the UK and beyond.

There is a reference in the Wikipedia page for the Hampshire's comment about Dracula, but it leads to the published case details for the trademark Hampshire registered for the Weekend. The submission may well have included some historical account for why she had chosen Whitby, but it does not appear to be included in the publicly available material on the UK Government's website. The story on Wikipedia is essentially correct, and shared by many other websites and news stories. It is also retold in Hodkinson (2002). The pen-pals are all goths, connected directly to Hampshire through email and old-fashioned post. Wikipedia seems to imply that the first Whitby Goth Weekend was when the 40 pen-pals of Hampshire all met up at the Elsinore, and this is the received wisdom of the genesis of the festival. However, there must have been some earlier planning and discussion to book the venue and the bands, and do all the work any event organiser has to do to ensure the event goes ahead. Hampshire must have been talking with bands and goths in her network for many months to make sure that the first festival happened. Whitby was already an attractive site for goths before Hampshire set up the festival there, so we can imagine goths telling her that she had to set it up in Whitby and use her local connections to make it happen. This history is correct, though. The festival was initially held at the Elsinore in 1994, and was a yearly event until 1997. The page shows how the Weekend grew year-on-year: it moved to the Pavilion venue in Whitby where it could host bigger bands and bigger crowds; it developed official and unofficial fringe events; and developed what became the Bizarre Bazaar.

The page is silent on the attempts to squeeze out Whitby Goth Weekend by rival promoters, and the struggle over ownership and control of the concept and brand itself. There is nothing about the criticism from goths unhappy at the takeover of the festival by fans of eighties pop and eighties pop bands: people far removed from anything alternative or subcultural. There is nothing about the recent struggle with the Bram Stoker International Film Festival over booking the Pavilion on the Halloween weekend. But, there is some controversy it is impossible to ignore or remove. The entry on Wikipedia continues:[10]

> In the mid-2000s the October weekend on or near Halloween began to attract large numbers of non-goths in Halloween, horror, historical, fantasy and Sci-Fi costume, which has led to an increase in photographers and visitors. The weekend now attracts other alternative subcultures, including Victorian vampires, rockers, punks and members of the steampunk subgenre. Some regulars consider it no longer a purely "Goth" weekend, and it was acknowledged by Hampshire in the 2014 Whitby Goth Weekend Guide that in order to survive the event would have to diversify into other areas that have influenced Goth. Concerns have grown about disrespect being shown to the graves in St. Mary's Churchyard by photographers using them for photographic purposes which has resulted in a petition to have the area closed during the event, an action that Whitby Goth Weekend fully supports. The Bram Stoker Film Festival, which also takes place in the town, have rehashed the proposal to build a film set graveyard which photographers would be charged to use.

We will discuss the problem of photographers and 'fancy dress' participants in a separate Section: Performing 'Alternative', Framing 'Alternative'. The issue of Whitby Goth Weekend no longer being a goth festival – which is related to the specific problem of photography – will be the subject of the rest of this part of the analysis.

The quote from Wikipedia hints at the shift in the audience at Whitby Goth Weekend. Increasing numbers of goths have decided not to buy tickets for the Weekend itself, though they still go to Whitby to meet friends in pubs and unofficial fringe events (Spracklen & Spracklen, 2014). In our earlier research on the Whitby Goth Weekend, this is how we reported and analysed the feelings of the respondents in that project (Spracklen & Spracklen, 2014, p. 99):

> All of the Goths in our research believe the festival has become something bigger than just a Goth festival. Most noted that the festival attracts a wider audience to gaze at the Goths (our Goth respondents called these people tourists, as opposed to the Goths as proper Goths attending a Goth event, which only accidentally makes them tourists) but also people who 'act' Goth, people who come to the Goth weekend to dress as Goths. Two female Goths highlighted this phenomenon in their reflections on attending the festival in the last few years, when it has become a mediatised event. One of them, Lucretia, told us the exasperation she felt

when she could not get in one Goth-friendly pub because it was 'full of people in Halloween fancy dress ... [I] can tell when people are dressed up in ... [they] don't look comfortable'. Tourists are coming to Whitby for the Goth Weekend for the postmodern play of performing Goth identities, but the performances are inauthentic and dependent on an instrumentalised notion of what a real Goth looks like: they come dressed as steampunks or Victorian vampires or something from a horror film, but they do not have the right hair or the right makeup, or the right combination of jewellery or piercings or tattoos. Authenticity is still important to our respondents. The fake, inauthentic Goth-men look like a character from a Dickens adaption on a trashy TV channel; the fake Goth-women look like they are on a hen night. Despite attending the festival, some of the Goths we interviewed believe that it has over-commercialised and commodified Goth culture, that it has become more about the event than the music. For these respondents, Goth should be defined by its music and its alternative ideology: it is a reaction against the mainstream and should never be a part of that mainstream popular culture; as one suggested 'if anybody can be a Goth by buying the uniform it does stop being something else', that something else being the political, communicative edge the scene developed in the early 1980s. The same respondent questioned the loss of Goth's alternative spirit as a result of Whitby Goth Weekend normalising Goth style and opening Goth up from a counterculture to a part of the instrumentalised mainstream, where Goth becomes a brand to promote tourism: 'Goth' he told us, 'has lost its fuck-off punk attitude'.

In this earlier research, then, we were already mapping the change that Whitby Goth Weekend had made to itself, and the increasing number of people turning up in fancy dress: goths who do not bother with 'authentic' goth make-up; and steampunks and weekend vampires. Our respondents used the word 'tourist' to describe the people who were turning up and were not goth-like. That is, the people dressing up are seen as not serious, as people on holiday, people coming to Whitby to view the goths, or as people on package holidays who take photographs of the sights (Cohen, 1979; Mehmetoglu, 2004; Spracklen, Laurencic, & Kenyon, 2013). Although everybody visiting Whitby could be argued to be a tourist, the goths attending the goth festival were becoming part of the attraction, and feeling the need to distinguish their leisure and tourism from that of the people who were coming to view them. Further, the goths' regular attendance at the festival made them feel more than passing tourists: they had invested huge amounts of time, money and cultural capital in the festival and in Whitby, making it a goth 'home from home', a space safe to be a goth. For the people we interviewed in 2013, people who had attended the festival every year twice a year, the changes were worrying. They had not stopped attending Whitby because it was their festival and their space, but they were showing a range of negative feelings about the 'take over'. This feeling of potentially losing the festival and Whitby is repeated in the interviews we have done for this book. Over half of our respondents did go to the Weekend, but they recognised that the nature of the bands and the participants in the Pavilion had shifted. It was no longer solely a space for traditional goths, and they expressed many concerns about the way in which it had become a festival for someone else: steampunks, people in fancy dress, weekend goths, people trying to get their picture in the news or people who listened to and liked eighties pop music who wanted to re-live their mis-spent youth dancing to Toyah. Increasingly, large numbers of the people who want to dress up have stopped attending the festival and just turn up at Whitby to walk around on show. In the 2000s, the festival sold out very quickly: in recent years, tickets have still been for sale right up until the event itself. A small number of our respondents have stopped attending the festival and Whitby altogether, preferring instead to spend their money supporting local events or to travel to Germany for Wave-Gotik-Treffen. These trends are a dilemma for Hampshire and the Weekend's management team: they have expanded the kind of music played at the festival to try to attract a broader range of alternative people (such as steampunks, who we analyse in Chapter 11), as they have seen these people already attending in previous years. But, the more non-goth music is scheduled, the less likely it is that goths will buy a ticket.

A review of the line-ups of the last 10 Whitby Goth Weekends (October 2015–October 2017) reveals that about half of the acts are goth bands: first-generation goth rock bands such as The Mission and Skeletal Family, for example, as well as more recent goth bands such as The Birthday Massacre and Bad Pollyanna. About a quarter are alternative rock of some kind, or steampunk: such as the April 2016 headliners Therapy? (rock); and Abney Park and The Men That Will Not Be Blamed For Nothing (steampunk). Then, the remainder are pop or pop/post-punk bands from the eighties, all as headliners: Altered Images and Spear of Destiny in October 2015; Heaven 17 in November 2016; Toyah in April 2017; and Theatre of Hate in October 2017. This non-goth element has definitely appeared in the last few years. In the 2000s, there are a few bands that fall out of the goth genre, but they do not constitute around half of the line-ups. Now, it may well be that many of the bands that played Whitby Goth Weekend in the 1990s and 2000s are no longer performing, and some of the bigger goth rock bands such as Fields of the Nephilim and The Sisters of Mercy are probably out of the budget for the Weekend. However, we believe there are plenty of older goth bands from the full range of the history of goth – and plenty of new bands – to have an interesting, diverse but 100% goth-sounding (and goth-looking) line-up. If the festival is not selling out despite having these pop acts headlining, and if goths have stopped buying tickets for the festival, then its long-term future is not guaranteed.

All of the respondents we interviewed for this book want Whitby Goth Week-end to continue. It was an important place for goth to survive and thrive out of the gaze of the mainstream in the nineties and first years of the new century. All our respondents recognise the importance of Whitby and the festival in their own personal lives and histories as goths, and all of them hope that the festival will continue to be a place in their lives as goths. Two respondents seemed happy that the festival had attracted a wider audience, but the rest expressed ambivalence. On the one hand, one cannot ban people from attending the festival for wearing clothing one does not like, and goth fashions have always been more colourful and playful than the stereotype suggests (as we discuss in Chapter 11). However, on the other hand, this festival is a goth festival, and one expects to be able to share the festival space with other people who have resisted the mainstream, and embraced the goth aesthetic and communicative alternativity. If people turning up at the goth festival are the football hooligans and bullies who beat up the goth kids at school, is that okay? We suggest that once mainstream bands are booked for the goth festival, there is a real chance that people buying tickets have mainstream views about difference and alternativity.

Performing 'Alternative', Framing 'Alternative'

The biggest criticism of the festival comes from the local residents of the town, who are exasperated by the streets packed with people in fancy dress – and the dozens of amateur and professional photographers who are drawn to Whitby Goth Weekend to take pictures. They mainly take pictures on the old side of town, swarming around Church Street on the cobbles and the narrow spaces in between the gift shops and tea rooms. It has become a staple of national, local and international media to display these pictures: the funny goths eating cake and drinking tea in china cups at the Marie Antoinette café; the steampunks talking to their own young children dressed in similarly brown uniforms; the Victorian brides in their sixties; and the young goth women revealing their skin and their cleavage. In the early years of the goth festival, these pictures were bought and sold and used by news corporations around the world, making those who took them a bit of money and a bit of publicity. This had the effect of making other photographers make their way to Whitby to try to take pictures that got picked up by the media. In turn, some people saw the pictures as an opportunity to sell themselves as goths or alternative types. The presence of the photographers and the possibility of being seen at Whitby brought many people to the festival just to dress up and see if they would be in the newspapers or on the television. The pictures that proved the most popular in the newspapers were always the ones with attractive young women in them, although some left-wing newspapers such as *The Guardian* have seemingly made a conscious effort not to use photos that replicate male desire and heteronormative ideas of female sexuality (Butler, 2006). So, attractive young women started to turn up at Whitby when the goth festival was taking place just to be photographed: some came with tickets for the festival, and were photographed outside the Pavilion in heteronormative sex-fantasy costumes; others simply paraded up and down the old town.

As we saw in the entry on the Weekend on Wikipedia, the town is particularly concerned about the way in which the old graveyard at the top of the famous Church Steps has become used as a space for taking these pictures – without any regard for the fact that the churchyard is a sacred space. Tourists visit Whitby almost every day of the year, and on a summer weekend the graveyard can feel desecrated by people walking around it eating ice creams and chips. We have seen people having their photos taken among the graves in the summer season, so it is not just people at the Whitby Goth Weekend. But, the huge numbers of photographers at the festival are problematic, combined with the desire for some people to be photographed in a stereotypically 'gothic' situation. The graveyard is the perfect backdrop to someone wanting to look spooky and sexy, and the combination of female exhibitionists and careerists – looking for something for their Instagram feed so they can make a career as an 'alternative' babe-model – and creepy male photographers is egregious. Our respondents have heard rumours of gravestones being pushed to make shots look better, and rumours that some stones have been damaged (though we have not been able to prove any of this). Locals believe these things have happened, however, and even went as far as organising a petition to stop the church graveyard being used for these purposes. The petition reads:[11]

> Whitby Goth Weekend was started by Jo Hampshire and a group of like minded music lovers, 22 years ago. Now, besides the fabulous music events and alternative market, Whitby is inundated with thousands of people wanting to dress up and take photographs. Unfortunately, despite pleas from the event organisers, and from St Mary's Church themselves, people are still disrespecting the graves of the ancestors of the Whitby residents, by using their graves as props for a cheap photo opportunity. Not only is this disrespectful to the families and the church, it is giving goths a bad name, causing tension in the community for those who are goth all year round, not just for the weekend. We are asking St Mary's church to close their churchyard for the goth weekend, to avoid the disrespect of the graves, damage to the grounds and publicity of the undesirable behaviour. A appointment system is suggested for those two days, for family and parish members to visit the church and graves of their loved ones in peace, without the area being made into a spectacle. Whitby is a beautiful town and there are plenty of places suitable for a photo opportunity which does not disrespect the wishes of residents and family members.

The petition reached over a thousand supporters before it was closed and delivered to Whitby Parish Office in 2015. It was at this point that the issue reached the local and regional press, and the organisers of the rival Bram Stoker International Film Festival suggested that a special fake graveyard 'film set' was created for people wanting to take these pictures, though this did not happen, as far as we are aware. We are not aware of any attempt to close the graveyard following the petition in the way the petitioners suggest. There are already notices up in the graveyard asking people to treat families and the buried with respect by not taking photographs. Closing a graveyard may be difficult under Anglican canon law. And, closing the graveyard would potentially create more upset and concern among other tourists. It would be difficult as well to demonstrate how exactly one might have a connection to someone buried in the graveyard. Finally, there are many informal shrines to people who have had their ashes scattered at the end of the path close to the cliff – it would be impossible to demonstrate you wanted to enter the graveyard to remember your mother where you scattered her ashes.

The petition itself reveals what some local people think about how the festival has changed. The person who has started the petition obviously sympathises with the community and culture of goth. He praises Hampshire and her team for the 'fabulous music events and alternative market'. But, he says the consequence of the festival is an inundation of people 'wanting to dress up and take photographs'. These are people who are goth 'all year round', but goths just 'for the weekend'. He blames these people for using 'graves as props' for their photoshoots. He fears their disrespectful behaviour is angering people who have loved ones buried in the graveyard, and the wider town community who hear of the bad practice. He thinks that this is a bad thing for people who are proper goths who live in the town, or who visit it at other times, as the weekend goths, those who perform being alternative – and those who frame that alternative performance – cause damage and spread ill-will. He does not want goths to stop coming to Whitby, nor does he want local goths to be criticised or attacked, but he fears drastic action needs to take place to ensure the continued safety of goths in the town – and the continued success of the festival.

It is not just angry goth sympathisers and locals who are frustrated. Even people who are partly responsible for making the Weekend into a parade of people in fancy dress think the spectacle of heteronormative performativity (Butler, 2006) – the photographers and the photographed – has gone too far. The steampunk movement has been central to the embodiment of fancy dress and cosplay in the festival. Their costumes have been increasingly prominent in town in the festival days, and increasingly visible in the media representation of the festival. Even their bands have started to appear more frequently in the last few years, when there is no steampunk music genre as such, just clothes and lyrical themes. Yet one prominent steampunk blogger writes critically on this issue:[12]

> The other issue that concerns me and many others – and is especially annoying to the residents of Whitby – is photographers and their constant need to take pictures on gravestones at the Abbey and hounding people on Church Street. I'm still yet to climb up there and see what happens for myself but I may go next time and cause a fuss if need be... But who is to blame? Goths are generally not really up for having their photograph taken. They don't attend Whitby Goth Weekend to be models for all and sundry; they go for the atmosphere, the gigs and to meet up with friends in a mutual environment. Steampunks are arguably more willing to have their picture taken, but our subculture is one built on etiquette and we observe the need to respect the families of the deceased buried there. Most likely it is newcomers to each culture who will be young, looking to boost a portfolio and easily

manipulated by pushy photographers. One important thought occurred to me though. Where are all these pictures? We see some of them on Flickr and some Facebook pages, but the sheer volume of photographers and the amount of photographs they take should have us swamped in pictures. But we aren't. So where are the pictures? If they're not being published anywhere then why are people's memories being trampled on for that oh-so-important shot? Why are other photographers being pushed and shoved out of the way because they're not taking a picture at that particular moment? Why was a girl chased through town a few years ago just for some photographs?

This steampunk recognises that goths do not necessarily want to be photographed, which we recognise and our respondents do: as goths they are not there to perform for anyone, they are there to have a pleasant evening surrounded by people they know share our views and tastes. This is how we viewed Whitby when we visited the festival. The steampunk blogger suggests that steampunks may well be more open to having their photographs taken because they are dressed in their fancy best and want to show off to everyone – but not in a way that is based on bad 'etiquette' or ethics. We suspect many steampunks may not want their photographs taken either: people who dress up may have many good reasons for saying no to a photograph being taken. Simple rules about consent always need to be followed.

The blogger blames the problem of the spectacle on younger steampunks and goths – newcomers – who do not understand the significance of the graveyard and the distress they might cause. We suspect that is true, but we also believe many of them know they are in a space that is sacred, and they do not really care about it. He is right to say the people being photographed are driven only by a desire to build up a portfolio. In this world of social media and virtual celebrity, people see building photographs as a career choice: the racier the shots, the more followers and likes, and the more likely one can get advertising for one's channel/page/feed (Pearl & Polan, 2015; Spracklen, 2015a, 2015b; Stapleton, Luiz, & Chatwin, 2017). Alternative models are still highly sought after, and the hope that the pictures might help one get some kind of contract in the wider entertainment industry – or even just some paid work on the cover of a goth-metal band's album – remains a powerful motivation for the young women who have their picture taken. For the photographers, their motivation is partly economic and scene-based cultural capital accumulation, as we have discussed, but the blogger hints at something else going on – the photographers are amateurs who never publish anything, and they manipulate the women for their own private satisfaction.

On the Whitby Goth Weekend website, the team has responded to these growing concerns. In their FAQs is a section about being an amateur photographer that starts 'I'm a hobby photographer who's looking to take some interesting photos of visitors to the town. Is there anything I need to know?', before the festival answers:[13]

> Many Goths are becoming increasingly despondent at the sheer number of photographers visiting the event, and it sometimes seems that there are more photographers than attendees. Here are a few pointers to ensure everyone has a more positive experience:
>
> St Mary's Church have installed a sign requesting that people do not use the graves or gravestones for photographic purposes. As well as finding it incredibly disrespectful both WGW and the Church are very mindful of the Health and Safety implications of these 200 year old grave sites which are subject to subsidence and are consequently cracked and broken.
>
> Please don't assume all Goths are attention seeking exhibitionists. Despite what you may assume from their appearance many don't wish to have their photograph taken. Please ask the subject before taking the shot.

This is a very polite response, and very measured. The festival has fuelled the arrival of all these hobby photographers. Goths are getting very angry at the photographers taking photos without permission and taking photos in the graveyard. Goths are also getting angry at the hordes of people who have turned up to be photographed, fuelled by the previous years' framing of the spectacle, and the evolution of the festival into a fancy-dress or cosplay parade. On Facebook there is a more revealing exchange of messages between the Whitby Goth Weekend and an owner of holiday accommodation in Whitby. The discussion begins with the owner of the holiday accommodation reflecting on complaints he has seen personally on the website about the spectacle of people watching people taking photographs of other people:[14]

> **Paul Wicks:** Hi. I am a multiple holiday cottage owner who has been happily letting to visitors to The Weekend since the first one you did. I don't charge any extra for that weekend and I have mostly let to the same people year after year. No problems there. This year there have been some nasty comments on Facebook about the crowds and the fancy dressers who also attend. I think you are getting the blame for something out of your control. Question. Would it make any difference if your weekend was a week later? You would avoid the half term week. There would be less folk about so it would be easier to get accommodation which should be cheaper. You would even have less problems booking venues in advance. What do you think? Paul. Whitbycottagesdotcom. A fan by the way.
>
> **Whitby Goth Weekend:** Hi Paul It began that way because it ties in with Halloween but to most goths thats now inconsequential when compared with the premium accom price & lack of beds that battling with photographers and costume dressers inevitably brings (thank you for being one of the few that don't price hike).

However I think I speak for all of us when i say that we are for-ever in debt to the people of Whitby for embracing our commu-nity and we love the fact that we bring extra revenue to the town at off peak times of the season. In going a week later (as we were made to last year) means that for one the Park and Ride is closed which impacts on the amount of daytime footfall in town which is so crucial for small businesses. I was also very aware that Whit-bys community Bonfire had to be moved from Sat 5th Nov to Thurs 3rd Nov last year again to accommodate us (SBC wouldnt grant the road closures essential to such an event whilst we were all up on West Cliff) On top of all of this Whitby Pavilion has a festival calendar bursting at the seams with Musicport and the Blues Fest also in October we dont always have much room to change.

Paul Wicks: Fair point. I was just wondering if it was possible to distance it from what is possibly becoming too popular. Could all the fancy dressers and the Pervy photographers spoil it? What do you think?

According to Wicks, the town has become too crowded in the October Whitby Goth Weekend because of the people in fancy dress, the photographers, and the hordes of people wanting it all. He says that there are people on Facebook who blame the festival for the spectacle, and some locals are losing patience. He sug-gests that perhaps the October weekend should be moved away from the half-term holiday week, which he thinks is responsible for the large numbers of spectators and others getting in the way. The person running the Weekend account responds by pointing out the link with Halloween and the problem of the venue being booked on other desirable weekends. But, that person also talks about the 'pho-tographers and costume dressers' that have caused demand and prices for accom-modation in the weekend of the festival to increase. This is the root cause of the disquiet on Facebook, in goth spaces, and in Whitby itself. Wicks's response to the Weekend account is to ask them to explicitly distance themselves from the 'fancy dressers and pervy photographers'. This is the real moral issue at stake, not overcrowding per se. This question was asked over a year ago at the time of writ-ing – and no one responded to it publicly. Despite Wicks getting the issue exactly right, the Weekend has been too cautious: it has said the right thing about the graveyard and consent, but has not said anything to condemn the male gaze at the heart of the picture posing and taking.

Conclusion

In Spracklen and Spracklen (2014, p. 100), citing Edensor (2001) we ended with these words:

Edensor's (2001) ambivalence about the performance of tourism can be seen in the way Whitby has branded itself as a Dracula and

Goth town, and the way in which the Goth Weekend has become an established and well-known attraction. On the one hand, Whitby tourist chiefs are trying to stop the town becoming over-commercialised and are open to this (seemingly) strange subculture's presence in the town's streets. Goths created the festival as a communicative act among themselves, and use the Goth weekends as opportunities to perform authentic Goth identities in a communicative-shaped space (Habermas, 1984; Spracklen, 2009, 2011). But Whitby Goth Weekend has become a tourist event: the eventisation of tourism commodifies and instrumentalises the relationship between individuals 'at leisure' and the spaces around them (Smith, 2012). The Goth scene has become a commodity, a space where an industry (tourism) has taken over. People dress up (perform ambivalently) as Victorian Goths by hiring or buying expensive clothes, and the festival tries to promote itself beyond Goth music. The communicative freedom of the Goth scene is still present but it is limited. The struggle over the ownership of Whitby Goth Weekend, the attempts to control the fringes, and the evolution of the event as spectacle and popular carnival (when people become Goths for a weekend of inauthentic, fake performativity through the purchase of throw-away fancy dress) point away from that freedom.

In this new analysis of the Whitby Goth Weekend, we do not see any reason to change those words. Goths created the festival, and the wider weekend of events and informal get-togethers – but like all form of tourism, the festival has become part of a wider industry with its own interests. Furthermore, the weekend has attracted people who want to perform and dress alternative while carrying anti-alternative ideologies in their heads: they are the school bullies, not the bullied. They are people who see dressing up as a laugh, a chance to be wasted, or a chance to be noticed by agents who can offer modelling contracts. Goth survives at Whitby, but only as a ghost of festivals past.

Notes

1. Neither do we own any shares in Sykes Cottages or indeed any shares in anything; nor do we own property in Whitby or indeed any property other than our home.
2. Karl remembers going in one of the goth/alternative shops on holiday with his parents when he was at university, somewhere between 1990 and 1993.
3. http://draculaexperience.co.uk/. Accessed on 10 March 2018.
4. To be fair, the museum has a very real, spooky Hand of Glory: https://whitbymuseum.org.uk/whats-here/collections/special-collections/hand-of-glory/
5. http://www.whitbygothweekend.co.uk/about-wgw/. Accessed on December 13, 2017.
6. See review at http://www.terrorizer.com/dominion/dominionfeatures/title-85/. Accessed on December 13, 2017.

7. https://www.whitbygazette.co.uk/whats-on/arts/whitby-s-goth-festival-returns-in-subdued-style-1-3229272. Accessed on December 13, 2017.

8. In the name of transparency, Beverley was an invited performer at the 2016 Bram Stoker International Film Festival. We have no other connection to it, or interest in it. We have attended Whitby Goth Weekend.

9. https://en.wikipedia.org/wiki/Whitby_Goth_Weekend. Accessed on January 15, 2018.

10. https://en.wikipedia.org/wiki/Whitby_Goth_Weekend, accessed on 15 January 2018.

11. https://www.change.org/p/whitby-parish-office-close-st-mary-s-churchyard-in-whitby-over-the-goth-weekends. Accessed on December 18, 2017.

12. https://www.steampunkjournal.org/2016/04/30/whitby-goth-weekend-issues/. Accessed on December 19, 2017.

13. http://www.whitbygothweekend.co.uk/faq/. Accessed on January 19, 2018.

14. https://www.facebook.com/whitbygothweekend/. Accessed on December 13, 2017.

Chapter 11

Goth as Fashion Choice

Introduction

Coronation Street is one of the United Kingdom's most popular soap operas. Set in a fictional town/city on the edge of Manchester, *Coronation Street* ('Corrie' to its fans) has become a television programme that reflects the national mood and the fashions of the moment (Dunleavy, 2005; Weatherall, 1996). Its characters live though dramatic plots that are informed and constructed by the moral panics that shape the headlines of tabloid newspapers (Cohen, 2002). Even in this new century of digital television and online streaming, the soap opera retains its grip on the imaginations of millions of people in the country – and all over the world (Dunleavy, 2005). The return of a regular character called Rosie Webster – daughter of Sally and Kevin Webster – in 2017 had one website reflecting on the ways in which Rose had let her family down over the years. At the heart of this list of Rosie's 'biggest ever dramas' was the shocking turn to the dark side when Rosie was a still a young teenager:[1]

> Remember when Rosie morphed into a moody Goth, dyeing her hair jet black and discovering a love of heavy eyeliner? As fashion statements go, it was a pretty strong one. She spent all her time holed up in her bedroom with her boyfriend and fellow grunge enthusiast Craig Harris, where they listened to the not-so-dulcet tones of a heavy metal band called Stench of Death. But that's not all the randy teens were up to, and Sally and Kevin were horrified to learn their daughter was having underage sex. Rebellious Rosie ignored her parents' pleas to stop seeing Craig, but things eventually fizzled out between the young lovers in 2006 when she got cold feet over running away to Berlin with him.

The thing called goth in this recollection is that form of goth that is actually heavy metal, and, strangely grunge (which may well be the invention of the person writing the blog, as grunge is not something anyone we have spoken to would identify with goth). The band name mentioned seems to be an attempt to mimic the name of the real band Cradle of Filth. But, what is true is that Rosie Webster and her goth boyfriend were recognisable as a type in popular culture and society at the time. The creators of the soap had already noticed that many young teenagers were dying their hair black – perhaps, the writer of the Rosie Webster who becomes a goth plotline had such a child. At the start of this century, tabloid newspapers were becoming filled with stories of goth teenagers being a threat to the good order of British society: this was the age of the moral panic about emos in newspapers such as the right-wing, conservative *Daily Mail* (Brown, 2011). Like all moral panics, this led to more young people identifying as goths and emos as a way of identifying with a rebellious movement against the mainstream norms and values of their parents (Cohen, 2002). At first, Rosie Webster's conversion to goth was sympathetic to goth culture – she was seen dressed up in black clothes and make-up rarely seen on mainstream soap operas, and people around her seemed to respect her decision to be a goth, even if they tutted in the classic Corrie fashion about it.[2] But, as the recollection we have cited above shows, Rosie Webster's embrace of goth culture soon turned into a standard morality tale of domineering boyfriends and teenage sex and sexuality (Lancaster, 2011; Renold & Ringrose, 2011).

In this, our penultimate full chapter, we will look at the importance of fashion and style in the rise of goth. We will begin with a discussion of the change and continuity in goth fashions and goth aesthetics since the formative years of the nineteen-eighties. We will show how the goth aesthetic borrowed from punk, post-punk and hard rock; then, we will show how goth and metal have had a symbiotic relationship in terms of transgressive, alternative fashions (as we have already discussed previously). In the first section, we will show how goth in this century has become primarily a fashion choice, with gothness being performed as pantomime by amateurs, or as a professional career choice by models. We will briefly discuss the development of steampunk out of goth, and show how goths have resisted or embraced the steampunk aesthetic. In the final section and conclusion, we will then describe the ways in which goth fashions and styles have become co-opted by mainstream fashion, and mainstream popular culture.

The Early Goth Aesthetic

By the late eighties, the fashions of the goth culture had been pretty well established, as outlined in Hodkinson (2002) and Brill (2008), and popularised in the style guides of Mercer (1988, 1991, 1997, 2002) and Scharf (2011). We will discuss the popular understanding of the goth aesthetic – what people on the Internet believe it is – when we turn to exploring goth as a fashion choice later in this chapter. But essentially, the look of the early goth aesthetic was black, even if other colours were added to the blackness as the look evolved in the first years from post-punk (Harriman & Bontje, 2014). Hair was dyed black and kept long – for men and for women – with various ways of combing the hair back to build its shape. Of course, many people did not or could not stick to that dyed, long, transgressive look: men often did not bother with having long hair or black-dyed hair; and women often experiment with other colours. Men and women generally wore black clothes, though other colours would complement this colour palette, even after the post-punk period (Harriman & Bontje, 2014): purple tie-dye tops, for example, were very popular. For men, black jeans and black shirts or t-shirts were the standard uniform, and often those shirts carried the names of bands that were part of the wider alternative scene. For women, the clothes of choice depended on the context, and were often homemade or modified: going out to a nightclub might mean putting on a slinky black velvet dress, but going to a pub or a gig might mean choosing to wear black trousers and black tops that were more practical. On the feet, early goths wore a range of shoes and boots that reflected the fact that shoe designers and companies had yet to move into the goth market – there was no one goth boot as there was by the start of this century, when almost every goth had a pair of New Rocks. Our recollection of the period, combined with our respondents' memories, identify Kickers and Dr. Martens as brands that moved from indie and punk to goth, although most people seemed to wear ex-army boots or winkle-pickers of some kind. Women also had the opportunity to wear heels if they were wearing clothes suited for them, but the women we spoke to often wore boots with dresses. The early goth aesthetic was finished off with the application of white foundation and heavy make-up on the face. For many men, this might only be some eye-liner, and some men did not even bother with any make-up at all. For women, make-up was an essential part of becoming goth correctly – and the way the make-up is used is still seen by many of our respondents as the test for who is a proper goth and who is a fake (Spracklen & Spracklen, 2014). Essentially, the eyes need to be made striking, not pretty; scary, not meek. Eyeliner and eye-shadow need to be applied in a way that copies or adapts the layered effect seen infamously in the stage make-up of Siouxsie from the Banshees. This striking eye make-up is then contrasted with heavy blusher on the cheeks to make them look thin and almost cadaverous, and glossy lipstick that can be red, black or purple, or some other dark shade between them. Unlike goth in the nineties onwards, the early goth aesthetic did not embrace piercings and tattoos in any significant way: ear-piercing was fairly common among women because it was part of youth culture more generally at the time, and many goth men had one ear pierced, but that was all. And, tattoos were still associated with bikers, criminals and squaddies at this period (Yuen Thompson, 2015) – some metal musicians could be seen with tattoos but these were exceptions even in heavy metal (Winge, 2012).

The early goth aesthetic had a number of origins. The first and immediate origin is the wider aesthetic of the communicative alternativity at work in the eighties in the United Kingdom. In this alternative scene, wearing black was already a marker of being alternative, being transgressive and resisting the mainstream (Harriman & Bontje, 2014; Wilson, 1990). Black clothes – especially t-shirts – had been part of punk's sartorial code, and that had translated into post-punk and heavy metal by the middle of the eighties. Black band t-shirts were cool to wear, and projected one's taste and one's belonging and community to those who recognised the name of the band. Band t-shirts had a long history of being sold to and worn by fans, with official licensees battling bootleggers who sold shoddy versions of the t-shirts outside every gig (Larsen, 2013). Band t-shirts started out in all colours, but black became the colour of choice in the alternative scene because fans associated black with transgression and danger. More prosaically,

black t-shirts can be matched with a wider array of coloured clothes and accessories than other coloured t-shirts, so they are a practical choice. The wider alternative scene was also the site of biker culture, which had adopted black leather
jackets, long hair and black boots long before heavy metal and goth both adapted
those fashions for their own aesthetic (Schouten & McAlexander, 1995). Lemmy
of Motörhead channelled the biker style into his stage look, and he was a direct
influence on Andrew Eldritch, who took the black leather and black shirts and
added black-dye in his hair. Eldritch and the F-Club scene were also influenced
by Iggy Pop dressed all in black on stage (Spracklen, Henderson, & Procter, 2016;
Thompson, 2007), and the post-punk, proto-goth stage style of all the other
bands that shaped goth: Bauhaus, Killing Joke, Joy Division, Siouxsie and the
Banshees. This, in turn, tapped into the gothic horror of popular culture in the
sixties and seventies: for women, for example, there were already goth role models
in the form of the witches and vamps of Hollywood such as Morticia Addams
(Holland, 2004; Winge, 2012).

Another less-celebrated influence on the early goth aesthetic was Johnny Cash.
He wore a black shirt and black trousers on stage, and cultivated an image of
rebellion and political resistance. He became known as the Man in Black, and
stood on the side of prisoners, the poor and the oppressed in the United States
of America (Edwards, 2009). His songs had dark themes of murder and revenge,
though as a committed Christian in later life he wrote songs that were increasingly of a redemptive theme. Towards the end of his career, he worked with Rick
Rubin on the American series of albums that sold well among goth audiences
because of covers of songs by Nine Inch Nails and Depeche Mode. It was Cash
who made black clothes the fashion of resistance, rebellion and transgression –
even though his music was unfashionable in the seventies, he remained influential
among musicians who wanted to demonstrate they stood against the excesses
of the mainstream. So, Cash clearly inspired Iggy Pop and Lemmy, and almost
certainly inspired Andrew Eldritch, to wear black.

Goth and Metal as Darkwave Transgression

As we have discussed earlier, metal and goth influenced each other as forms of
communicative alternativity in the nineties and beyond. We have shown that they
were often perceived as belonging to the same transgressive sub-culture, even
though that sub-culture was actually part of the cultural industries – that is, part
of the hegemonic mainstream of popular culture (Adorno, 1991; Hebdige, 1979).
That perception of belonging to something called goth was sometimes a perception from within the sub-culture by individuals around the world who wanted to
be known as goths even though much of what they listed to was actually metal:
from the black metal underground all the way to festival headliners such as Marilyn Manson, Rammstein and My Dying Bride. In Germany, extreme metal and
goth rock all fell under the sub-cultural label of darkwave, and it was possible to
buy magazines that covered both genres alongside mittelalter, EBM, industrial
and neo-folk (Brill, 2008). In other countries, as we have shown, metal became

goth in the perception of the mainstream, from religious preachers fearing the end of the world to politicians and journalists worried about the gloomy-looking teenagers hanging around the shopping malls.

This confabulation of goth and metal led to changes in the goth aesthetic in the 1990s and in the 2000s. Goth became associated with tattoos and piercings, and there was an overtly heteronormative sexuality displayed by women. As Brill (2008) shows, fetish wear, corsets, short skirts and stockings became the fashionable form of clothing for goth women in night clubs. Transgression of gender roles in the wearing of clothes was permissible for men, but women's choices were limited to those that reproduced, rather than challenged, the gender order. This sexualisation of women goths came more from the industrial/metal part of goth in the nineties, and from North America and Germany, rather than the communicatively alternative underground in the United Kingdom. Metal had (and has) an ambiguous role in the gender order (Hill, 2016; Spracklen, 2015a). Parts of heavy metal were homosocial and homoerotic for men, but gender roles in metal were rigidly defined in this period (Walser, 1993). The heteronormative sexuality of the groupie dressed in sexy clothes became a staple of stories in songs, and was represented in the videos of the bands (Savigny & Sleight, 2015). Although heavy metal's sexism was challenged at this time by radical feminists aligned with the Riot Grrl movement and more progressive bands such as Sepultura, the 'sexy girl' in the video and on the album cover continued to mark metal as heteronormative (Hill, 2016). So, bands that were influenced by goth and which became seen as goth because they were played in goth nightclubs – Marilyn Manson, Type O Negative, Cradle of Filth, for example – all used heteronormative (Butler, 2006) goth-looking young women in their videos. The clothing and make-up on these models reflected the fashions in metal and goth spaces, and informed and shaped the future direction of those fashions. Men in the goth sub-culture also found themselves becoming more like metallers, but the fashion of male metallers and male goths were very similar all along: black boots, long hair, black shirt or black t-shirt and black trousers. Big boots with lots of buckles and heavy soles became the norm in goth and metal, and they probably came from the German darkwave scene. The only definite crossover from goth to metal for men was the widespread adoption of black jeans in extreme metal spaces.

More generally, goth and metal fashions – clothing, make-up and accessories – were often sold in the same spaces online and on the high street. Some independent retailers had separate sections inside their shops for goth and for metal – this was the way we remember from Hellraiser Records in Leeds, York and Wakefield in the first decade of this century. We could enter the shop in Leeds and turn one way to enter the goth section, which had its own name and cash register, or stay in the main shop to buy metal stuff. Many online retailers had separate goth and metal sections, and often used goth and metal as identifying tags for anyone browsing clothes and other accessories. But, more often than not, the shops sold products that were equally goth and metal. Beyond records and band merchandise, it was (and is) difficult for us to label, predict or confirm whether any particular dress or shirt was goth or metal. Both were dark aesthetics that played with transgression. Perhaps, something with a Celtic cross or knot pattern might be suggestive of goth; something with an upside-down cross is almost definitely metal. But, what about something with a pentagram? That could equally be something worn by a goth from the eighties who became a pagan in the nineties, or a metaller who associates the pentagram with the cartoon-version of the Devil made popular in extreme metal (Spracklen, 2014, 2017b; Spracklen & Spracklen, 2012). Or, what about something styled with fetish straps? Again, both goths and metallers could wear that and not be making a category mistake the next time they went out. Our respondents all note this fluidity at the boundary of metal and goth in the 1990s and 2000s.

A final confabulation of goth and metal was the rise of emo. Emo started out as sub-genre of hardcore, itself a sub-genre of punk (Brown, 2011; Hill, 2011). Emo was short for 'emotional hardcore', and was a label used to identify bands with lyrical and musical themes of anguish, heartbreak and despair. The sub-genre rapidly became popular in the 2000s as bands married the original hardcore form with pop and rock structures. My Chemical Romance became the biggest band of the movement, and they used many themes and aesthetics familiar in goth culture. Emos became synonymous with goths, and soon emos were dressing in goth fashions, and goths adopted emo fashions, especially the red colours and bracelets associated with My Chemical Romance and their fans. In turn, emo changed the metal scene, and challenged it, because emo fans were more likely to be women than metal fans, and emo ejected the sexism that was a part of metal (Hill, 2011). As such, many male metallers rejected emo and emo fashions, retreating to a more supposedly authentic metal aesthetic borrowed from the eighties (Hill, 2011). Goths meanwhile were more welcoming of emo, and My Chemical Romance songs became hits in goth clubs.

Goth as Fashion Choice(s)

In this contemporary age of globalisation and post-industrialisation, we seem to be living in a time of choice. Many sociologists, theorists and philosophers have made this claim about the world in which we live. This claim is at the heart of the theory of postmodernism and postmodernity: with the decline of Western power, and the dissolution of social structures, more people are given the freedom to explore and construct their place in the world (Lyotard, 1984). With the struggle against capitalism seemingly lost with the decline of the working-class political activism and the factories in which working-class people worked, postmodern theorists saw hope in identity politics (Lefebvre, 1991, 1996; Lyotard, 1984; Muggleton, 2000; Redhead, 1997; Winge, 2012). From having identity imposed on them by hegemonic elites, the people of this new age have supposedly been given the freedom to choose their identities – from online spaces all the way through to their brand of coffee and the leisure activities they take part in and the sports they support (Rojek, 2000, 2010). Furthermore, it is argued that in today's world of inter-connected spaces people become cosmopolitan, hybrid and global travellers (Urry, 2007). For Bauman (2000), for example, this is the world and society of liquid modernity, where capitalism has made people alienated, individualists, and makers of their own identity through consumption (where they are not the poor consumers of the global poor). Being alternative is one other fashion and identity choice provided in the postmodern, liquid society in which we supposedly lie.

We have argued earlier in this book that this theory of contemporary society is wrong. We have argued that the dissolution of social structures is over-stated in these postmodern accounts of the world, and actually that hegemonic power associated with elites remains crucial in constraining choice and perpetuating inequality and injustice. For the many people who are poor, the choice of post-industrial, global capitalism's cultural industries remains a choice between two kinds of whips, or two kinds of chains. For the many people who are not rich, white people from the global North, choices remain an illusion perpetuated by the invisibility of instrumental whiteness (Spracklen, 2013b). For women in the global North, there may be more freedoms to pick and choose identities and leisure lives this century compared with the first half of the last century; but, these choices remain constrained by hegemonic masculinity and conservative traditions about good women (who know their place, who dress in pretty clothes) and bad women (Butler, 2006). The alternative space constructed as a Habermasian lifeworld against the instrumentality of capitalism and nation-states was a space for identity-making, and for meaning and purpose for those who joined it (Habermas, 1984, 1984, 1989). But, in today's world, this lifeworld, like other communicative spaces, is in danger more than ever of being colonised by the logic of capitalism (Habermas, 1984; Spracklen, 2011). Alternativity is not a choice – it is an imperative for those who want to express their loathing of the mainstream. Unfortunately, alternativity today is almost just a choice, and all its communicative rationality has been all-but extinguished, as alternative fashion becomes a lifestyle choice.

For those who have the economic, social and capital, it is possible to dress up and be a goth – to play at being a goth for a night or a weekend – or perform the role of a goth for as long as one desires. The economic capital comes from the well-paid jobs many people in the global North have, relative to the rest of the world and the rest of their home nation's populations. There is a significant middle-class bourgeoisie that have flourished in the North despite (or because of) the rising inequalities in these nations, and the rise in numbers of people struggling to pay their bills (Bauman, 2000). This new bourgeoisie are the university-educated, liberal urban classes who have skills and knowledge that cannot be outsourced: lawyers, academics, accountants and systems analysts. Those who cannot afford to buy alternative fashion have to go into debt to keep up with these big-spending actors, or buy second-hand, or feel alienated and angry, as some of our respondents admitted. The social capital associated with being a goth comes from time spent connecting with other goth people, knowing what spaces are available where one can be a goth, and meet others who are goths. All this is easy to acquire online, though the spaces in the real world where goths can be goths are limited to the cities and towns where clubs-nights, festivals and gigs happen. Cultural capital is much harder to acquire: this is the crucial learned knowledge about what is real and fake, true and false, in the aesthetics and history of goth. In this limited sense, it is easy to be a goth, and to express identity with goth, through simply wearing the clothes and make-up. So long as no-one asks someone dressing as a goth about their favourite song on the first Rhombus EP, and one follows the accepted rules of the goth aesthetic, one can get away with being a goth. The rules of the goth aesthetic have been crafted by the communicative alternativity of the nineties underground scene. But, they have also become established rules drawn up and published on the Internet, especially on the collective memory of Wikipedia. Here is what that that website says about goth fashion some paragraphs down the main page on Goth sub-culture:[3]

> Gothic fashion is stereotyped as conspicuously dark, eerie, mysterious, complex and exotic. Goth fashion can be recognized by its stark black clothing. Typical gothic fashion includes dyed black hair, dark eyeliner, black fingernails and black period-styled clothing; goths may or may not have piercings. Styles are often borrowed from the Elizabethan, Victorian or medieval period and often express pagan, occult or other religious imagery. Ted Polhemus described goth fashion as a 'profusion of black velvets, lace, fishnets and leather tinged with scarlet or purple, accessorized with tightly laced corsets, gloves, precarious stilettos and silver jewelry depicting religious or occult themes'. Researcher Maxim W. Furek stated that 'Goth is a revolt against the slick fashions of the 1970s disco era and a protest against the colourful pastels and extravagance of the 1980s. Black hair, dark clothing and pale complexions provide the basic look of the Goth Dresser. One can paradoxically argue that the Goth look is one of deliberate overstatement as just a casual look at the heavy emphasis on dark flowing capes, ruffled cuffs, pale makeup and dyed hair demonstrate a modern-day version of late-Victorian excess'. Gothic fashion may also feature silver jewelry.

This is a simplistic view of goth fashion, although much of it is essentially correct. We note that the person who has written this part of the page is mixing up goth with Gothic, a common confusion, and one perpetrated by some writers (as we have mentioned earlier in the book) and many goths themselves. The first sentence of this description of the goth aesthetic is rather pathetic and meaningless: what is 'eerie, mysterious, complex and exotic'? The person who has written this sentence wants to be as inclusive as possible in identifying goth, but in doing so retreats to lazy, empty signifiers. The second sentence mentions some detail, black as a defining colour, which is correct, and uses the more precise word 'goth'. Then, there is some detail about hair and make-up, and piercings, which is correct but seems to be a simplified set of rules for a would-be goth to tick off before they go to their first club night. The paragraph proceeds to make a rather audacious claim that goth style borrows from three named time periods. Although goth has borrowed medieval style and from the Victorians, we have yet to see someone turn up at a goth event looking like the Elizabethan cad

Edward Blackadder,[4] complete with a big ruff round their neck. The authors of the paragraph are better informed when they suggest goth fashion uses religious imagery – both Christian and anti-Christian. They then provide an account of goth fashion from which they have clearly drawn this idea, which also provides a summary of the underground aesthetic of the nineties, when women started to dress more sexually provocatively. They then cite Furek (2008) who suggests goth is a revolt against the colours and excess of the eighties, which is hilariously wrong. Goths were wearing black in the eighties, but they embraced some of the colours and extravagance of the mainstream fashions of that decade: goths in the eighties had big hair and glossy lipstick, and experimented with other colours in the post-punk period that merged into goth in the early eighties. Furek then continues to write that goth fashion is basically a modern example of late-Victorian excess, conflating goth with Gothic and assuming the only correct form of goth is the goth that dresses like a Victorian, or the goth that dresses like a Victorian vampire. It is quite possible to be a goth and not be Victorian, but this paragraph assumes that is unlikely – so if you heading to Whitby, you can buy your Victorian funeral gear and think you are doing the right thing, and the only thing.

Elsewhere on Wikipedia, another attempt to define goth fashion can be found at a completely separate page unfortunately entitled 'Gothic fashion'. This shares some similarities with the paragraph cited above, but there are some points of difference:[5]

> Gothic fashion is a clothing style marked by conspicuously dark, mysterious, antiquated and homogeneous features. It is worn by members of the Goth subculture. A dark, sometimes morbid fashion and style of dress, typical gothic fashion includes a pale complexion with colored black hair, black lips and black clothes. Both male and female goths can wear dark eyeliner and dark fingernail polish most especially black. Styles are often borrowed from the punk fashion, Victorians and Elizabethans. Goth fashion is sometimes confused with heavy metal fashion and emo fashion.

As with the other paragraph, the first sentence is conspicuously dark and mysterious in its style and content, and was clearly written by someone whose only reference to goth was watching Rosie Webster having a big sulk on *Coronation Street*. The author has used Gothic, and mentions goth's antiquated features – presumably, the borrowing from medieval and Victorian periods, and not something that is old-fashioned or out-of-date. The paragraph continues to correctly identify the people who wear goth fashions as members of the goth culture, and even makes the claim that the culture is a sub-culture, something we have been careful to claim. The next sentence summarises the key markers of the goth aesthetic, though we are not sure that morbid is the right term, as it has pejorative connotations: goths are interested in death and transgression, but that does not make them or their clothes morbid. The penultimate sentences – notwithstanding the strange appearance of the Elizabethans again – are actually an accurate description of the influences on the goth aesthetic, as if they had read this chapter before they wrote the words. Goth fashion has its roots in punk and has borrowed from the Victorians, though it is more than just a product of punk and Victoriana as it draws on the wider alternative sub-culture of the eighties as well (as we have just said). And, as we have also said, goth has become confused and conflated with metal and emo, and has changed because of that interaction.

Goth as a modern-day fashion choice, then, is regulated, reduced and instrumentalised by the style guides and fashion tips that have grown on the Internet. Goth is now easier to perform and choose as a lifestyle, but what constitutes goth – what makes goth unique and alternative and transgressive – has been reduced to a few key aesthetical markers and symbols. In Spracklen (2014), the first of us discussed the 'heat-death' of goth and black metal as a consequence of the commodification of both scenes. The radical politics and experimentation that defined goth has be replaced by dresses bought in shopping malls and people trying to make careers out of dressing-up. Goth music and goth politics have been sidelined by young people trying to be the most popular goth on Twitter or Instagram, hoping to be spotted so that they could transform themselves into goth models and goth celebrities, just as many young people find validation in fame and celebrity (Renold & Ringrose, 2011). Pursuing the idea of goth as choice to its extent, these people only want to buy the right make-up, get the right tattoo and pay for the right professional photographer to get noticed. The career of one goth model can stand pretty much for any other. This is one we found carefully curated on Wikipedia:[6]

> Wednesday Mourning works primarily in the fields of acting and alternative modeling. She specializes in the Goth subculture and has been influential in goth fashion, as well as being the celebrity spokesmodel for Atelier Gothique and appearing as a model for the band My Chemical Romance's CD *Welcome To The Black Parade*. She was awarded 2010 Goth Day Model of the year, LA Weekly's Goth Girl of the Week, and since 2012, Mourning has been a co-star on *Oddities: San Francisco*, a Science Channel program. Mourning is also curator of an esoteric bookstore, Orphic Vellum Books, the only one of its kind in the U.S., and has appeared in several publications including Gothic Beauty, Elle Magazine and writing contributor for Celtic Family Magazine.

From what we can gather from its website, *Gothic Beauty* is a magazine aimed at women who want to learn how to dress and look like women like Wednesday Mourning, and at men who want to look at pictures of goth women. The competitions and lists referred to in the career biography are also essentially about the male gaze, although we are sure Wednesday believes all these things are empowering for her (Butler, 2006; Holland, 2004; Winge, 2012; Yuen Thompson, 2015). She has had a good career, after all, which has led to all sorts of opportunities to get her name known and her product sold. She has managed to get herself on the front cover of a CD by the emo band My Chemical Romance, and has acquired the real fame of these times – a regular appearance on a reality TV programme.

The existence of goth models as a category of celebrity goes against the radical feminist politics eighties goth, and the wider alternative sub-culture of those times. Still, many goths retain a commitment to feminism, so again this trend seems to be troubling to some of our respondents. All the women we spoke to expressed concern about hyper-sexuality and younger goth women entering the scene feeling pressured to dress in a heteronormative, hyper-sexual style – a conclusion reached of course by Brill (2008). More worryingly, the normalisation of the idea that being a goth means being a successful goth model feeds the narcissism of social media, and the frenzy of Whitby Goth Weekend. Becoming a goth is becoming seen to be just one other way of becoming rich and famous, which of course is just one way people without power are fooled into accepting the inequality of the world.

Steampunk

Steampunk has become one of the most instantly recognisable tribes of modern society. It has spread from its sub-cultural roots to become a form of cosplay: dressing up in a fictive, alternative universe in which the British Empire had space ships powered by steam. The word steampunk was first applied by to a sub-genre of science fiction novels and comics that explored this idea of an alternative Victorian Britain (Cherry & Mellins, 2011; Onion, 2008; Rose, 2009). As a science-fiction sub-genre, steampunk borrowed its name from cyberpunk, which had been coined to describe the dark, dystopian, virtual spaces of the work of William Gibson, especially his novel *Neuromancer*. This work was cyber because it dealt with cybernetics, the idea of the Internet and the way in which humans would be plugged into (and lost in) cyberspace in the imagined future. Gibson's work was punk because he wrote against the ponderous world building and optimism of mainstream science fiction: he was a rebel attacking the establishment and using science fiction to say something about the politics of the day, capitalism and the human condition (McCaffery, 1991). Steampunk replaced the cyber with steam, which is a reasonable one-world destruction of the sub-genre, but the punk part of the name is more problematic, especially because steampunk is a celebration of the racism, sexism, nationalism and imperial hegemony of late Victorian and Edwardian Britain. Steampunk literature imagines the British Empire's successful colonisation of other worlds, with its soldiers waving the flag and defending the interests of Queen and Country against aliens and foreigners alike.

A number of authors have been claimed as the first person to write steampunk (Onion, 2008). In our view, the most important precursor to the steampunk writers of the eighties was Michael Moorcock. Through the seventies and eighties, Moorcock's novels were enormously popular, read by hippies and alternative types all the way to young teenagers. Moorcock was a friend of members of the band Hawkwind, and even wrote and performed with them. He had a huge, inter-connected set of stories ranging across what he called the Multiverse, with the same struggle for humanity and the Cosmic Balance taking place in each of these stories. In each of them, there was an aspect of the Eternal Champion fighting to save an imagined world (Greenland, 2013). In the early seventies, Moorcock wrote *The Warlord of the Air* (1971), the first of a series of three novels called '*A Nomad of the Time Streams*'. This particular series within the wider Multiverse introduced an officer of the British Empire called Oswald Bastable, who was a stereotype of British upper-class masculinity from the beginning of the twentieth century. Bastable started out chasing an enemy of the Empire in Afghanistan in this world, but fell through a gap in the Multiverse to find an Earth where airships were used to secure imperial power. In this book and its two sequels, Moorcock is trying to make a point about the evils of the British Empire and totalitarian states, but he also captures perfectly the style, fashions and manners of the late Victorian and Edwardian periods. Reading the book one finds oneself become enculturated to their ways and their world-view, wanting to drink tea from a china cup while reading Kipling. These books, then, are a direct influence on K. W. Jeter, the author who coined steampunk to describe his own work, and the work of the other authors Jeter identified with steampunk (Rose, 2009). In this steampunk literature, there is an enormous amount of authentic detail, and inventions that fit the Victorian and Edwardian aesthetic, as well as plots and characters lifted from the popular fiction of the time superimposed on the steam-engine spaceship hybrid technologies (Onion, 2008; Rose, 2009).

From its invention as science fiction, steampunk took some time to transform into a fashion. The origins steampunk aesthetics can be found in the nineties in the underground goth scene, when goths started to dress as vampires, as we have described earlier. This led to a number of goths borrowing clothes and accessories from Victorian Gothic, including some of our respondents, and then some of those goths became interested in dressing as authentic Victorians. The Victorian aesthetic adopted was that of elite Victorians – upper-class or urban bourgeoisie – but at least it was an attempt to recreate a style believed to be true of the period. Steampunks were the people who wanted to dress Victorian, but who were not bothered about authenticity. They were influenced by the literature of alternative Victoriana, and saw goth as a place where one could dress as a steampunk without anyone complaining (Cherry & Mellins, 2011). So, steampunks started to appear at Whitby, as we have discussed earlier; very soon, steampunk became a fixed fashion choice with a set of rules about how to dress. The style of steampunk as a fashion borrowed very heavily from the resurrected *Doctor Who*, as well as video games and movies set in Victorian times, or games that already had a steampunk theme (Scharf, 2011). The style of steampunk is described and defined on Wikipedia:[7]

> Steampunk fashion has no set guidelines but tends to synthesize modern styles with influences from the Victorian era. Such influences may include bustles, corsets, gowns, and petticoats; suits with waistcoats, coats, top hats and bowler hats (themselves originating in 1850 England), tailcoats and spats; or military-inspired garments. Steampunk-influenced outfits are usually accented

with several technological and 'period' accessories: timepieces, parasols, flying/driving goggles, and ray guns. Modern accessories like cell phones or music players can be found in steampunk outfits, after being modified to give them the appearance of Victorian-era objects. Post-apocalyptic elements, such as gas masks, ragged clothing, and tribal motifs, can also be included. Aspects of steampunk fashion have been anticipated by mainstream high fashion, the Lolita and aristocrat styles, neo-Victorianism, and the romantic goth subculture. In 2005, Kate Lambert, known as 'Kato', founded the first steampunk clothing company, 'Steampunk Couture', mixing Victorian and post-apocalyptic influences. In 2013, IBM predicted, based on an analysis of more than a half million public posts on message boards, blogs, social media sites, and news sources, 'that "steampunk", a subgenre inspired by the clothing, technology and social mores of Victorian society, will be a major trend to bubble up and take hold of the retail industry'. Indeed, high fashion lines such as Prada, Dolce & Gabbana, Versace, Chanel, and Christian Dior had already been introducing steampunk styles on the fashion runways. And in episode 7 of Lifetime's 'Project Runway: Under the Gunn' reality series, contestants were challenged to create avant-garde 'steampunk chic' look.

The aesthetic is described correctly here. It is essentially the actual clothes worn by elite civilians and the military in the British Empire combined with a number of fanciful elements drawing on the idea of Britain ruling the space waves. Steampunk is predominantly brown in its aesthetic, not black, which is why we are reluctant to call steampunk a part of goth. Our respondents are also wary of identifying steampunk as goth, but all recognise that steampunk emerged in the goth scene, and still shares some of the same spaces. Indeed, some goths dress up as steampunks and goths – we have seen people we know dress in both fashions to attend different events. And, some goth aesthetic has been influenced by steampunk. But, steampunk has its own followers, many of whom do not seem to be goths anymore, and many of whom seem never to have been goths at all. More research is needed to explore this issue, of course, but we believe it is possible that many steampunks have become steampunks through being interested in dressing up and re-enacting different vintage periods (as part of the vintage fashion scene more generally: Holland, 2017), rather than coming to it through the goth scene becoming more Victorian in its clothing choices. Whatever the origins of individual steampunks, it is clear from the preceding long quote that steampunk has become another form of commodificiation and instrumentality in modern popular culture. Steampunk has become an Instagram look, a way of presenting and showing off marketed instrumental alternativity in shops, on television and in movies.

Steampunk's problem as a youth culture, sub-culture or tribe is its lack of a defined genre of music with which it is associated (Hebdige, 1979; Hodkinson,

2002). It is not goth. It is not punk. But, it comes out of goth spaces and it has punk in its name. There are musicians trying to define their music as steampunk music. Wikipedia continues:[8]

> Steampunk music is very broadly defined. Abney Park's lead singer Robert Brown defined it as 'mixing Victorian elements and modern elements'. There is a broad range of musical influences that make up the Steampunk sound, from industrial dance and world music to folk rock, dark cabaret to straightforward punk, Carnatic to industrial, hip-hop to opera (and even industrial hip-hop opera), darkwave to progressive rock, barbershop to big band. Joshua Pfeiffer (of Vernian Process) is quoted as saying, 'As for Paul Roland, if anyone deserves credit for spearheading Steampunk music, it is him. He was one of the inspirations I had in starting my project. He was writing songs about the first attempt at manned flight, and an Edwardian airship raid in the mid-80s long before almost anyone else…' Thomas Dolby is also considered one of the early pioneers of retro-futurist (i.e., Steampunk and Dieselpunk) music. Amanda Palmer was once quoted as saying, 'Thomas Dolby is to Steampunk what Iggy Pop was to Punk!' Steampunk has also appeared in the work of musicians who do not specifically identify as Steampunk. For example, the music video of 'Turn Me On', by David Guetta and featuring Nicki Minaj, takes place in a Steampunk universe where Guetta creates human droids. Another music video is 'The Ballad of Mona Lisa', by Panic! at the Disco, which has a distinct Victorian Steampunk theme. A continuation of this theme has in fact been used throughout the 2011 album Vices & Virtues, in the music videos, album art, and tour set and costumes. In addition, the album Clockwork Angels (2012) and its supporting tour by progressive rock band Rush contain lyrics, themes, and imagery based around Steampunk. Similarly, Abney Park headlined the first 'Steamstock' outdoor steampunk music festival in Richmond, California, which also featured Thomas Dolby, Frenchy and the Punk, Lee Presson and the Nails, Vernian Process, and others.

This is a very strange attempt to re-invent the history of alternative, avant-garde music as the roots of steampunk music. There is no steampunk music until self-styled steampunk bands started to make music inspired by the look and the stories of steampunk. Abney Park are indeed a steampunk band, the first one to emerge, but their music is not a mix of Victorian music hall with futurist electronica and angry punk. Their music is just pop rock or indie-rock. These steampunk musicians have their own musical heroes and their own styles of writing and performing, but these are not steampunks. As we have already mentioned earlier in the book, the only truly alternative punk-ish steampunk band is The Men That Will Not Be Blamed For Nothing, and they started out as a joke against steampunks and their desire to be elite Victorians fighting for the Empire. While steampunks and playmate steampunk festivals have adopted them, The Men That Will Not Be Blamed For Nothing reject the ambivalence about hegemony at the heart of steampunk. The band's albums actually have more metal than punk, as guitarist Andrew O'Neill is also a well-known heavy metal stand-up comedian with roots in extreme metal. Steampunk, then, is as punk as Ed Sheeran, and as goth as Ed Sheeran and has as much alternativity as Ed Sheeran. It is a form of dressing-up for people who want to think they are alternative by dressing up, and a form of dressing up the Empire that resonates problematically in an age of post-colonialism and forgetting about the past (Spracklen, 2013b).

Conclusion: Goth in the Mainstream Today

The seeming end of times for the goth aesthetic has come with its embrace in mainstream fashions. This is how Wikipedia approvingly explores the many instances of the goth aesthetic being embraced by the kinds of well-known designers who have become celebrities and brands in the Adornian culture industries of our day (Adorno, 1991):[9]

> Goth fashion has a reciprocal relationship with the fashion world. In the later part of the first decade of the 21st century, designers such as Alexander McQueen, Anna Sui, Rick Owens, Gareth Pugh, Ann Demeulemeester, Philipp Plein, Hedi Slimane, John Richmond, John Galliano, Olivier Theyskens and Yohji Yamamoto brought elements of goth to runways. This was described as 'Haute Goth' by Cintra Wilson in the New York Times. Thierry Mugler, Claude Montana, Jean Paul Gaultier and Christian Lacroix have also been associated with a gothic style. In Spring 2004, Riccardo Tisci, Jean Paul Gaultier, Raf Simons and Stefano Pilati dressed their models as 'glamorous ghouls dressed in form-fitting suits and coal-tinted cocktail dresses'. Swedish designer Helena Horstedt and jewelry artist Hanna Hedman also practice a goth aesthetic.

Just as steampunk has become a style to be worn in music videos and movies because it looks quirky yet acceptably conservative, so goth has become the look the managers of the culture industries impose on their models and stars when they want to look dangerous and slightly transgressive. This was already happening as early as 1998, when the pop star Madonna released the song 'Frozen' from the album *Ray of Light* (Prieto-Arranz, 2012). The song itself is a standard pop ballad with some spooky effects and electronic beats. In the video to the song, Madonna is playing the role of a goth: she has a long black goth dress on, with black costume jewellery and her hair is long and black. Her make-up is not particularly goth, but her face is shot in such a way that is difficult to see her eyes clearly. In the video, she chants the mournful lyrics to the song and moves her body and especially her hands in a goth manner. This feels like cultural appropriation to us. Madonna has flirted with goth fashions on a number of other public outings, but she was never a goth, is not a goth, and never released any music or videos that suggested she was a goth. Our respondents who mentioned this song said they liked it, and it is an interesting pastiche of goth tropes, from the lyrics to the strings to the henna paint on Madonna's fingers. However, it has become the moment when it was permissible for anyone to play at being a goth for one video, or one album, or just for one weekend.

Since Madonna's temporary flirtation with the goth aesthetic, many other celebrities, or would-be celebrities, have dabbled in the goth look. Dressing up as a goth – or rather, borrowing some goth fashions and making them more palatable for the mainstream – has become something managers and agents encourage their acts to do to make them look edgy and transgressive. This embrace of the goth aesthetic extends beyond the celebrity designers and their models into all aspects of fashion in mainstream popular culture. When goths started to get tattoos and piercings,[10] it was a way of marking themselves as being unacceptable to the mainstream (Yuen Thompson, 2015; Winge, 2012). Now, almost every person on television has a tattoo with a 'gothic' rose pattern, and almost every woman on television has red or green hair – colours that have come from the goth-emo aesthetic and re-tooled to be scary and safe at the same time: all representing the entropic 'heat death' of the goth aesthetic (Spracklen, 2014). People wear black dresses, skirts, jeans and tops on the way to work; and when they are going out to socialise. Wearing black is no longer dangerous: now, it is the safe colour that ensures one does not stand out, it is the colour that matches everything and make everybody feel special yet invisible. Dressing like a goth is now very easy, unless you live in a place ruled by conservative reactionaries or crazy autocrats. Goth fashions, then, come into fashion in a regular cycle that serves the interests of the culture industries and the media that feeds them.

Notes

1. http://www.digitalspy.com/soaps/coronation-street/feature/a820677/coronation-street-rosie-webster-biggest-ever-dramas-on-the-cobbles/. Accessed on January 16, 2018.
2. *Coronation Street* is famous for its older, working-class women who spend their time gossiping and making tutting noises about the people and the things of which they disapprove (Weatherall, 1996). They do not like anyone with fancy ideas, flashy clothes or loose morals.
3. https://en.wikipedia.org/wiki/Goth_subculture. Accessed on January 23, 2018.
4. Edward Blackadder was a fictional comedy character played by Rowan Atkinson, made famous in a BBC series in the eighties. We both remember seeing the second series of the programme (the one set in Elizabethan times) around the same time goth rock was becoming supported by the British music media, and being impressed by the immoral nature of the character – but we are sure he had little influence on the early British goth rock scene.
5. https://en.wikipedia.org/wiki/Gothic_fashion. Accessed on January 25, 2018.
6. https://en.wikipedia.org/wiki/Wednesday_Mourning. Accessed on January 21, 2018.

7. https://en.wikipedia.org/wiki/Steampunk. Accessed on January 23, 2018.
8. https://en.wikipedia.org/wiki/Steampunk. Accessed on January 23, 2018.
9. https://en.wikipedia.org/wiki/Gothic_fashion. Accessed on January 31, 2018.
10. Borrowing from the wider alternative scene.

Chapter 12

The End of Goth?

Introduction

This is the most controversial chapter in the book. In this final substantive chapter, we will take the pulse of the goth scene today, and show how its commitment to alternativity, and its self-imposed marginalisation, is being threatened existentially and materially by the forces of instrumentality that govern the late modern-global capitalism. We will explore how goths today make sense of goth ideology and style through interviews with our goths and online ethnography, and argue that although goth is alive and well in its radical, communicative state, it is at risk of becoming sidelined, or taken over and changed into something more corporate.

Goth Not Dead?

All our goth respondents unsurprisingly argued that goth was alive and well. As all our goths are involved in goth culture, we would be shocked to hear anything different. But, they had different views about the evolution of goth culture, and its eventual demise. Most of them argued that goth would always exist, at least for the near future. They argued that that are still significant numbers of goths around the world, evidenced by the thousands of active social media accounts about goth, for example. The sustainability and vitality of the goth culture can be seen in the numbers of bands, goth club nights and the thousands of goths who turn up at festivals such as Whitby Goth Weekend. The total number of goths might have shrunk compared to the previous century, but goth culture had become more global, and goths seem to be enthusiastic about remaining part of goth culture. For two of our goth respondents, there was a fear that goth has shrunk to a point where it may not be sustainable. Now that the last of the teddy boys have passed away, the sub-culture associated with them has pretty much disappeared completely, remembered only as a footnote in popular cultural history. The fear of our goth respondents who think goth will fade away is analogous to the story of the teddy boys. Teddy boys continued to listen to their music and dress in their fashions, but they did not pass on their rituals, clothes and songs to their children. Eventually, teddy boys disappeared from the streets as they fell ill, were retired and moved into care homes. There are a few echoes of the style and music of teddy boys, but these are fake revivals played out in front of hipsters. If goth does not recruit new members to the sub-culture, it will, say our two pessimists, fade away and die when the older generation of goths die.

Our respondents, then, are broadly optimistic about the future of goth. They have seen the goth culture evolve from a sub-culture into a globalised, inter-connected set of fashions and music sub-genres. They have seen goth become changed through its interaction with metal and with other alternative culture. They have seen goth shaped by the Internet, and nurtured by the early gen-eration of websites. They have seen goth become the subject of moral panics, and then the focus of different expressions of faith: from Christianity through paganism to Islam. They have seen goth become part of popular culture, one form of living among a myriad other forms. They have seen goth move from a sub-culture that was mocked and reviled to one that is accepted by people in the mainstream society. They have seen goth become a scene that prides itself on its inclusion and its willingness to embrace change, and as a result the big goth festivals attract huge numbers and huge interest, even if much of that interest is from people who are not only at the festivals to dress up and take pictures of other people dressed up. Irked by music journalists who claim goth rose and col-lapsed in the eighties, and by the strange re-writing of the history of The Sisters of Mercy by Andrew Eldritch, our goths identify a long, unbroken chain of goth music and culture that connects this new age with the origin and early deeds of goth. Thus is the Whig interpretation of goth history, a collective memory of continuity that gives goths today a sense of place and belonging through the construction of the past in goth narratives. This is a view of goth that we recog-nise from our own experiences and recollections. We share the collective memory of our goths: goth has survived to this day, even if it has changed and become mainstream.

Goth Not Dead

A search of the Internet finds that most stories published in the last few years have been positive about the current and future state of goth culture. Goth is clearly shown to be alive and thriving, and the negativity attached to some of the media coverage in the 1990s and 2000s has disappeared. No longer do we find journalists mocking goths or mis-reading the origin and evolution of goth culture, as we have highlighted in earlier chapters of this book. In an age of social media, it has become easier for journalists to find sources and information, and much easier for sub-cultures and campaign groups to respond to bad press and force it to be taken down (Aaker & Smith, 2010). One article published on 22 May 2017 in the British newspaper, *The Independent*, starts with a problematic, click-bait headline ('World Goth Day: Shedding Some Light on the Darkness of a Much-Maligned Sub-Culture') that sounds like it is going to be an attack. But, the author, Kashmira Gander, has a more measured take on the essence and future of goth. She begins by making the claim that goth is not like other sub-cultures (Gander, 2017):

> Most pop subcultures are doomed to die - or if not, to persist
> in tragic parody like a bunch of middle-aged mods at a But-
> lin's reunion... They tend to coalesce around clusters of young

people in reaction to the prevailing zeitgeist, then fade away...
However, there is an exception. Goth has, rather ironically, survived to become one of a handful of subcultures fully established in the mainstream.

Gander provides the standard cultural studies argument about sub-cultures
that stems from Williams (1977) and Hebdige (1979): all sub-cultures are born
from the anger and rebellion of youth, who reject the norms and values of the
mainstream; but all sub-cultures fade away through the pressure of mainstream-
ing, before they become residual. We have taken a similar line on sub-cultures and
identified communicative alternativity with the first form of this Williamsian sub-
culture. Following Habermas (1984, 1987), however, we have argued throughout
this book that there is always an interaction in the lifeworld between communicative rationality and action – the sub-cultural imperative to choose to resist – and
the colonisation of the lifeworld with the instrumental logic of capitalism and
nation-states. Goth, then, has survived into the contemporary age because a part
of it still works as a site for communicative alternativity, for its goth inhabitants
and for others who want to identify with goth. In the first sentences above, Gander (2017) seems to be associating goth with the rise and fall of sub-cultures, and
she cleverly draws on myths and stereotypes that continue to be made about goth:
it is just a phase, teenagers grow up and leave goth behind, just like Rosie Webster
in *Coronation Street*. But, even though she says goth has survived being part of
a teen phase, she is her own example of teenage gothness, in the next paragraph
(Gander, 2017):

> It was a time when fashion favoured "glamazon"... As a teenage
> girl... Goth culture seemed instead to value intelligence... The
> music was disturbing and sometimes shocking... With hindsight,
> I can see I was more of a part-timer, just as taken with the tight
> jeans and vision-impairing hairstyles of emo (a dirty word in
> Goth circles).

Gander's own narrative of growing-up threatens to subvert her claim that
goth is not a teen phase, and that goth has somehow been able to be something truly alternative. She tells us that she was attracted to goth because of the
dark aesthetic. She believed goth to be something set up in opposition to the
mainstream fashions and music, which was true. She describes goth music as
disturbing and shocking, which sounds like something a concerned parent or
a Christian preacher would say. Then, she admits that she was only ever half-
engaged with it, and says she was actually an emo, using that term to become a
stereotype of confused teen rebellion (Brown, 2011; Cohen, 2002; Hill, 2011).
This is all very confusing for Gander's main argument. She is vaguely aware
that many goths do not like to be associated with emo, although emos were
part of the mainstream version of goth that merged with metal in the nineties.
Being emo is seen as being transient and conformist by some goths because it has
emerged from the metal and rock part of the music industry. Gander's narrative

of finding goth and emo as transient lifestyle choices within the mainstream of the Adornian culture industries (Adorno, 1991) seems to show that goth has ceased to be goth after all.

The article, however, continues to present evidence that goth is alive and well. In the entire article, she sets out to assure her readers that goth did not disappear in the nineties, goths are not dangerous Devil-worshippers and they are alive and well. She talks with some people who are confused about goth and Gothic, and spends some time telling us about the evolution of her goth friends. She discusses the continued interest in goth festivals, clubs and acts, and interviews a number of important people who tell her goth is thriving. The most significant respondent in the article is Paul Hodkinson himself, who says, reflecting on the outcry over the murder in Bacup (Gander, 2017):

> I think the Sophie Lancaster incident has probably helped many people to realise that, rather than being a 'threat', Goths often are more likely to be on the receiving end of hostility... Although the culture is subversive in some respects, I think it is very important to note that Goths are very 'normal'.

Hodkinson has taken the line he has always taken about goths. For him, goths are not a danger to the norms and values of mainstream society (Hodkinson, 2002). They are not the sexual transgressors of Siegel's (2005) fantasy; nor are they the folk devils of religious denunciations. He wants to say that goth is a transgressive sub-culture, an alternative sub-culture; however, while defending goth from its critics, he has to say that they are just ordinary people who just dress up in strange clothes. Goths for Hodkinson are as mundane as any other person in the street. They might only wear their goth clothes when performing as goths; otherwise, they go to work with just an acceptable hint of goth aesthetic on their bodies. This mundaneness has removed the communicative alternativity that roused goths to reject the mainstream and replaced it with the compromise of being accepted and valued by society. Gander (2017) continues the article by arguing that the death of Sophie Lancaster brought goths closer together, as well as providing sympathy for goths among the mainstream. She then says that goth fashions have become well-known in the mainstream, and cites a range of people such as Kim Kardashian and Victoria Beckham who have been inspired to dress as goths. She also says that goth has crossed over with aspects of punk and metal.

Again, this sounds like Gander is moving towards making the point that goth has ceased to be alternative. If anybody can be a goth, and goth crosses over into punk and metal, goth as sub-culture and counter-culture and site of resistance is no more. And, if it stops being alternative, it stops being anything other than a lifestyle choice. But, she rapidly forgets the logic of her argument and tells us that:

> People in their fifties - the original Goths - continue to enjoy the scene alongside its newest members. "Put simply, Goth isn't a 'phase'" says Tim Sinister, who runs The Blogging Goth website.

We note that she thinks young people are still becoming goths, which is certainly true, though we wonder whether they are arriving in sufficient numbers to replace the older goths who are dying off. We note as well that the sustained commitment of the older goths to their culture is something younger people joining goth might replicate. For the older goths, being goth in the eighties and nineties was to be transgressive, alternative, and a political and cultural danger to the norms and values of the mainstream. Older goths have earned their status as goths through years of ridicule and attacks. Tim Synyster (not Sinister as Gander has it) is right to say that goth is not a phase, but it is impossible to say what younger people will do in this new age of individualism and choice. That is, younger people in the global melting pot of pick-and-mix, liquid culture and liquid leisure (Bauman, 2000; Rojek, 2000, 2010) may well see goth as just one of a range of identities they are allowed to collect and consume in the digital marketplace. Alternatively, they may see the word goth to mean metal. On the other hand, they may think goth is only for the weird kids who are bullied, like the alternative schoolchildren mocked for their gothness in the cartoon *South Park* (Thorogood, 2016). If goths are figures of fun, they lose their transgressive status, and young people do not want be the focus of the joke because they want to be individuals who are accepted because they look like every other individual. Gander (2017) herself has shown us how she dabbled with goth and emo because it was a cool thing, a space to dress up and not be like the women on television – but at the same time, it was something that could be performed and discarded as she grew older. She is quite happy to reduce goth to a few safe symbols and myths: goth music being disturbing; goth being about vampires and werewolves. She seems to know nothing about the radical politics of goth other than some of its feminist beliefs about being non-judgemental about body shapes. If Gander is typical of the generation growing up into adulthood in the last decade, there is no future for goth because there is no sense of what being goth actually means. That said, Gander (2017) ends with another important UK-based goth, DJ Cruel Britannia, who says:

> Goth endures because it's the very nature of most people to have a 'dark side'; be it a curiosity in the macabre through books... or music... Goth in itself has evolved constantly like... other music-based subculture, such as... metal or... dance.

DJ Cruel Britannia is correct. Goth music has evolved into a wide range of sub-genres, just like metal and dance. However, those two music genres are much bigger than goth. There are dozens of metal sub-genres because there are thousands of metal bands around the world, and millions of metal fans (Brown, Spracklen, Kahn-Harris, & Scott, 2016; Clifford-Napoleone, 2015). Dance is equally huge in contemporary popular culture, so again the Byzantine complexities of its sub-genres reflect its popularity and the need for musicians to find creative niches and audiences (McLeod, 2001). Goth does not have the same amount of bands as metal, and does not have the same amount of active fans as metal (Brill, 2008; van Elferen & Weinstock, 2016), as a cursory analysis of Facebook shows. So, when goths splinter into sub-genres, they are reliant on a handful of musicians to keep them alive, and on hundreds of fans dedicated enough to keep buying records and other stuff associated with the sub-genre. This is not sustainable, and goth music as a consequence has become less diverse in recent years, as goth festivals rely on the established bands to fill them, or book in bands that are not really goth at all.

The DJ's comment about what keeps goth attracting new people is interesting. Humans do indeed have a dark side. Much of contemporary goth culture revolves around the macabre. There is something fundamental about the human condition that appeals to goths, that is, we live, we fall in love and we die. Being human is tragic. We want to believe that we have a meaning and purpose; that life has meaningful and the losses we suffer will be temporary. At the same time, we all see the passing of years, and see that humans die just like animals. All religions and most classic philosophers grapple with making sense of death and our place in the world. Goth in its first iteration embraced nihilism and existentialism as an answer: goths danced and took amphetamine because they wanted to rage at the injustice of human existence. In doing that, they also saw hope in finding community and a space to resist the mainstream in goth. The danger with the latest iteration of goth is the only thing it has left to define itself is a space that is marked as 'macabre' or spooky: and being spooky just means every goth just seems to be taking part in an American Halloween party in a terrible Hollywood movie.

The End of Goth

There are signs that goth has reached an endpoint. In our own experience, we have seen the number of goth nights in Leeds and the north of England shrink, especially since the high-point of the mid-2000s (Spracklen, Richter, & Spracklen, 2013). Some of this shrinkage has been forced on the goth scene, as clubs and venues face the squeeze of gentrification and what we have called eventisation (Spracklen, Richter, & Spracklen, 2013). Promoters who want to put on music they love to their friends have been forced to make tough decisions about how much money they can lose, as landlords increase rents and costs in city centres become ridiculously high. Even so, some of the decline in goth nights is related to falling numbers. When the Wendy House club night at Leeds University was at its height, it was attracting coach parties from across the north of England. Getting into the venue was a hard work because it was very busy, and finding a way to one of the dancefloors involved patience and much gentle pushing to get round the crowds. The Wendy House was the biggest monthly goth night in Leeds at the time, but there were other nights in a number of other venues. At the time we are writing this, goth has been reduced to just one event per month in Leeds, in a venue above a pub out of the city centre in the goth heartlands of Leeds 6 (Spracklen, Henderson, & Procter, 2016). Similar reductions in the scale and number of nights have happened in York, as far as we can see from our more limited interaction with goths in York. Goth is just about surviving in Leeds and the north of England, but the numbers of goths and the number of goth spaces are shrinking.

The evidence on the Internet for the end of goth is thin, but there are some places in which a decline of goth activity is evident or discussed. All the goth spaces that used to be hives of net.goth activity show marked declines in use in the last 10 years, as we have discussed earlier in the book. The number of active users and posts and threads on websites such as MyHeartland have reduced, and some popular sites such as goth.net have stopped having any posts altogether. This decline may be because everybody now uses social media accounts (Spracklen, 2015b), but it may also be caused by a decline worldwide in the number of goths. There are still plenty of people interacting in online forums for other fan cultures; for instance, and in our own experience we can see people still using such spaces to talk about *Star Trek* and science fiction fandom (Spracklen, 2015b).

We have found three stories posted on the Internet that suggest or claim goth is in its final stages. There may well be more like them, but we feel each of them serves as an evidence for alternative visions about the end of goth now, or the future of goth. They are not meant to be representative about what people think about the end of goth. They are not in any evidence or proof that goth is dead, they are merely discourse about goth's decline. The first was posted on 22 October 2015 by a blogger on gothic Lolita called Chelsea Lovelace, who wrote a despairing complaint of the decline of goth:[1]

> I'd been planning on writing a blog entry about this for a while. This document had been sitting half-finished on my desktop for weeks until I had a conversation with some other nostalgic Moitié fans. Brace yourself, it's a long one. Gothic lolita isn't dead yet, but it's definitely on life support. The slow death of Moitié (and gothic lolita in general) reminds me of what's currently happening in the goth scene. As any real goth would tell you, goth is dead. The heyday of goth is long gone – most people have moved onto a new scene, leaving behind an ever-shrinking number of hardcore (and rapidly ageing) devotees. The younger newcomers to the scene are starting to redefine what it means to be a goth, causing splintering within the subculture. Admittedly, I don't know jack about Japan, but I don't think that Mana or Moitié (or gothic lolita/aristocrat/ visual kei music and fashion) are as influential and popular anymore. There's still a base of hardcore older fans but there's not much new blood coming in. Plenty of Japanese gothic brands have disappeared or wound down – BPN is a good example (RIP). Outside of the usual suspects – Atelier Boz, Atelier Pierrot, Moitié, h. Naoto, and a few small Japanese indie brands – gothic is pretty much nonexistent. People just aren't really interested in goth anymore…even though old school is starting to come back, old school gothic is pretty much nonexistent on this side of the pond. I hear that in Europe, especially Germany and France, gothic lolita has maintained a strong presence. I'd probably attribute that to the fact that goth subculture and schwarze szhene in general are much bigger in Europe, since almost all of the big-name bands, stores, and festivals are based there.

Lovelace has posted this long rant because she is concerned specifically about the decline and disappearance of shops and designers who service the goth Lolita style. This style had its origins in Japan and is associated with the wider sub-culture of *visual kei* (McLeod, 2013). Goth Lolita combines the goth aesthetic with hyper-sexualised female costumes inspired by Japanese films and comics (Mattar, 2008; Skutlin, 2016). The poster is not sure about how popular visual kei is in Japan, but she thinks it is not very popular anymore.[2] She thinks this because the designers she lists are closing down or changing the clothes they sell. Love-lace is unhappy that people are no longer buying enough goth Lolita clothing to keep the industry going. She sees the decline in goth Lolita as a direct result of a decline in goth in general, at least in the United States of America where she lives. She tells us that she sees goth shrinking as its tiny number of fans get older and new goths do not join the scene. She thinks the Japanese goth scene has shrunk just as the American scene has, and she thinks people are just not interested in being goths or listening to goth music. She tells us she has heard 'old-school' goth is on the way back but it is 'non-existent' in the States. She has heard that goth thrives in Europe, especially France and Germany. She does not mention the United Kingdom, and her use of German suggests she is really thinking only of Germany when she writes about Europe.

Now, it might be argued that goth Lolita is a pretty obscure sub-genre, and hence it is one subject to collapse if its handful of fans move on to something else. One might say we cannot move from one sub-genre to the entire goth culture. However, it is clear that Lovelace sees the decline in her part of goth culture as a result of a wider collapse in goth culture in the United States of America and Japan. One might say that goth Lolita has only ever been a space of commodifica-tion and instrumentality, filled with people buying expensive clothes and posting pictures of themselves. Again, Lovelace shows that she knows that there is a wider goth culture that is associated somehow with the 'old-school', a culture that was or is part of the wider alternative scene in Germany (van Elferen & Weinstock, 2016). Her devotion to the performativity of goth Lolita does not make her any less connected to and aware of the wider goth culture, as she shows so clearly. Finally, we are aware that Lovelace recovered from her fear of the end of goth and the end of goth Lolita, and has since posted updates to her blog with new pictures and information about other sellers and designers. Perhaps, her blog on the end of goth was an attempt to convince the key designers to continue to make goth Lolita fashions. But, it certainly reads like an authentic cry of despair about goth in the United States of America, and the warning about the shrinking num-ber of ageing members could be a warning for other parts of the goth world, too.

The second of our stories that herald the end of goth comes from nerdist.com, and is very recent to the time we were finishing this book. On 12 January 2018, under the headline '2018 Will Sadly See The Final "Bats Day" At Disneyland', Eric Diaz writes:[3]

> If you live in Southern California and are a frequent visitor to Disneyland, then you might have noticed a dark cloud descending on the Magic Kingdom on certain days of the year. For the past

20 years, 'Bats Day' has been the occasion for the goth community to get together and spend the day at the Happiest Place on Earth. Sadly, it will now be coming to an end, at least for now. According to Inside The Magic, the 20th annual Bats Day in the Fun Park will be the last, the group announced earlier this month. Why the end to all the spooky fun? Well, according to a press release on the Bats Day Facebook page, the problem of rising costs have made it too much of a hassle to continue the event past this year. From their press release: 'Due to the new 2018 tax plan, the struggling economy and ever-rising costs, we can no longer run Bats Day in the Fun Park on the grand scale that it has had for the past 15 years. What most people don't realize is that Bats Day is a labor of love; we don't make money on it. Bats Day has never had any corporate funding or sponsorship, either: It is an event we do for the community. It is something our crew donates varying amounts of time and energy toward without seeing any kind of pay or profit from it'.

Bat Day was an annual get-together at Disney for goths, organised by goths. Its success was proof that there were sufficient numbers of goths in the United States of America for the event to run in the first year and the first few years. Its success was also proof that goths in the United States of America had become acceptable, and part of the mainstream. Disney was happy to support goths as a form of its community outreach. The organisation saw goths as just one of the many forms of American community it wanted to be seen to be supporting. Of course, the existence of goths at Bat Day at Disney seems on reflection to be an egregious commodification and compromise, and clearly an example of how goth lost its communicative alternativity. Disney has supported the construction of a vacuous goth identity through its relentless push of merchandising and branding associated with Tim Burton's *The Nightmare Before Christmas*. We recall seeing the merchandise in the front window of a Disney shop in the centre of Leeds, and feeling sad at this cultural appropriation of black and purple, and skeletons (even if we like the film). Goths congratulating at Disney because of Tim Burton's film and the *Pirates of the Caribbean* franchise seems to us to be something that proves Andrew Eldritch's claim that goths are fashion victims.[4] There is nothing communicative or transgressive about dressing up like Jack Sparrow and having your photograph taken eating a Disney-branded hot dog.[5] Being well-respected by Disney is a million miles from the positive punk, anti-capitalist ideology of the scene in the early eighties. However, there is no denying that Bat Day happened because Disney and the organisers saw nothing wrong in having it at Disney; and both Disney and the organisers could see there were goths all over the United States of America, enough to ensure the event's success.

On the surface, this news story does not look like anything to worry about. Having an event at Disney is bound to be difficult to run, even if Disney has allowed the goths to congregate at the park for free or on a reduced rate. Running anything costs money these days, and finances are complex and tricky for organisations that are run by enthusiasts. The people who organise the Bat Day hint that there may be something replacing the event, something less 'grand scale'. But, contemplating this story more carefully, there is the fact that someone in the management of the event does not think the numbers of goths attending are sustainable. That is, someone thinks that the costs associated with the event will not be recouped by goths spending money in the park, because someone thinks there will be fewer goths attending the event. That prophet of doom may be someone involved at Disney, looking at the global picture and making a rush to judgement. Alternatively, it may be that the organisers have seen numbers at the day dropping as well as the amount of spend dropping; thus, they can no longer guarantee income that covers the costs. Whoever has made the decision, they have made it because the numbers do not add up anymore: there are not enough goths in the United States of America, and there were not enough goths at the Bat Day in the last few years, to make the event sustainable.

Our third and final story is a piece of click-bait, which nonetheless has a lot of truth to it. The story is entitled 'Meet The Elderly Women Who Will Not Stop Being Goth, No Matter What Anyone Says', and was published on 08 December 2017:[6]

> At some point or another, we've all gone through different 'phases' in our lives. Some of us were punks, others might have been really into taxidermy, and then there were the goths. You know, the ones who walked down the hallways covered in chains and wearing all black. Eventually though, everyone grew out of their phases and moved on to become boring accountants and real estate agents. The only exception? The small group of elderly women who have maintained their goth lifestyle and refuse to give it up, no matter how old they get.

The anonymous author of the blog is not very good at writing. The title of the piece, though, is a classic of the genre. The title implies that these older women are wrong for being goths, because they stick with the culture 'no matter what anyone says' – anyone being a word used here to mean anyone sensible. The title also works to attract the jaded millennial flicking through Instagram and wanting to get a cheap hit by laughing at the 'elderly' women who look stupid by dressing like goths when they should not be dressing as goths. As well as attracting people who want cheap laughs at goths, the title may also attract people who want to look at pictures of goth women in heteronormative clothing and make-up – and indeed, there are some of these goth women posted in the blog alongside other photos of older goth women.

The opening paragraph cited above works to situate goth as a teen phase that anyone who is sensible will have passed through with a measure of relief and embarrassment. Goth is something that is relegated to the past, in societal terms and in personal narratives of growing up and changing. The author weirdly compares goth to taxidermy, which they want us to think of as the nerdiest yet creepiest thing anyone might want to as a childhood hobby. Being a goth is reduced in this imaginary past as wearing 'chains' and being clothed 'all in black' in hallways.

Presumably, the author means school hallways, as the image of goths walking in a group does not work in a hallway in a house. While referring to school, then, the author situates goth as something done at school, before the goths grew up to get normal – boring – jobs. The author then tells us all goths have given up goth apart from this weird bunch of 'elderly women' who have continued to be goths. There is no mention here of older men, though some appear in the pictures that accompany the blog. The opening paragraph marks these older goth women out as strange survivors of this culture that has all-but disappeared. The author in this opening paragraph wants us to think these goth women are something abnormal and weird. The author also wants us to think these goth women are all that remains of goth, because goth is at an end.

In the rest of the article, the author interviews a woman who provides support and advice online to older goths and especially older goth women who want to continue to be goth. There is some sympathetic reporting of the woman's opinions and some of the advice she gives to women who are older and who want to remain goth. There is some badly worded discussion about being a parent goth and a goth at work, then the article ends with a cheery, American individualist thought:

> At the end of the day, it's all about being true to yourself… It's all about doing what makes you happy.

If it was all about being true to oneself, the blog would not have started with the assumption that these older women are freaks who should not be doing what makes them happy. Instead, the blog implies that they should grow up and dress like adults.

Conclusion

The three stories about the end of goth, and our reflections on what is happening in the north of England, do not outweigh the evidence from elsewhere that goth is still thriving. Goth is not dead; but, it has changed so much that it is danger of losing its meaning and purpose. Through the history of goth, as we have shown in this book, its essential ideological core has been about transgression and resistance. The Whig interpretation of goth history depends on the idea that goth is transgressive and never becomes normal, or acceptable. This ideology is what we have identified as its commitment to communicative alternativity. Now, as we have shown in this chapter, this alternativity and goth's self-imposed marginalisation to the liminal spaces of society, is being threatened existentially and materially by the forces of instrumentality that govern late modern global capitalism (Habermas, 1987; Spracklen, 2009). Without that alternativity, goth becomes part of everyday society, and goth becomes something young people choose to reject because they do not see it as dangerous or transgressive. Our goths and our ethnography show that goth is alive and well in its radical, communicative state, but it is at risk of becoming sidelined, or taken over and changed into something more corporate. Goth is at risk of everybody getting old and dying off, and the numbers of goths seem to be on the decline, as goth spaces in the United States of America and the United Kingdom seem to be shrinking in size.

At the same time, goths are perfectly acceptable members of society, protected by hate crime legislation and able to hold down professional jobs while wearing their corporate-goth black suits. Goths are school governors and local councillors, soccer coaches and social workers, doing good in their community and demonstrating they are not evil Satanists or deviants. Goths are anyone who wants to dress up at the weekend, because anyone can be what they want to be, for as short or as long time as they desire. Goths do not have to be that bothered about the music and the history of goth because goths want to be welcoming and tolerant of others, so they allow anyone to be a goth. Goths have worked hard to prove they are respectable members of the Habermasian public sphere (Habermas, 1989), but in doing so they have forgotten that goth needs to reject the mainstream and be radical in its transgression, because that is how it has attracted its members over time. If goth is only a lifestyle choice, it is not a form of communicative alternativity, it is a form of instrumental rationality, something bought and sold by global capitalism. If goth is only a lifestyle choice, it is no different from any other form of culture, and it becomes just one other form of culture that is co-opted, commodified and controlled by the hegemons of the world. There is, then, a paradox at the centre of goth at this moment in time and space: goth needs to be transgressive to have a future and attract new goths, but goths want goth to be an acceptable lifestyle choice. We will return to this theme in the conclusion of the book.

Notes

1. http://rosenocturnalia.blogspot.co.uk/2015/10/goth-is-dead-end-of-moi-meme-moitie.html. Accessed on February 6, 2018.
2. It is still very popular – see Skutlin (2016).
3. https://nerdist.com/final-last-bats-day-disneyland/. Accessed on February 12, 2018.
4. We have paraphrased this, of course: Eldritch never mentions goths. See our chapter on The Sisters of Mercy for the details.
5. We have never been to a Disney park so we have no idea if such a thing exists. Actually, we have looked on the Internet and apparently, it does (https://collinsrace1. wordpress.com/2015/05/20/the-best-hot-dogs-at-disney-world/, accessed on February 13, 2018). We apologise for confirming that fact.
6. http://www.rebelcircus.com/blog/meet-elderly-women-refuse-stop-goth/. Accessed on February 13, 2018.

Chapter 13

Conclusion

Introduction

This is our short conclusion. Here, we return to discuss the big themes of goth's radical politics and its communicative leisure and culture. We hope you have followed our argument and our attempt to provide a history, philosophy and sociology of goth culture. We have explored the genesis and deeds of the goths, and the evolution and globalisation of the culture. We have shown how the goth scene emerged from punk and post-punk, and was shaped by the wider alternative sub-culture that existed around it in the early eighties. We have shown that goth has a Whig history of its own, which shows how goth emerged from post-punk and became a counter-culture and sub-culture. We have shown that goth defined itself as radical and transgressive, a Habermasian communicative action (Habermas, 1984), and a sub-culture that operated as a counter-culture against the mainstream. But, the mainstream of society and the Adornian culture industries (Adorno, 1991) have imposed themselves on goth for many years. Over its evolution, goth has gone underground and become unfashionable, while shaping heavy metal sub-culture to such an extent that a large part of metal came to be identified as goth. We have shown how goth has been the focus of moral panics, as goth globalised in the wake of the Internet and digital leisure. Then, in this century, goth has become an accepted lifestyle choice, with goths appearing in popular culture, and in the everyday spaces of life. Goth has become normal, something people dress up as for a weekend, a fashion season or forever. All goths are welcome in society, and goths welcome anyone into the culture.

In the first section of this conclusion, we want to show how goths were – and are – actively engaged in resisting attempts to subvert their alternative space, and they were – and are – involved in boundary work, memory-making and community action to maintain that. But, there is a danger that such work will fail as the idea of the alternative changes in wider society. In the final section of this concluding chapter, we make a short return to our new theory of communicative alternativity, and explore what it suggests what the future of goth may be.

Resistance and Communicative Action

In the early 1980s, as post-punk moved through positive punk to become goth, the sub-culture became identifiable as goth by insiders and outsiders. In the collective memory of goths today, this moment has become a founding myth – even if different versions of it exist. For our goth respondents, Leeds and The Sisters of Mercy play a crucial founding role in the myth. We ourselves have argued that this is the case, that the Sisters were the musicians who defined and popularised for a moment what goth was and became: radical politics; a disregard for the mainstream; black clothes; black hair; black merchandise; amphetamines; drum machines and big bass lines; dry ice; jangly guitars; minor chords and deep mournful voices, deep meaningful lyrics. The first generation of goth rock bands emerged with an aesthetic that matched the template set by the Sisters, but their commitment to communicative alternativity was more fluid. The chance to make money and live a life of sex, drugs and rock-and-roll was too tempting for many of the musicians and their managers and entourage. The Cult abandoned the goth rock aesthetic altogether in their pursuit of success; others such as The Mission maintained the goth look and sound, but only for as long as they could make it a career. Goth in the late eighties in the United Kingdom and Europe was the subject of much instrumentality and commodification, as people realised there was a market of fans wanting to be part of the goth movement. Goth was fashionable and in the mainstream media in the United Kingdom and Europe, and gathering notice in the United States of America. This commodification led to bands signing to major labels, bands headlining tours and festivals and fans being able to buy clothes and merchandise.

In the early nineties, goth rock reached a peak in the mainstream; then, like all music genres and fashions, it became yesterday's music (Frith, 1998). In the nineties, goths existed in large numbers in the global North, and continued to act in a communicative way to ensure the sub-culture survived. Goths organised and supported nightclubs, small labels, fanzines and websites. Being ignored by the mainstream, and abandoned by the major labels who had commodified goth rock, goth musicians played for their love of the music, or went on to find over jobs or other projects. Goth fans found community and identity in the goth spaces that were available to them, especially independent record and clothing shops. Goths found communicative alternativity by exploring the more esoteric and transgressive elements of the goth aesthetic, and through being goth in the face of mockery on buses, trains and pavements.

At the same time as goth was finding meaning in its underground, abject status, other forms of alternative culture were taking on the fashions and the claims of goth. These were various sub-genres of heavy metal. For black metal, identifying with goth made it transgressive and a space for communicative alternativity, rejecting the mainstream because black metal believed the mainstream was impure and soft (Kahn-Harris, 2007; Spracklen, 2006, 2014). For industrial metal and death-doom metal bands, associating with goth allowed them to feel cool and transgressive, while simultaneously reaching out to the huge number of goths and former goths still looking for a dark vibe. Goth metal was not goth; it was inspired by goth, but it became goth to a new generation of fans. Marilyn Manson, despite not being a goth band, were a goth band because everybody called them a goth band, and their fans called themselves goths. In this period, then, goth existed in two connected spaces, with fans and songs moving from one to the other: the underground made by goths for goths as a Habermasian lifeworld in defence of the instrumentality and the mainstream (Habermas, 1984, 1987, 1989); and the mainstream of the culture industries (Adorno, 1991), where Marilyn Manson sold out venues, had hits around the world, and generated lurid headlines as their singer became a celebrity.

In this century, the Internet has accelerated the dispersal of goth music and goth fashion around the world. While goth music became emo and metal, goth fashion became something anyone can buy in a shopping mall, a matter of play and choice so long as one does not go too far in challenging the norms and values of society. Goth has become a meme, a trope of popular culture, the troubled teen exemplified by Rosie Webster in *Coronation Street* who leaves goth when she becomes an adult. Goths have been associated with crime and disorder, and sex, by right-wing tabloids and preachers. Goths have reacted to moral panics by making a big show of being normal, everyday folk. They have reacted to stereotypes of being something for troubled teenagers to get into by demonstrating that goth is a long-term, sustainable leisure lifestyle choice. Goths point to the generations of families that are all goths as evidence that goth is attractive and suitable for all ages. Goth festivals and other spaces are family-friendly, inclusive and welcoming of others. This is communicative action at its best, being open to change and tolerating difference. As some goths spaces have become popular, this has proven to be a challenge. Whitby Goth Weekend, for example, now attracts far more steampunks, fancy-dressers and exhibitionists than traditional goths. This means for some goths at least, there is resentment that their favourite festival – where they used to go to be themselves, to meet their friends and to listen to their music – has been colonised by people who have no sustained interest in goth music or goth culture. While it is impossible – and morally undesirable – to have a goth test to ensure only goths get tickets to Whitby Goth Weekend, it is sad to see the festival has lost its allure for people like us. The event has become an example of how goth's tolerance of difference has allowed that contested goth *space* (Lefebvre, 1991) to be re-shaped by commodification and instrumentality, removing any of the communicative alternativity and performativity (Butler, 2006) that made it in the first instance.

There are some signs emerging that people in goth culture are reclaiming it as a counter-culture bound by the radical politics of punk and post-punk. In Leeds, we have seen the excellent work by the people behind Goth City Festival[1] in 2016 and 2017 to construct goth as radical, from the careful choice of bands chosen to the fringe events and donations to the group Positive Action for Refugees & Asylum Seekers. This is a goth festival based around goth music, with a strong sense of the history of goth in Leeds and the north of England. One of us (Karl) was invited to be on a panel at the 2016 event, but we have no formal connection to it. Its continued success shows there are still people willing to identify with the communicative alternativity of goth, and who understand the origins of goth in Leeds and the north of England. It also shows there are new bands emerging in the goth scene in the area that identify with goth's politics and aesthetics. So, goth is alive and still being alternative, here and in other places around the world.

The Future of Goth

The only certain thing about making predictions about the future is how futile they are. History is filled with people confidently making claims about one thing or another, and when the prediction is shown to be false the person who has written the claims is made to look foolish. Confidently predicting the future from observing historical trends is notoriously dangerous (Popper, 2002). We know saying goth will die, or goth will survive, puts us on a dangerous episte-mological parity with the utopians and dystopians of the last century. How-ever, we cannot end this conclusion and book without making our contribution to what goths and non-goths talk about among themselves. Does goth have a future?

Goth will survive only if it becomes a radical, transgressive and counter-cul-tural space again (Butler, 2006; Lefebvre, 1991). If it rejects the mainstream and uses its communicative action to construct communicative alternativity, it will meet the need of everyone who feels the mainstream – its popular culture, its normal and values that constrain its society – is oppressive and alienating. In this horrible world of global capitalism and global culture industries, the existential crisis against modernity is felt even more than it was last century (Spracklen, 2009, 2011). To feel human, we need to resist the inequalities and the injustices of modernity, even if in resisting all we can do is find a space where we can be alternative among others like us. This human desire to find meaning and purpose in leisure, in the liminal spaces where we can be free, is at the root of the search by young people and others to find something that feels like it is outside the main-stream. Goth fulfilled that needs all through its history. To keep attracting those new members, goth has to reject as many compromises with the instrumentality of the mainstream as possible.

If goth does not return fully to its communicative alternativity, it will not recruit new members alienated by society. Its members will drift in and out of goth in between other acts and performances and fashions. Goth music will become unknown or reduced to one or two songs played in adverts. Another youth culture will emerge that meets the needs of those who know the mod-ern world is cruel. Goth aesthetic will become something that comes in and out of fashion, revived in stage shows, films and television programmes when outsiders want to laugh at how strange the goths were. Goth will then die with the last old goths, just like the original Goths of the first millennium died off. Like the Barbarians, the new goths will leave artefacts for archaeologists to dig up, and texts (and music) for historians to explore. Like the old goths or the teddy boys, the new goths may well leave a few ideas and words in what comes after; but no one will think like the new goths after the last goth dies. This is a potential future. Given the colonisation, commodification and appropriation of goth culture by the mainstream, we suspect it is a likely future. The only way to stop it happening is for goths of the world to unite, to paraphrase Marx and Engels (2015) in *The Communist Manifesto*: they have nothing to lose but their chains, black jeans and buckles. Together, they can try to stop goth being stolen from them.

Note

1. http://www.gothcity.co.uk/.

References

Aaker, J., & Smith, A. (2010). *The dragonfly effect: Quick, effective, and powerful ways to use social media to drive social change*. London: John Wiley & Sons.

Adorno, T. (1991). *The culture industry*. Abingdon: Routledge.

Adorno, T. (2002). *The jargon of authenticity*. Abingdon: Routledge.

Adorno, T. (2005). *Minima moralia: Reflections on damaged life*. London: Verso.

Adorno, T. (2016). *Philosophy of modern music*. London: Bloomsbury.

Adorno, T., & Horkheimer, M. (2016). *Dialectic of enlightenment*. London: Verso.

Ashaalan, L., Alsukah, A., & Algadheeb, N. A. (2013). Prevalence of the emotional (emo) subculture among university students in Saudi Arabia. *Journal of International Education Research*, *9*(4), 351–358.

Baddeley, G. (1999). *Lucifer rising: A book of sin, devil worship and rock n' roll*. London: Plexus.

Baddeley, G. (2000). *Dissecting Marilyn Manson*. London: Plexus.

Baddeley, G. (2002). *Goth chic: A connoisseur's guide to dark culture*. London: Plexus.

Baddeley, G. (2006). *The gospel of filth: A black metal bible*. London: FAB Press.

Bale, T. (2015). In life as in death? Margaret Thatcher (mis)remembered. *British Politics*, *10*(1), 99–112.

Bamford, T. (2017). The history of Nightbreed. Retrieved from http://www.nightbreedrecordings.org/the-history-of-nightbreed.html. Accessed on January 25, 2018.

Barnes, R. (2018). *Uncovering online commenting culture: Trolls, fanboys and lurkers*. London: Springer.

Bataille, G. (1985). *Visions of excess: Selected writings 1927–1939*. Manchester: Manchester University Press.

Bataille, G. (1988). *The accursed share: An essay on general economy*. New York, NY: Zone Books.

Bauman, Z. (1992). *Intimations of postmodernity*. London: Routledge.

Bauman, Z. (2000). *Liquid modernity*. Cambridge: Polity.

Bell, M. (1979). Joy Division: Unknown Pleasures. New Musical Express. Retrieved from http://www.rocksbackpages.com/Library/Article/joy-division-iunknown-pleasuresi-factory. Accessed on August 30, 2017.

Benjamin, W. (2015). *Illuminations*. London: Bodley Head.

Bennett, A. (1999). Subcultures or neo-tribes? Rethinking the relationship between youth, style and musical taste. *Sociology*, *33*(3), 599–617.

Bennett, A. (2000). *Popular music and youth culture: Music, identity and place*. New York, NY: Macmillan.

Bestley, R. (2011). From 'London's Burning' to 'Sten Guns in Sunderland'. *Punk and Post Punk*, *1*(1), 41–71.

Bourdieu, P. (1986). *Distinction*. London: Routledge.

Braund, S. (2004). *Juvenal and Persius*. Cambridge, MA: Loeb Classical Library.

Bridson M. (2017). Getting to grips with Whitby Goth Weekend. *Sykes Cottages*. Retrieved from https://www.sykescottages.co.uk/blog/guide-whitby-goth-weekend/. Accessed on January 30, 2018.

Brill, D. (2006). *Subversion of stereotype? The Gothic subculture as a case study of gendered identities and representations*. Giessen: Ulme-mini-Verlag.

Brill, D. (2008). *Goth culture: Gender, sexuality and style*. Oxford: Berg.

Brown, A. R. (2008). Popular music cultures, media and youth consumption: Towards an integration of structure, culture and agency. *Sociology Compass*, *2*(2), 388–408.

Brown, A. R. (2011). Suicide solutions: Or, how the emo class of 2008 were able to contest their media demonization, whereas the headbangers, burnouts or 'children of ZoSo' generation were not. *Popular Music History, 6*(1/2), 19–37.

Brown, A. R. (2015a). Explaining the naming of heavy metal from rock's 'Back Pages': A dialogue with Deena Weinstein. *Metal Music Studies, 1*(2), 233–261.

Brown, P. R. (2015b). Meet the Mekons: Popular music, art, and cultural critique. *Rock Music Studies, 2*(1), 22–45.

Brown, A. R., Spracklen, K., Kahn-Harris, K., & Scott, N. (Eds.). (2016). *Global metal music and culture: Current directions in metal studies*. Abingdon: Routledge.

Burchill, J., & Parsons, T. (1978). *'The boy looked at Johnny': The obituary of rock and roll*. London: Pluto.

Burns, R. G. (2008). German symbolism in rock music: National signification in the imagery and songs of Rammstein. *Popular Music, 27*(3), 457–472.

Butler, J. (2006). *Gender trouble*. Abingdon: Routledge.

Butterfield, H. (1968). *The Whig interpretation of history*. London: Bell.

Cadwalladr, C. (2015). Marilyn Manson: 'I created a fake world because I didn't like the one I was living in'. *The Guardian*. Retrieved from https://www.theguardian.com/music/2015/jan/18/marilyn-manson-i-created-a-fake-world. Accessed on March 9, 2017.

Camus, A. (1946). *The outsider*. London: Hamish Hamilton.

Carpenter, A. (2012). The 'ground zero' of goth: Bauhaus, 'Bela Lugosi's Dead' and the origins of gothic rock. *Popular Music and Society, 35*(1), 25–52.

Castells, M. (1996). *The information age, volume one: The rise of the network society*. Oxford: Blackwell.

Cherry, B., & Mellins, M. (2011). Negotiating the punk in steampunk: subculture, fashion & performative identity. *Punk & Post Punk, 1*(1), 5–25.

Clifford-Napoleone, A. R. (2015). *Queerness in heavy metal music: Metal bent*. Abingdon: Routledge.

Cohen, E. (1979). A phenomenology of tourist experiences. *Sociology, 13*(2), 179–201.

Cohen, S. (1991). *Rock culture in Liverpool: Popular music in the making*. Oxford: Oxford University Press.

Cohen, S. (2002). *Folk devils and moral panics: The creation of the mods and rockers*. London: Psychology Press.

Cope, A. L. (2016). *Black Sabbath and the rise of heavy metal music*. Abingdon: Routledge.

Corry, H. (1983). Two days down in gothic city. *Yorkshire Evening Post*.

Crossley, N. (2015). *Networks of sound, style and subversion: The punk and post-punk worlds of Manchester, London, Liverpool and Sheffield, 1975–80*. Oxford: Oxford University Press.

Dahlberg, L. (2001). The Internet and democratic discourse: Exploring the prospects of online deliberative forums extending the public sphere. *Information, Communication & Society, 4*(4), 615–633.

Deleuze, G., & Guattari, F. (1983). *Anti-Oedipus: Capitalism and schizophrenia*. Minneapolis, MN: University of Minnesota Press.

Deleuze, G., & Guattari, F. (2013). *A thousand plateaus*. London: Bloomsbury.

Derrida, J. (1976). *Of grammatology*. Baltimore, MD: Johns Hopkins University Press.

Donaghey, J. (2017). Punk Indonesia: A brief introduction. *Punk & Post Punk, 6*(2), 181–187.

Dunkle, R. (2008). *Gladiators: Violence and spectacle in ancient Rome*. London: Longman.

Dunleavy, T. (2005). Coronation Street, Neighbours, Shortland Street: Localness and universality in the primetime soap. *Television & New Media, 6*(4), 370–382.

Dunn, K. (2012). Anarcho-punk and resistance in everyday life. *Punk & Post Punk, 1*(2), 201–218.

Edensor, T. (2001). Performing tourism, staging tourism: (Re)producing tourist space and practice. *Tourist Studies, 1*(1), 59–81.

Edwards, L. H. (2009). *Johnny Cash and the paradox of American identity.* Bloomington, IN: Indiana University Press.

Elden, S. (2004). *Understanding Henri Lefebvre: Theory and the possible.* London: Continuum.

Evans, E. J. (2013). *Thatcher and Thatcherism.* Abingdon: Routledge.

Farnell, G. (2009). The gothic and the thing. *Gothic Studies, 11*(1), 113–123.

Ferrarese, M. (2014). Kami semua headbangers: Heavy metal as multiethnic community builder in Penang Island, Malaysia. *International Journal of Community Music, 7*(2), 153–171.

Feyerabend, P. (1975). *Against method.* London: Verso.

Foucault, M. (1973). *The birth of the clinic.* London: Tavistock.

Fraser, B., & Fuoto, A. (2012). Manchester, 1976: Documenting the urban nature of Joy Division's musical production. *Punk & Post Punk, 1*(2), 139–154.

Foucault, M. (1986). Of other spaces. *Diacritics, 16*(1), 22–27.

Foucault, M. (1991). *Discipline and punish: The birth of the prison.* Harmondsworth: Penguin.

Foucault, M. (1998a). *The history of sexuality, volume one: The will to knowledge.* Harmondsworth: Penguin.

Foucault, M. (1998b). *The history of sexuality, volume two: The use of knowledge.* Harmondsworth: Penguin.

Foucault, M. (2002). *The archaeology of knowledge.* Abingdon: Routledge.

Foucault, M. (2006). *The history of madness.* Abingdon: Routledge.

Friedman, M. (2009). *Capitalism and freedom.* Chicago, IL: University of Chicago Press.

Frith, S. (1986). Art versus technology: The strange case of popular music. *Media, Culture and Society, 8*(3), 263–279.

Frith, S. (1998). *Performing rites: On the value of popular music.* Cambridge, MA: Harvard University Press.

Furek, M. W. (2008). *The death proclamation of Generation X: A self-fulfilling prophesy of goth, grunge and heroin.* Bloomington, IN: Indiana University Press.

Futrell, R., Simi, P., & Gottschalk, S. (2006). Understanding music in movements: The white power music scene. *The Sociological Quarterly, 47*(2), 275–304.

Gander, K. (2017). World Goth Day: Shedding some light on the darkness of a much-maligned sub-culture. *The Independent.* Retrieved from http://www.independent.co.uk/life-style/world-goth-day-2017-pop-sub-culture-what-is-it-darkness-music-clothes-style-cure-dracula-tim-burton-a7038176.html. Accessed on March 5, 2018.

Garland, J. (2010). 'It's a mosher just been banged for no reason': Assessing targeted violence against goths and the parameters of hate crime. *International Review of Victimology, 17*(2), 159–177.

Giroux, H. A. (2004). Beyond belief: Religious fundamentalism and cultural politics in the age of George W. Bush. *Cultural Studies-Critical Methodologies, 4*(4), 415–425.

Goffman, E. (1971). *The presentation of self in everyday life.* Harmondsworth: Penguin.

Goodlad, A. C. (2004). So full of myself as a chick: Goth women, sexual independence, and gender egalitarianism. *Gender and Society, 18*(3), 328–349.

Goodlad, L. M., & Bibby, M. (Eds.). (2007). *Goth: Undead subculture.* Durham, NC: Duke University Press.

Goodman, J., Lovejoy, P. E., & Sherratt, A. (2007). *Consuming habits: Global and historical perspectives on how cultures define drugs.* New York, NY: Psychology Press.

Goulding, C., & Saren, M. (2009). Performing identity: An analysis of gender expressions at the Whitby Goth Festival'. *Consumption, Markets and Culture, 12*(1), 27–46.

Goulding, C., & Saren, M. (2010). Immersion, emergence and reflexivity: Grounded theory and aesthetic consumption. *International Journal of Culture, Tourism and Hospitality Research, 4*(1), 70–82.

Gracyk, T. (1992). Adorno, Jazz, and the aesthetics of popular music. *The Musical Quarterly, 76*(4), 526–542.

Gramsci, A. (1971). *Selections from prison notebooks*. London: Lawrence and Wishart.

Grant, M. (1994). *Propaganda and the role of the state in inter-war Britain*. Oxford: Oxford University Press.

Greenland, C. (2013). *Entropy exhibition: Michael Moorcock and the British new wave in science fiction*. Abingdon: Routledge.

Griffiths, R. (2010). The gothic folk devils strike back! Theorizing folk devil reaction in the post-Columbine era. *Journal of Youth Studies, 13*(3), 403–422.

Gunn, J. (1999). Marilyn Manson is not goth: Memorial struggle and the rhetoric of subcultural identity. *Journal of Communication Inquiry, 23*(4), 408–431.

Habermas, J. (1981). Modernity versus postmodernity. *New German Critique, 22*, 3–14.

Habermas, J. (1984). *The theory of communicative action, volume one: Reason and the rationalization of society*. Cambridge: Polity Press.

Habermas, J. (1987). *The theory of communicative action, volume two: The critique of functionalist reason*. Cambridge: Polity Press.

Habermas, J. (1989). *The structural transformation of the public sphere*. Cambridge: Polity Press.

Habermas, J. (1990). *The philosophical discourse of modernity*. Cambridge: Polity Press.

Habermas, J. (2006). Political communication in media society: Does democracy still enjoy an epistemic dimension? The impact of normative theory on empirical research. *Communication Theory, 16*(4), 411–426.

Habermas, J. (2008). *Between naturalism and religion*. Cambridge: Polity Press.

Hall, S. (2016). *Cultural studies 1983: A theoretical history*. Durham, NC: Duke University Press.

Hanks, R. R. (2016). Narratives of Islam in Uzbekistan: Authoritarian myths and the Janus-state syndrome. *Central Asian Survey, 35*(4), 501–513.

Harriman, A., & Bontje, M. (2014). *Some wear leather, some wear lace: A worldwide compendium of postpunk and goth in the 1980s*. Bristol: Intellect Books.

Harron, M. (1979a). Gang of four: Dialectics meet disco. *Melody Maker*. Retrieved from http://www.rocksbackpages.com/Library/Article/gang-of-four-dialectics-meet-disco. Accessed on August 30, 2017.

Harron, M. (1979b). Factory records: Food for thought. Melody maker. Retrieved from http://www.rocksbackpages.com/Library/Article/factory-records-food-for-thought. Accessed on August 29, 2017.

Heather, P. (1989). Cassiodorus and the rise of the Amals: Genealogy and the goths under Hun domination. *The Journal of Roman Studies, 79*, 103–128.

Heather, P. (1996). *The goths*. Oxford: Blackwell.

Hebdige, D. (1979). *Subculture: The meaning of style*. London: Routledge.

Hesmondhalgh, D. (1997). Post-Punk's attempt to democratise the music industry: The success and failure of Rough Trade. *Popular Music, 16*(3), 255–274.

Hesmondhalgh, D. (2013). *Why music matters*. London: John Wiley & Sons.

Hill, R. L. (2011). Is emo metal? Gendered boundaries and new horizons in the metal community. *Journal for Cultural Research, 15*(3), 297–313.

Hill, R. L. (2016). *Gender, metal and the media: Women fans and the gendered experience of music*. London: Palgrave.

Hill, K. A., & Hughes, J. E. (1997). Computer-mediated political communication: The USENET and political communities. *Political Communication, 14*(1), 3–27.

Hodkinson, P. (2002). *Goth*. Oxford: Berg.

Holland, S. (2004). *Alternative femininities: Body, age and identity*. Oxford: Berg.

Holland, S. (2017). *Modern vintage homes and leisure lives: Ghosts and glamour*. London: Palgrave.

Hopkins, L. (2007). *Bram Stoker: A literary life*. Basingstoke: Palgrave.

Horkheimer, M. (2013). *Critique of instrumental reason*. London: Verso.

Huey, S. (2017). The Sisters of Mercy. Retrieved from https://itunes.apple.com/gb/artist/the-sisters-of-mercy/id702929. Accessed on December 7, 2017.

Hunter, M. (1993). Mourning jewellery: A collector's account. *Costume, 27*(1), 9–22.

Ibrahimova, D. (2012). The last goths of Tashkent. *BBC*. Retrieved from http://www.bbc.co.uk/news/world-asia-19009188. Accessed on November 19, 2017.

Inglis, F. (2010). *A short history of celebrity*. Princeton, NJ: Princeton University Press.

Israel, J. (2001). *Radical enlightenment: Philosophy and the making of modernity, 1650–1750*. Oxford: Oxford University Press.

Jackson, G. (2017). *The British whaling trade*. Oxford: Oxford University Press.

Kahn-Harris, K. (2007). *Extreme metal*. Oxford: Berg.

Kahnke, C. (2013). Transnationale teutonen: Rammstein representing the Berlin republic. *Journal of Popular Music Studies, 25*(2), 185–197.

Kallioniemi, K. (2017). 'The sound of Thatcherism on vinyl': New pop, early neo-right aspirations and Spandau Ballet. *Journal of European Popular Culture, 8*(2), 125–138.

Kayany, J. M. (1998). Contexts of uninhibited online behavior: Flaming in social newsgroups on Usenet. *Journal of the American Society for Information Science, 49*(12), 1135–1141.

Khair, T., & Höglund, J. (Eds.). (2013). *Transnational and postcolonial vampires: Dark blood*. Basingstoke: Palgrave Macmillan.

Khalid, A. (2015). *Making Uzbekistan: Nation, empire, and revolution in the early USSR*. Ithaca, NY: Cornell University Press.

Klee, H. (1998). The love of speed: An analysis of the enduring attraction of amphetamine sulphate for British youth. *Journal of Drug Issues, 28*(1), 33–55.

Kruse, H. (1993). Subcultural identity in alternative music culture. *Popular Music, 12*(1), 33–41.

Kuhn, T. (1962). *The structure of scientific revolutions*. Chicago, IL: University of Chicago Press.

Kummer, J. (2017). 'I Remember You': Exploring glam metal's re-emergence in contemporary metal music markets. *Metal Music Studies, 3*(3), 421–436.

Lacan, J. (2007). *Ecrits*. London: W. W. Norton & Company.

Laing, R. D. (1990). *The divided self*. Harmondsworth: Penguin.

Lancaster, R. N. (2011). *Sex panic and the punitive state*. Oakland, CA: University of California Press.

Larsen, A. (2013). Fast, cheap and out of control: The graphic symbol in hardcore punk. *Punk & Post Punk, 2*(1), 91–106.

Latham, R. (2014). Goths and God: Theological reflections on a subculture. *Practical Theology, 7*(4), 280–292.

Latour, B. (1987). *Science in action*. Cambridge, MA: Harvard University Press.

Latour, B. (2005). *Reassembling the social*. Oxford: Oxford University Press.

Lefebvre, H. (1991). *The production of space*. Oxford: Blackwell.

Lefebvre, H. (1996). *Writings on cities*. Oxford: Blackwell.

Lefebvre, H. (2014). *Critique of everyday life*. London: Verso.

LeGreco, M., & Tracy, S. (2009). Discourse tracing as qualitative practice. *Qualitative Inquiry, 15*(9), 1516–1543.

Lindgren, S. (2013). Pirate panics: Comparing news and blog discourse on illegal file sharing in Sweden. *Information, Communication & Society, 16*(8), 1242–1265.

Lindsey, L. L. (2015). *Gender roles: A sociological perspective*. Abingdon: Routledge.

Longhurst, B. (2007). *Popular music and society*. Cambridge: Polity Press.

Luckhurst, R. (Ed.). (2017). *The Cambridge companion to Dracula*. Cambridge: Cambridge University Press.

Lyotard, J. F. (1984). *The postmodern condition: A report on knowledge*. Manchester: Manchester University Press.

Maffesoli, M. (1996). *The time of the tribes: The decline of individualism in mass society*. London: Sage.

Mahoney, M. S., & Haigh, T. (2011). *Histories of computing*. Cambridge, MA: Harvard University Press.

Marx, K., & Engels, F. (2015). *The communist manifesto*. London: Penguin.

Mattar, Y. (2008). Miso soup for the ears: Contemporary Japanese popular music and its relation to the genres familiar to the Anglophonic audience. *Popular Music and Society*, *31*(1), 113–123.

Matthee, R. (2014). Alcohol in the Islamic Middle East: Ambivalence and ambiguity. *Past and Present*, *222*(9), 100–125.

McCaffery, L. (Ed.). (1991). *Storming the reality studio: A casebook of cyberpunk and postmodern science fiction*. Durham, NC: Duke University Press.

McLeod, K. (2013). Visual Kei: Hybridity and gender in Japanese popular culture. *Young*, *21*(4), 309–325.

Mears, D. P., Moon, M. M., & Thielo, A. J. (2017). Columbine revisited: Myths and realities about the bullying-school shootings connection. *Victims & Offenders*, *12*(6), 939–955.

Mehmetoglu, M. (2004). Tourist or traveller? A typological approach. *Tourism Review*, *59*(3), 33–39.

Mercer, M. (1988). *Gothic rock black book*. London: Omnibus Press.

Mercer, M. (1991). *Gothic rock: All you ever wanted to know…but were too gormless to ask*. London: Pegasus Publishing.

Mercer, M. (1997). *Hex files: The goth Bible*. London: Overlook Press.

Mercer, M. (2002). *Twenty-first century goth*. London: Reynolds & Hearn.

Mercer, M. (2009). *Music to die for*. London: Cherry Red Books

Meriwether, M. L. (2018). *A social history of women and gender in the modern Middle East*. Abingdon: Routledge.

Moberg, M. (2015). *Christian metal: History, ideology, scene*. London: Bloomsbury.

Moberg, M. (2017). *Church, market, and media: A discursive approach to institutional religious change*. London: Bloomsbury.

Morley, P. (1982). Southern death cult: The last tribe. *New Musical Express*. Retrieved from http://www.rocksbackpages.com/Library/Article/southern-death-cult-the-last-tribe. Accessed on August 30, 2017.

Muggleton, D. (2000). *Inside subculture: The postmodern meaning of style*. Oxford: Berg.

Nehring, N. (2007). Everybody's given up and just wants to go dancing: From punk to rave in the Thatcher era. *Popular Music and Society*, *30*(1), 1–18.

North, R. (1983). Positive punk: blood and roses. *New Musical Express*. Retrieved from http://www.rocksbackpages.com/Library/Article/positive-punk-blood-and-roses. Accessed on August 30, 2017.

Ogg, A. (2009). Don't fear the reaper – Mick Mercer on goth. *The Quietus*. Retrieved from http://thequietus.com/articles/01452-don-t-fear-the-reaper-mick-mercer-on-goth. Accessed on March 1, 2018.

Onion, R. (2008). Reclaiming the machine: An introductory look at steampunk in everyday practice. *Neo-Victorian Studies*, *1*(1), 138–163.

O'Reilly, D., & Doherty, K. (2006). Music b(r)ands online and constructing community: The case of New Model Army. In M. D. Ayers (Ed.), *Cybersounds: Essays on virtual music culture* (pp. 137–160). New York, NY: Peter Lang.

Osman, T. (2016). *Islamism: What it means for the Middle East and the world*. New Haven, CT: Yale University Press.

Partridge, C. (2014). *The lyre of Orpheus: Popular music, the sacred and the profane*. Oxford: Oxford University Press.

Pearl, S., & Polan, D. (2015). Bodies of digital celebrity. *Public Culture*, *27*(1), 185–192.

Phillipov, M. (2012). *Death metal and music criticism: Analysis at the limits*. New York, NY: Lexington Books.

Phillips, L. (1998). Hegemony and political discourse: The lasting impact of Thatcherism. *Sociology*, *32*(4), 847–867.

Pigliucci, M., & Boudry, M. (Eds.). (2013). *Philosophy of pseudoscience: Reconsidering the demarcation problem*. Chicago, IL: University of Chicago Press.

Pini, M. (2001). *Club cultures and female subjectivity: The move from home to house*. Basingstoke: Palgrave.

Popper, K. (2002). *The poverty of historicism*. Abingdon: Routledge.

Prescott, C. E., & Giorgio, G. A. (2005). Vampiric affinities: Mina Harker and the paradox of femininity in Bram Stoker's Dracula. *Victorian Literature and Culture*, *33*(2), 487–515.

Prieto-Arranz, J. I. (2012). The semiotics of performance and success in Madonna. *The Journal of Popular Culture*, *45*(1), 173–196.

Rabinowitz, P. (2016). *American pulp: How paperbacks brought modernism to Main Street*. Princeton, NJ: Princeton University Press.

Redhead, S. (1997). *Subcultures to clubcultures*. Oxford: Blackwell.

Regev, M. (1996). *Musica mizrakhit*, Israeli rock and national culture in Israel. *Popular Music*, *15*(3), 275–284.

Reijnders, S. (2011). Stalking the count: Dracula, fandom and tourism. *Annals of Tourism Research*, *38*(1), 231–248.

Renold, E., & Ringrose, J. (2011). Schizoid subjectivities? Re-theorizing teen girls' sexual cultures in an era of 'sexualization'. *Journal of Sociology*, *47*(4), 389–409.

Retallack, D. (1973). *The sound of music and plants*. Camarillo, CA: DeVorss & Company.

Reyes, I. (2013). Blacker than death: Recollecting the 'black turn' in metal aesthetics. *Journal of Popular Music Studies*, *25*(2), 240–257.

Rix, R. W. (2012). Northumbrian angels in Rome: Religion and politics in the anecdote of St. Gregory. *Journal of Medieval History*, *38*(3), 257–277.

Robinson, L. (2016). Collaboration in, collaboration out: The eighties in the age of digital reproduction. *Cultural and Social History*, *13*(3), 403–423.

Rojek, C. (2000). *Leisure and culture*. London: Sage.

Rojek, C. (2010). *The labour of leisure*. London: Sage.

Rose, M. (2009). Extraordinary pasts: Steampunk as a mode of historical representation. *Journal of the Fantastic in the Arts*, *20*(3), 319–333.

Roy, O., & Boubekeur, A. (2012). *Whatever happened to the Islamists? Salafis, heavy metal Muslims and the lure of consumerist Islam*. New York, NY: Columbia University Press.

Runkel, G. (1998). Sexual morality of Christianity. *Journal of Sex and Marital Therapy*, *24*(2), 103–122.

Saeed, A. (2017). *Freedom of religion, apostasy and Islam*. Abingdon: Routledge.

Savage, J. (2002). *England's dreaming, revised edition: Anarchy, Sex Pistols, punk rock, and beyond*. Basingstoke: Macmillan.

Savigny, H., & Sleight, S. (2015). Postfeminism and heavy metal in the United Kingdom: Sexy or sexist? *Metal Music Studies*, *1*(3), 341–357.

Scharf, N. (2011). *Worldwide gothic: A chronicle of a tribe*. Church Stretton: IMP.

Schouten, J. W., & McAlexander, J. H. (1995). Subcultures of consumption: An ethnography of the new bikers. *Journal of Consumer Research*, *22*(1), 43–61.

Shekhovtsov, A. (2009). Apoliteic music: Neo–Folk, martial industrial and 'metapolitical fascism'. *Patterns of Prejudice*, *43*(5), 431–457.

Siegel, C. (2005). *Goth's dark empire*. Bloomington, IN: Indiana University Press.

Simpson, D. (2006). Back in black. *The Guardian*. Retrieved from https://www.theguardian.com/music/2006/sep/29/popandrock. Accessed on December 13, 2017.

Sinclair, D. (1988). Sisters of Mercy: Floodland. *Q*. Retrieved from http://www.rocksbackpages.com/Library/Article/sisters-of-mercyi-floodlandi. Accessed on December 3, 2017.

Skutlin, J. (2016). Goth in Japan: Finding identity in a spectacular subculture. *Asian Anthropology*, *15*(1), 36–51.

Spracklen, K. (2006). Leisure, consumption and a blaze in the northern sky: Developing an understanding of leisure at the end of modernity through the Habermasian framework of communicative and instrumental rationality. *World Leisure Journal*, *48*(3), 33–44.

Spracklen, K. (2009). *The meaning and purpose of leisure: Habermas and leisure at the end of modernity*. Basingstoke: Palgrave Macmillan.

Spracklen, K. (2011). *Constructing leisure: Historical and philosophical debates*. Basingstoke: Palgrave Macmillan.

Spracklen, K. (2013a). Nazi punks folk off: Leisure, nationalism, cultural identity and the consumption of metal and folk music. *Leisure Studies*, *32*(4), 415–428.

Spracklen, K. (2013b). *Whiteness and leisure*. Basingstoke: Palgrave Macmillan.

Spracklen, K. (2014). There is (almost) no alternative: The slow 'heat death' of music subcultures and the instrumentalization of contemporary leisure. *Annals of Leisure Research*, *17*(3), 252–266.

Spracklen, K. (2015a). To Holmgard… and beyond: Folk metal fantasies and hegemonic white masculinities. *Metal Music Studies*, *1*(3), 354–377.

Spracklen, K. (2015b). *Digital leisure, the internet and popular culture: Communities and identities in a digital age*. London: Palgrave.

Spracklen, K. (2016). Theorising northernness and northern culture: The north of England, northern Englishness, and sympathetic magic. *Journal for Cultural Research*, *20*(1), 4–16.

Spracklen, K. (2017a). Leisure, instrumentality and communicative action. In K. Spracklen, B. Lashua, E. Sharpe, & S. Swain (Eds.), *The Palgrave handbook of leisure theory* (pp. 523–538). London: Palgrave.

Spracklen, K. (2017b). Sex, drugs, Satan and rock and roll: Re-thinking dark leisure, from theoretical framework to an exploration of pop-rock-metal music norms. *Annals of Leisure Research*, 1–17. doi:10.1080/11745398.2017.1326156

Spracklen, K., Henderson, S., & Procter, D. (2016). Imagining the scene and the memory of the F-Club: Talking about lost punk and post-punk spaces in Leeds. *Punk and Post-Punk*, *5*(2), 147–162.

Spracklen, K., & Lamond, I. (2016). *Critical event studies*. Abingdon: Routledge.

Spracklen, K., Laurencic, J., & Kenyon, A. (2013). 'Mine's a pint of bitter': Performativity, gender, class and representations of authenticity in real-ale tourism. *Tourist Studies*, *13*(3), 304–321.

Spracklen, K., Richter, A., & Spracklen, B. (2013). The eventization of leisure and the strange death of alternative Leeds. *City*, *17*(2), 164–178.

Spracklen, K., & Spracklen, B. (2012). Pagans and Satan and goths, oh my: Dark leisure as communicative agency and communal identity on the fringes of the modern goth scene. *World Leisure Journal*, *54*(4), 350–362.

Spracklen, K., & Spracklen, B. (2014). The strange and spooky battle over bats and black dresses: The commodification of Whitby Goth Weekend and the loss of a subculture. *Tourist Studies*, *14*(1), 86–102.

Stapleton, P., Luiz, G., & Chatwin, H. (2017). Generation validation: The role of social comparison in use of Instagram among emerging adults. *Cyberpsychology, Behavior, and Social Networking*, *20*(3), 142–149.

Sutcliffe, P. (1980). Bauhaus: University of Surrey, Guildford. Sounds. Retrieved from http://www.rocksbackpages.com/Library/Article/bauhaus-university-of-surrey-guildford. Accessed on August 30, 2017.

Swank, E., & Fahs, B. (2016). Resources, masculinities, and gender differences among pro-life activists. *Sexuality & Culture*, *20*(2), 277–294.

Tagg, P. (2011). Caught on the back foot: Epistemic inertia and visible music. *IASPM@ Journal*, *2*(1–2), 3–18.

Thompson, D. (2007). *The dark reign of gothic rock: In the reptile house with the 'Sisters of Mercy', 'Bauhaus' and 'The Cure'*. London: Helter Skelter.

Thornton, S. (1995). *Club cultures: Music, media and subcultural capital*. Cambridge: Polity.

Thorogood, J. (2016). Satire and geopolitics: Vulgarity, ambiguity and the body grotesque in South Park. *Geopolitics, 21*(1), 215–235.

Tkacz, N. (2014). *Wikipedia and the politics of openness*. Chicago, IL: University of Chicago Press.

Triggs, T. (2006). Scissors and glue: Punk fanzines and the creation of a DIY aesthetic. *Journal of Design History, 19*(1), 69–83.

Turner, V. (1969). *The ritual process: Structure and anti-structure*. Ithaca, NY: Cornell University Press.

Unsworth, C. (1989). Exit the '80s – goth: Bats out of hell. Sounds. Retrieved from http://www.rocksbackpages.com/Library/Article/exit-the-80s--goth-bats-out-of-hell. Accessed on August 30, 2017.

Urry, J. (2007). *Mobilities*. Cambridge: Polity Press.

van Elferen, I. (2012). *Gothic music: The sounds of the uncanny*. Cardiff: University of Wales Press.

van Elferen, I., & Weinstock, J. A. (2016). *Goth music: From sound to subculture*. New York, NY: Routledge.

Walser, R. (1993). *Running with the devil: Power, gender, and madness in heavy metal music*. Middletown, CT: Wesleyan University Press.

Walton, J. (2000). *The British seaside: Holidays and resorts in the twentieth century*. Manchester: Manchester University Press.

Wang, O. (2014). Hear the drum machine get wicked. *Journal of Popular Music Studies, 26*(2–3), 220–225.

Weatherall, A. (1996). Language about women and men: An example from popular culture. *Journal of Language and Social Psychology, 15*(1), 59–75.

Weber, M. (1964). *Theory of social and economic organization*. London: Macmillan.

Wegner, P. E. (2009). *Life between two deaths, 1989–2001: US culture in the long nineties*. Durham, NC: Duke University Press.

Weinstein, D. (1991). *Heavy metal: A cultural sociology*. New York, NY: Lexington Books.

Whittaker, J. (2007). Dark webs: Goth subcultures in cyberspace. *Gothic Studies, 9*(1), 35–45.

Wickham, C. (2009). *The inheritance of Rome: A history of Europe from 400 to 1000*. London: Penguin.

Wilde, J. (1982). Sex gang children. *ZigZag*. Retrieved from http://www.rocksbackpages.com/Library/Article/sex-gang-children. Accessed on August 30, 2017.

Wilkins, A. C. (2004). So full of myself as a chick: Goth women, sexual independence, and gender egalitarianism. *Gender and Society, 18*(3), 328–349.

Williams, D. J. (2009). Deviant leisure: Rethinking 'the good, the bad, and the ugly. *Leisure Sciences, 31*(2), 207–213.

Williams, R. (1977). *Marxism and literature*. Oxford: Oxford University Press.

Wilson, E. (1990). Deviant dress. *Feminist Review, 35*(1), 67–74.

Winge, T. M. (2012). *Body style*. London: Bloomsbury.

Wright, R. (2000). 'I'd sell you suicide': Pop music and moral panic in the age of Marilyn Manson. *Popular Music, 19*(3), 365–385.

Yardley, M. (2010). Under the rose: Goth in the 1990s. *Terrorizer: Dominion*. Retrieved from http://www.terrorizer.com/dominion/dominionfeatures/under-the-rose-goth-in-the-1990s/. Accessed on March 6, 2018.

Yavuz, M. S. (2017). 'Delightfully depressing': Death/doom metal music world and the emotional responses of the fan. *Metal Music Studies, 3*(2), 201–218.

Yeomans, H. (2014). *Alcohol and moral regulation: Public attitudes, spirited measures and Victorian hangovers*. Bristol: Policy Press.

Yuen Thompson, B. (2015). *Covered in ink: Tattoos, women and the politics of the body*. New York, NY: NYU Press.

Index

Note: Page numbers followed by "*n*" with numbers indicate notes.

Printed and bound by CPI Group (UK) Ltd, Croydon, CR0 4YY

28/01/2025

14634076-0001